DAN-4   DANTES SUBJECT STANDARDIZED TESTS (DSST)

This is your
PASSBOOK for...

Principles of Basic Statistics

Test Preparation Study Guide
Questions & Answers

COPYRIGHT NOTICE

This book is SOLELY intended for, is sold ONLY to, and its use is RESTRICTED to individual, bona fide applicants or candidates who qualify by virtue of having seriously filed applications for appropriate license, certificate, professional and/or promotional advancement, higher school matriculation, scholarship, or other legitimate requirements of education and/or governmental authorities.

This book is NOT intended for use, class instruction, tutoring, training, duplication, copying, reprinting, excerption, or adaptation, etc., by:

1) Other publishers
2) Proprietors and/or Instructors of "Coaching" and/or Preparatory Courses
3) Personnel and/or Training Divisions of commercial, industrial, and governmental organizations
4) Schools, colleges, or universities and/or their departments and staffs, including teachers and other personnel
5) Testing Agencies or Bureaus
6) Study groups which seek by the purchase of a single volume to copy and/or duplicate and/or adapt this material for use by the group as a whole without having purchased individual volumes for each of the members of the group
7) Et al.

Such persons would be in violation of appropriate Federal and State statutes.

PROVISION OF LICENSING AGREEMENTS – Recognized educational, commercial, industrial, and governmental institutions and organizations, and others legitimately engaged in educational pursuits, including training, testing, and measurement activities, may address request for a licensing agreement to the copyright owners, who will determine whether, and under what conditions, including fees and charges, the materials in this book may be used them. In other words, a licensing facility exists for the legitimate use of the material in this book on other than an individual basis. However, it is asseverated and affirmed here that the material in this book CANNOT be used without the receipt of the express permission of such a licensing agreement from the Publishers. Inquiries re licensing should be addressed to the company, attention rights and permissions department.

All rights reserved, including the right of reproduction in whole or in part, in any form or by any means, electronic or mechanical, including photocopying, recording, or by any information storage and retrieval system, without permission in writing from the Publisher.

Copyright © 2025 by
National Learning Corporation

212 Michael Drive, Syosset, NY 11791
(516) 921-8888 • www.passbooks.com
E-mail: info@passbooks.com

PASSBOOK® SERIES

THE *PASSBOOK® SERIES* has been created to prepare applicants and candidates for the ultimate academic battlefield – the examination room.

At some time in our lives, each and every one of us may be required to take an examination – for validation, matriculation, admission, qualification, registration, certification, or licensure.

Based on the assumption that every applicant or candidate has met the basic formal educational standards, has taken the required number of courses, and read the necessary texts, the *PASSBOOK® SERIES* furnishes the one special preparation which may assure passing with confidence, instead of failing with insecurity. Examination questions – together with answers – are furnished as the basic vehicle for study so that the mysteries of the examination and its compounding difficulties may be eliminated or diminished by a sure method.

This book is meant to help you pass your examination provided that you qualify and are serious in your objective.

The entire field is reviewed through the huge store of content information which is succinctly presented through a provocative and challenging approach – the question-and-answer method.

A climate of success is established by furnishing the correct answers at the end of each test.

You soon learn to recognize types of questions, forms of questions, and patterns of questioning. You may even begin to anticipate expected outcomes.

You perceive that many questions are repeated or adapted so that you can gain acute insights, which may enable you to score many sure points.

You learn how to confront new questions, or types of questions, and to attack them confidently and work out the correct answers.

You note objectives and emphases, and recognize pitfalls and dangers, so that you may make positive educational adjustments.

Moreover, you are kept fully informed in relation to new concepts, methods, practices, and directions in the field.

You discover that you are actually taking the examination all the time: you are preparing for the examination by "taking" an examination, not by reading extraneous and/or supererogatory textbooks.

In short, this PASSBOOK®, used directedly, should be an important factor in helping you to pass your test.

NONTRADITIONAL EDUCATION

Students returning to school as adults bring more varied experience to their studies than do the teenagers who begin college shortly after graduating from high school. As a result, there are numerous programs for students with nontraditional learning curves. Hundreds of colleges and universities grant degrees to people who cannot attend classes at a regular campus or have already learned what the college is supposed to teach.

You can earn nontraditional education credits in many ways:
- Passing standardized exams
- Demonstrating knowledge gained through experience
- Completing campus-based coursework, and
- Taking courses off campus

Some methods of assessing learning for credit are objective, such as standardized tests. Others are more subjective, such as a review of life experiences.

With some help from four hypothetical characters – Alice, Vin, Lynette, and Jorge – this article describes nontraditional ways of earning educational credit. It begins by describing programs in which you can earn a high school diploma without spending 4 years in a classroom. The college picture is more complicated, so it is presented in two parts: one on gaining credit for what you know through course work or experience, and a second on college degree programs. The final section lists resources for locating more information.

Earning High School Credit

People who were prevented from finishing high school as teenagers have several options if they want to do so as adults. Some major cities have back-to-school programs that allow adults to attend high school classes with current students. But the more practical alternatives for most adults are to take the General Educational Development (GED) tests or to earn a high school diploma by demonstrating their skills or taking correspondence classes.

Of course, these options do not match the experience of staying in high school and graduating with one's friends. But they are viable alternatives for adult learners committed to meeting and, often, continuing their educational goals.

GED Program

Alice quit high school her sophomore year and took a job to help support herself, her younger brother, and their newly widowed mother. Now an adult, she wants to earn her high school diploma – and then go on to college. Because her job as head cook and her family responsibilities keep her busy during the day, she plans to get a high school equivalency diploma. She will study for, and take, the GED tests. Every year, about half a million adults earn their high school credentials this way. A GED diploma is accepted in lieu of a high school one by more than 90 percent of employers, colleges, and universities, so it is a good choice for someone like Alice.

The GED testing program is sponsored by the American Council on Education and State and local education departments. It consists of examinations in five subject areas: Writing, science, mathematics, social studies, and literature and the arts. The tests also measure skills such as analytical ability, problem solving, reading comprehension, and ability to understand and apply information. Most of the questions are multiple choice; the writing test includes an essay section on a topic of general interest.

Eligibility rules for taking the exams vary, but some states require that you must be at least 18. Tests are given in English, Spanish, and French. In addition to standard print, versions in large print, Braille, and audiocassette are also available. Total time allotted for the tests is 7 1/2 hours.

The GED tests are not easy. About one-fourth of those who complete the exams every year do not pass. Passing scores are established by administering the tests to a sample of graduating high school seniors. The minimum standard score is set so that about one-third of graduating seniors would not pass the tests if they took them.

Because of the difficulty of the tests, people need to prepare themselves to take them. Often, they start by taking the Official GED Practice Tests, usually available through a local adult education center. Centers are listed in your phone book's blue pages under "Adult Education," "Continuing Education," or "GED." Adult education centers also have information about GED preparation classes and self-study materials. Classes are generally arranged to accommodate adults' work schedules. National Learning Corporation publishes several study guides that aim to thoroughly prepare test-takers for the GED.

School districts, colleges, adult education centers, and community organizations have information about GED testing schedules and practice tests. For more information, contact them, your nearest GED testing center, or:

GED Testing Service
One Dupont Circle, NW, Suite 250
Washington, DC 20036-1163
1(800) 62-MY GED (626-9433)
(202) 939-9490

Skills Demonstration

Adults who have acquired high school level skills through experience might be eligible for the National External Diploma Program. This alternative to the GED does not involve any direct instruction. Instead, adults seeking a high school diploma must demonstrate mastery of 65 competencies in 8 general areas: Communication; computation; occupational preparedness; and self, social, consumer, scientific, and technological awareness.

Mastery is shown through the completion of the tasks. For example, a participant could prove competency in computation by measuring a room for carpeting, figuring out the amount of carpet needed, and computing the cost.

Before being accepted for the program, adults undergo an evaluation. Tests taken at one of the program's offices measure reading, writing, and mathematics abilities. A take-home segment includes a self-assessment of current skills, an individual skill evaluation, and an occupational interest and aptitude test.

Adults accepted for the program have weekly meetings with an assessor. At the meeting, the assessor reviews the participant's work from the previous week. If the task has not been completed properly, the assessor explains the mistake. Participants continue to correct their errors until they master each competency. A high school diploma is awarded upon proven mastery of all 65 competencies.

Fourteen States and the District of Columbia now offer the External Diploma Program. For more information, contact:

External Diploma Program
One Dupont Circle, NW, Suite 250
Washington, DC 20036-1193
(202) 939-9475

Correspondence and Distance Study

Vin dropped out of high school during his junior year because his family's frequent moves made it difficult for him to continue his studies. He promised himself at the time he dropped out that he would someday finish the courses needed for his diploma. For people like Vin, who prefer to earn a traditional diploma in a nontraditional way, there are about a dozen accredited courses of study for earning a high school diploma by correspondence, or distance study. The programs are either privately run, affiliated with a university, or administered by a State education department.

Distance study diploma programs have no residency requirements, allowing students to continue their studies from almost any location. Depending on the course of study, students need not be enrolled full time and usually have more flexible schedules for finishing their work. Selection of courses ranges from vo-tech to college prep, and some programs place different emphasis on the types of diplomas offered. University affiliated schools, for example, allow qualified students to take college courses along with their high school ones. Students can then apply the college credits toward a degree at that university or transfer them to another institution.

Taking courses by distance study is often more challenging and time consuming than attending classes, especially for adults who have other obligations. Success depends on each student's motivation. Students usually do reading assignments on their own. Written exercises, which they complete and send to an instructor for grading, supplement their reading material.

A list of some accredited high schools that offer diplomas by distance study is available free from the Distance Education and Training Council, formerly known as the National Home Study Council. Request the "DETC Directory of Accredited Institutions" from:

The Distance Education and Training Council
1601 18th Street, NW.
Washington, DC 20009-2529
(202) 234-5100

Some publications profiling nontraditional college programs include addresses and descriptions of several high school correspondence ones. See the Resources section at the end of this article for more information.

Getting College Credit For What You Know

Adults can receive college credit for prior coursework, by passing examinations, and documenting experiential learning. With help from a college advisor, nontraditional students should assess their skills, establish their educational goals, and determine the number of college credits they might be eligible for.

Even before you meet with a college advisor, you should collect all your school and training records. Then, make a list of all knowledge and abilities acquired through experience, no matter how irrelevant they seem to your chosen field. Next, determine your educational goals: What specific field do you wish to study? What kind of a degree do you want? Finally, determine how your past work fits into the field of study. Later on, you will evaluate educational programs to find one that's right for you.

People who have complex educational or experiential learning histories might want to have their learning evaluated by the Regents Credit Bank. The Credit Bank, operated by Regents College of the University of the State of New York, allows people to consolidate credits earned through college, experience, or other methods. Special assessments are available for Regents College enrollees whose knowledge in a specific field cannot be adequately evaluated by standardized exams. For more information, contact the Regents Credit Bank at:

Regents College
7 Columbia Circle
Albany, NY 12203-5159
(518) 464-8500

Credit For Prior College Coursework

When Lynette was in college during the 1970s, she attended several different schools and took a variety of courses. She did well in some classes and poorly in others. Now that she is a successful business owner and has more focus, Lynette thinks she should forget about her previous coursework and start from scratch. Instead, she should start from where she is.

Lynette should have all her transcripts sent to the colleges or universities of her choice and let an admissions officer determine which classes are applicable toward a degree. A few credits here and there may not seem like much, but they add up. Even if the subjects do not seem relevant to any major, they might be counted as elective credits toward a degree. And comparing the cost of transcripts with the cost of college courses, it makes sense to spend a few dollars per transcript for a chance to save hundreds, and perhaps thousands, of dollars in books and tuition.

Rules for transferring credits apply to all prior coursework at accredited colleges and universities, whether done on campus or off. Courses completed off campus, often called extended learning, include those available to students through independent study and correspondence. Many schools have extended learning programs; Brigham Young University, for example, offers more than 300 courses through its Department of Independent Study. One type of extended learning is distance learning, a form of correspondence study by technological means such as television, video and audio, CD-ROM, electronic mail, and computer tutorials. See the Resources section at the end of this article for more information about publications available from the National University Continuing Education Association.

Any previously earned college credits should be considered for transfer, no matter what the subject or the grade received. Many schools do not accept the transfer of courses graded below a C or ones taken more than a designated number of years ago. Some colleges and universities also have limits on the number of credits that can be transferred and applied toward a degree. But not all do. For example, Thomas Edison State College, New Jersey's State college for adults, accepts the transfer of all 120 hours of credit required for a baccalaureate degree – provided all the credits are transferred from regionally accredited schools, no more than 80 are at the junior college level, and the student's grades overall and in the field of study average out to C.

To assign credit for prior coursework, most schools require original transcripts. This means you must complete a form or send a written, signed request to have your transcripts released directly to a college or university. Once you have chosen the schools you want to apply to, contact the schools you attended before. Find out how much each transcript costs, and ask them to send your transcripts to the ones you are applying to. Write a letter that includes your name (and names used during attendance, if different) and dates of attendance, along with the names and addresses of the schools to which your transcripts should be sent. Include payment and mail to the registrar at the schools you have attended. The registrar's office will process your request and send an official transcript of your coursework to the colleges or universities you have designated.

Credit For Noncollege Courses

Colleges and universities are not the only ones that offer classes. Volunteer organizations and employers often provide formal training worth college credit. The American Council on Education has two programs that assess thousands of specific courses and make recommendations on the amount of college credit they are worth. Colleges and universities accept the recommendations or use them as guidelines.

One program evaluates educational courses sponsored by government agencies, business and industry, labor unions, and professional and voluntary organizations. It is the Program on Noncollegiate Sponsored Instruction (PONSI). Some of the training seminars Alice has participated in covered topics such as food preparation, kitchen safety, and nutrition. Although she has not yet earned her GED, Alice can earn college credit because of her completion of these formal job-training seminars. The number of credits each seminar is worth does not hinge on Alice's current eligibility for college enrollment.

The other program evaluates courses offered by the Army, Navy, Air Force, Marines, Coast Guard, and Department of Defense. It is the Military Evaluations Program. Jorge has never attended college, but the engineering technology classes he completed as part of his military training are worth college credit. And as an Army veteran, Jorge is eligible for a service that takes the evaluations one step further. The Army/American Council on Education Registry Transcript System (AARTS) will provide Jorge with an individualized transcript of American Council on Education credit recommendations for all courses he completed, the military occupational specialties (MOS's) he held, and examinations he passed while in the Army. All Army and National Guard enlisted personnel and veterans who enlisted after October 1981 are eligible for the transcript. Similar services are being considered by the Navy and Marine Corps.

To obtain a free transcript, see your Army Education Center for a 5454R transcript request form. Include your name, Social Security number, basic active service date, and complete address where you want the transcript sent. Mail your request to:
AARTS Operations Center
415 McPherson Ave.
Fort Leavenworth, KS 66027-1373

Recommendations for PONSI are published in *The National Guide to Educational Credit for Training Programs;* military program recommendations are in *The Guide to the Evaluation of Educational Experiences in the Armed Forces.* See the Resources section at the end of this article for more information about these publications.

Former military personnel who took a foreign language course through the Defense Language Institute may request course transcripts by sending their name, Social Security number, course title, duration of the course, and graduation date to:

    Commandant, Defense Language Institute
    Attn: ATFL-DAA-AR
    Transcripts
    Presidio of Monterey
    Monterey, CA 93944-5006

Not all of Jorge's and Alice's courses have been assessed by the American Council on Education. Training courses that have no Council credit recommendation should still be assessed by an advisor at the schools they want to attend. Course descriptions, class notes, test scores, and other documentation may be helpful for comparing training courses to their college equivalents. An oral examination or other demonstration of competency might also be required.

There is no guarantee you will receive all the credits you are seeking – but you certainly won't if you make no attempt.

Credit By Examination

Standardized tests are the best-known method of receiving college credit without taking courses. These exams are often taken by high school students seeking advanced placement for college, but they are also available to adult learners. Testing programs and colleges and universities offer exams in a number of subjects. Two U.S. Government institutes have foreign language exams for employees that also may be worth college credit.

It is important to understand that receiving a passing score on these exams does not mean you get college credit automatically. Each school determines which test results it will accept, minimum scores required, how scores are converted for credit, and the amount of credit, if any, to be assigned. Most colleges and universities accept the American Council on Education credit recommendations, published every other year in the 250-page *Guide to Educational Credit by Examination*. For more information, contact:

    The American Council on Education
    Credit by Examination Program
    One Dupont Circle, Suite 250
    Washington, DC 20036-1193
    (202) 939-9434

Testing programs:

You might know some of the five national testing programs by their acronyms or initials: CLEP, ACT PEP: RCE, DANTES, AP, and NOCTI. (The meanings of these initialisms are explained below.) There is some overlap among programs; for example, four of them have introductory accounting exams. Since you will not be awarded credit more than once for a specific subject, you should carefully evaluate each program for the subject exams you wish to take. And before taking an exam, make sure you will be awarded credit by the college or university you plan to attend.

CLEP (College-Level Examination Program), administered by the College Board, is the most widely accepted of the national testing programs; more than 2,800 accredited schools award credit for passing exam scores. Each test covers material taught in basic undergraduate courses. There are five general exams – English composition, humanities, college mathematics, natural sciences, and social sciences and history – and many subject exams. Most exams are entirely multiple-choice, but English composition exams may include an essay section. For more information, contact:

    CLEP
    P.O. Box 6600
    Princeton, NJ 08541-6600
    (609) 771-7865

ACT PEP: RCE (American College Testing Proficiency Exam Program: Regents College Examinations) tests are given in 38 subjects within arts and sciences, business, education, and nursing. Each exam is recommended for either lower- or upper-level credit. Exams contain either objective or extended response questions, and are graded according to a standard score, letter grade, or pass/fail. Fees vary, depending on the subject and type of exam. For more information or to request free study guides, contact:

    ACT PEP: Regents College Examinations
    P.O. Box 4014
    Iowa City, IA 52243
    (319) 337-1387
    (New York State residents must contact Regents College directly.)

DANTES (Defense Activity for Nontraditional Education Support) standardized tests are developed by the Educational Testing Service for the Department of Defense. Originally administered only to military personnel, the exams have been available to the public since 1983. About 50 subject tests cover business, mathematics, social science, physical science, humanities, foreign languages, and applied technology. Most of the tests consist entirely of multiple-choice questions. Schools determine their own administering fees and testing schedules. For more information or to request free study sheets, contact:

    DANTES Program Office
    Mail Stop 31-X
    Educational Testing Service
    Princeton, NJ 08541
    1(800) 257-9484

The AP (Advanced Placement) Program is a cooperative effort between secondary schools and colleges and universities. AP exams are developed each year by committees of college and high school faculty appointed by the College Board and assisted by consultants from the Educational Testing Service. Subjects include arts and languages, natural sciences, computer science, social sciences, history, and mathematics. Most tests are 2 or 3 hours long and include both multiple-choice and essay questions. AP courses are available to help students prepare for exams, which are offered in the spring. For more information about the Advanced Placement Program, contact:

    Advanced Placement Services
    P.O. Box 6671
    Princeton, NJ 08541-6671
    (609) 771-7300

NOCTI (National Occupational Competency Testing Institute) assessments are designed for people like Alice, who have vocational-technical skills that cannot be evaluated by other tests. NOCTI assesses competency at two levels: Student/job ready and teacher/experienced worker. Standardized evaluations are available for occupations such as auto-body repair, electronics, mechanical drafting, quantity food preparation, and upholstering. The tests consist of multiple-choice questions and a performance component. Other services include workshops, customized assessments, and pre-testing. For more information, contact:

NOCTI
500 N. Bronson Ave.
Ferris State University
Big Rapids, MI 49307
(616) 796-4699

Colleges and universities:

Many colleges and universities have credit-by-exam programs, through which students earn credit by passing a comprehensive exam for a course offered by the institution. Among the most widely recognized are the programs at Ohio University, the University of North Carolina, Thomas Edison State College, and New York University.

Ohio University offers about 150 examinations for credit. In addition, you may sometimes arrange to take special examinations in non-laboratory courses offered at Ohio University. To take a test for credit, you must enroll in the course. If you plan to transfer the credit earned, you also need written permission from an official at your school. Books and study materials are available, for a cost, through the university. Exams must be taken within 6 months of the enrollment date; most last 3 hours. You may arrange to take the exam off campus if you do not live near the university.

Ohio University is on the quarter-hour system; most courses are worth 4 quarter hours, the equivalent of 3 semester hours. For more information, contact:

Independent Study
Tupper Hall 302
Ohio University
Athens, OH 45701-2979
1(800) 444-2910
(614) 593-2910

The University of North Carolina offers a credit-by-examination option for 140 independent study (correspondence) courses in foreign languages, humanities, social sciences, mathematics, business administration, education, electrical and computer engineering, health administration, and natural sciences. To take an exam, you must request and receive approval from both the course instructor and the independent studies department. Exams must be taken within six months of enrollment, and you may register for no more than two at a time. If you are not near the University's Chapel Hill campus, you may take your exam under supervision at an accredited college, university, community college, or technical institute. For more information, contact:

Independent Studies
CB #1020, The Friday Center
UNC-Chapel Hill
Chapel Hill, NC 27599-1020
1(800) 862-5669 / (919) 962-1134

The Thomas Edison College Examination Program offers more than 50 exams in liberal arts, business, and professional areas. Thomas Edison State College administers tests twice a month in Trenton, New Jersey; however, students may arrange to take their tests with a proctor at any accredited American college or university or U.S. military base. Most of the tests are multiple choice; some also include short answer or essay questions. Time limits range from 90 minutes to 4 hours, depending on the exam. For more information, contact:

Thomas Edison State College
TECEP, Office of Testing and Assessment
101 W. State Street
Trenton, NJ 08608-1176
(609) 633-2844

New York University's Foreign Language Program offers proficiency exams in more than 40 languages, from Albanian to Yiddish. Two exams are available in each language: The 12-point test is equivalent to 4 undergraduate semesters, and the 16-point exam may lead to upper level credit. The tests are given at the university's Foreign Language Department throughout the year.

Proof of foreign language proficiency does not guarantee college credit. Some colleges and universities accept transcripts only for languages commonly taught, such as French and Spanish. Nontraditional programs are more likely than traditional ones to grant credit for proficiency in other languages.

For an informational brochure and registration form for NYU's foreign language proficiency exams, contact:

New York University
Foreign Language Department
48 Cooper Square, Room 107
New York, NY 10003
(212) 998-7030

Government institutes:

The Defense Language Institute and Foreign Service Institute administer foreign language proficiency exams for personnel stationed abroad. Usually, the tests are given at the end of intensive language courses or upon completion of service overseas. But some people – like Jorge, who knows Spanish – speak another language fluently and may be allowed to take a proficiency exam in that language before completing their tour of duty. Contact one of the offices listed below to obtain transcripts of those scores. Proof of proficiency does not guarantee college credit, however, as discussed above.

To request score reports from the Defense Language Institute for Defense Language Proficiency Tests, send your name, Social Security number, language for which you were tested, and, most importantly, when and where you took the exam to:

Commandant, Defense Language Institute
Attn: ATFL-ES-T
DLPT Score Report Request
Presidio of Monterey
Monterey, CA 93944-5006

To request transcripts of scores for Foreign Service Institute exams, send your name, Social Security number, language for which you were tested, and dates or year of exams to:

Foreign Service Institute
Arlington Hall
4020 Arlington Boulevard
Rosslyn, VA 22204-1500
Attn: Testing Office (Send your request to the attention of the testing office of the foreign language in which you were tested)

Credit For Experience

Experiential learning credit may be given for knowledge gained through job responsibilities, personal hobbies, volunteer opportunities, homemaking, and other experiences. Colleges and universities base credit awards on the knowledge you have attained, not for the experience alone. In addition, the knowledge must be college level; not just any learning will do. Throwing horseshoes as a hobby is not likely to be worth college credit. But if you've done research on how and where the sport originated, visited blacksmiths, organized tournaments, and written a column for a trade journal – well, that's a horseshoe of a different color.

Adults attempting to get credit for their experience should be forewarned: Having your experience evaluated for college credit is time-consuming, tedious work – not an easy shortcut for people who want quick-fix college credits. And not all experience, no matter how valuable, is the equivalent of college courses.

Requesting college credit for your experiential learning can be tricky. You should get assistance from a credit evaluations officer at the school you plan to attend, but you should also have a general idea of what your knowledge is worth. A common method for converting knowledge into credit is to use a college catalog. Find course titles and descriptions that match what you have learned through experience, and request the number of credits offered for those courses.

Once you know what credit to ask for, you must usually present your case in writing to officials at the college you plan to attend. The most common form of presenting experiential learning for credit is the portfolio. A portfolio is a written record of your knowledge along with a request for equivalent college credit. It includes an identification and description of the knowledge for which you are requesting credit, an explanatory essay of how the knowledge was gained and how it fits into your educational plans, documentation that you have acquired such knowledge, and a request for college credit. Required elements of a portfolio vary by schools but generally follow those guidelines.

In identifying knowledge you have gained, be specific about exactly what you have learned. For example, it is not enough for Lynette to say she runs a business. She must identify the knowledge she has gained from running it, such as personnel management, tax law, marketing strategy, and inventory review. She must also include brief descriptions about her knowledge of each to support her claims of having those skills.

The essay gives you a chance to relay something about who you are. It should address your educational goals, include relevant autobiographical details, and be well organized, neat, and convey confidence. In his essay, Jorge might first state his goal of becoming an engineer. Then he would explain why he joined the Army, where he got hands-on training and experience in developing and servicing electronic equipment.

This, he would say, led to his hobby of creating remote-controlled model cars, of which he has built 20. His conclusion would highlight his accomplishments and tie them to his desire to become an electronic engineer.

Documentation is evidence that you've learned what you claim to have learned. You can show proof of knowledge in a variety of ways, including audio or video recordings, letters from current or former employers describing your specific duties and job performance, blueprints, photographs or artwork, and transcripts of certifying exams for professional licenses and certification – such as Alice's certification from the American Culinary Federation. Although documentation can take many forms, written proof alone is not always enough. If it is impossible to document your knowledge in writing, find out if your experiential learning can be assessed through supplemental oral exams by a faculty expert.

Earning a College Degree

Nontraditional students often have work, family, and financial obligations that prevent them from quitting their jobs to attend school full time. Can they still meet their educational goals? Yes.

More than 150 accredited colleges and universities have nontraditional bachelor's degree programs that require students to spend little or no time on campus; over 300 others have nontraditional campus-based degree programs. Some of those schools, as well as most junior and community colleges, offer associate's degrees nontraditionally. Each school with a nontraditional course of study determines its own rules for awarding credit for prior coursework, exams, or experience, as discussed previously. Most have charges on top of tuition for providing these special services.

Several publications profile nontraditional degree programs; see the Resources section at the end of this article for more information. To determine which school best fits your academic profile and educational goals, first list your criteria. Then, evaluate nontraditional programs based on their accreditation, features, residency requirements, and expenses. Once you have chosen several schools to explore further, write to them for more information. Detailed explanations of school policies should help you decide which ones you want to apply to.

Get beyond the printed word – especially the glowing words each school writes about itself. Check out the schools you are considering with higher education authorities, alumni, employers, family members, and friends. If possible, visit the campus to talk to students and instructors and sit in on a few classes, even if you will be completing most or all of your work off campus. Ask school officials questions about such things as enrollment numbers, graduation rate, faculty qualifications, and confusing details about the application process or academic policies. After you have thoroughly investigated each prospective college or university, you can make an informed decision about which is right for you.

Accreditation

Accreditation is a process colleges and universities submit to voluntarily for getting their credentials. An accredited school has been investigated and visited by teams of observers and has periodic inspections by a private accrediting agency. The initial review can take two years or more.

Regional agencies accredit entire schools, and professional agencies accredit either specialized schools or departments within schools. Although there are no national accrediting standards, not just any accreditation will do. Countless "accreditation associations" have been invented by schools, many of which have no academic programs and sell phony degrees, to accredit themselves. But 6 regional and about 80 professional accrediting associations in the United States are recognized by the U.S. Department of Education or the Commission on Recognition of Postsecondary Accreditation. When checking accreditation, these are the names to look for. For more information about accreditation and accrediting agencies, contact:

    Institutional Participation Oversight Service Accreditation and State Liaison Division
    U.S. Department of Education
    ROB 3, Room 3915
    600 Independence Ave., SW
    Washington, DC 20202-5244
    (202) 708-7417

Because accreditation is not mandatory, lack of accreditation does not necessarily mean a school or program is bad. Some schools choose not to apply for accreditation, are in the process of applying, or have educational methods too unconventional for an accrediting association's standards. For the nontraditional student, however, earning a degree from a college or university with recognized accreditation is an especially important consideration. Although nontraditional education is becoming more widely accepted, it is not yet mainstream. Employers skeptical of a degree earned in a nontraditional manner are likely to be even less accepting of one from an unaccredited school.

Program Features

Because nontraditional students have diverse educational objectives, nontraditional schools are diverse in what they offer. Some programs are geared toward helping students organize their scattered educational credits to get a degree as quickly as possible. Others cater to those who may have specific credits or experience but need assistance in completing requirements. Whatever your educational profile, you should look for a program that works with you in obtaining your educational goals.

A few nontraditional programs have special admissions policies for adult learners like Alice, who plan to earn their GEDs but want to enroll in college in the meantime. Other features of nontraditional programs include individualized learning agreements, intensive academic counseling, cooperative learning and internship placement, and waiver of some prerequisites or other requirements – as well as college credit for prior coursework, examinations, and experiential learning, all discussed previously.

Lynette, whose primary goal is to finish her degree, wants to earn maximum credits for her business experience. She will look for programs that do not limit the number of credits awarded for equivalency exams and experiential learning. And since well-documented proof of knowledge is essential for earning experiential learning credits, Lynette should make sure the program she chooses provides assistance to students submitting a portfolio.

Jorge, on the other hand, has more credits than he needs in certain areas and is willing to forego some. To become an engineer, he must have a bachelor's degree; but because he is accustomed to hands-on learning, Jorge is interested in getting experience as he gains more technical skills. He will concentrate on finding schools with strong cooperative education, supervised fieldwork, or internship programs.

Residency Requirements

Programs are sometimes deemed nontraditional because of their residency requirements. Many people think of residency for colleges and universities in terms of tuition, with in-state students paying less than out-of-state ones. Residency also may refer to where a student lives, either on or off campus, while attending school.

But in nontraditional education, residency usually refers to how much time students must spend on campus, regardless of whether they attend classes there. In some nontraditional programs, students need not ever step foot on campus. Others require only a very short residency, such as one day or a few weeks. Many schools have standard residency requirements of several semesters but schedule classes for evenings or weekends to accommodate working adults.

Lynette, who previously took courses by independent study, prefers to earn credits by distance study. She will focus on schools that have no residency requirement. Several colleges and universities have nonresident degree completion programs for adults with some college credit. Under the direction of a faculty advisor, students devise a plan for earning their remaining credits. Methods for earning credits include independent study, distance learning, seminars, supervised fieldwork, and group study at arranged sites. Students may have to earn a certain number of credits through the degree-granting institution. But many programs allow students to take courses at accredited schools of their choice for transfer toward their degree.

Alice wants to attend lectures but has an unpredictable schedule. Her best course of action will be to seek out short residency programs that require students to attend seminars once or twice a semester. She can take courses that are televised and videotape them to watch when her schedule permits, with the seminars helping to ensure that she properly completes her coursework. Many colleges and universities with short residency requirements also permit students to earn some credits elsewhere, by whatever means the student chooses.

Some fields of study require classroom instruction. As Jorge will discover, few colleges and universities allow students to earn a bachelor's degree in engineering entirely through independent study. Nontraditional residency programs are designed to accommodate adults' daytime work schedules. Jorge should look for programs offering evening, weekend, summer, and accelerated courses.

Tuition and Other Expenses

The final decisions about which schools Alice, Jorge, and Lynette attend may hinge in large part on a single issue: Cost. And rising tuition is only part of the equation. Beginning with application fees and continuing through graduation fees, college expenses add up.

Traditional and nontraditional students have some expenses in common, such as the cost of books and other materials. Tuition might even be the same for some courses, especially for colleges and universities offering standard ones at unusual times. But for nontraditional programs, students may also pay fees for services such as credit or transcript review, evaluation, advisement, and portfolio assessment.

Students are also responsible for postage and handling or setup expenses for independent study courses, as well as for all examination and transcript fees for transferring credits. Usually, the more nontraditional the program, the more detailed the fees. Some schools charge a yearly enrollment fee rather than tuition for degree completion candidates who want their files to remain active.

Although tuition and fees might seem expensive, most educators tell you not to let money come between you and your educational goals. Talk to someone in the financial aid department of the school you plan to attend or check your library for publications about financial aid sources. The U.S. Department of Education publishes a guide to Federal aid programs such as Pell Grants, student loans, and work-study. To order the free 74-page booklet, *The Student Guide: Financial Aid from the U.S. Department of Education,* contact:

Federal Student Aid Information Center
P.O. Box 84
Washington, DC 20044
1 (800) 4FED-AID (433-3243)

Resources

Information on how to earn a high school diploma or college degree without following the usual routes is available from several organizations and in numerous publications. Information on nontraditional graduate degree programs, available for master's through doctoral level, though not discussed in this article, can usually be obtained from the same resources that detail bachelor's degree programs.

National Learning Corporation publishes study guides for all of these exams, for both general examinations and tests in specific subject areas. To order study guides, or to browse their catalog featuring more than 5,000 titles, visit NLC online at www.passbooks.com, or contact them by phone at (800) 632-8888.

Organizations

Adult learners should always contact their local school system, community college, or university to learn about programs that are readily available. The following national organizations can also supply information:

American Council on Education
One Dupont Circle
Washington, DC 20036-1193
(202) 939-9300

Within the American Council on Education, the Center for Adult Learning and Educational Credentials administers the National External Diploma Program, the GED Program, the Program on Noncollegiate Sponsored Instruction, the Credit by Examination Program, and the Military Evaluations Program.

DANTES Subject Standardized Tests

INTRODUCTION

The DANTES (Defense Activity for Non-Traditional Education Support) subject standardized tests are comprehensive college and graduate level examinations given by the Armed Forces, colleges and graduate schools as end-of-subject course evaluation final examinations or to obtain college equivalency credits in the various subject areas tested.

The DANTES Examination Program enables students to obtain college credit for what they have learned on the job, through self-study, personal interest, correspondence courses or by any other means. It is used by colleges and universities to award college credit to students who demonstrate that they know as much as students completing an equivalent college course. It is a cost-efficient, time-saving way for students to use their knowledge to accomplish their educational goals.

Most schools accept the American Council on Education (ACE) recommendations for the minimum score required and the amount of credit awarded, but not all schools do. Be sure to check the policy regarding the score level required for credit and the number of credits to be awarded.

Not all tests are accepted by all institutions. Even when a test is accepted by an institution, it may not be acceptable for every program at that institution. Before considering testing, ascertain the acceptability of a specific test for a particular course.

Colleges and universities that administer DANTES tests may administer them to any applicant – or they may administer the tests only to students registered at their institution. Decisions about who will be allowed to test are made by the school. Students should contact the test center to determine current policies and schedules for DANTES testing.

Colleges and universities authorized to administer DANTES tests usually do so throughout the calendar year. Each school sets its own fee for test administration and establishes its own testing schedule. Contact the representative at the administering school directly to make arrangements for testing.

Checklist For Students

✓ Visit **www.getcollegecredit.com** to obtain a list of tests, fact sheets, test preparation materials, participating colleges and universities, and much more.

✓ Contact your school advisor to confirm that the DSST you selected will fit into your curriculum.

✓ Consult the ***DSST Candidate Information Bulletin*** for answers to specific questions.

✓ Contact the test site to schedule your test.

✓ Prepare for your examination by using the fact sheet as a guide.

✓ Take the test.

If you would like a score report sent to your college or university, it is a good idea to bring the four-digit code with you. You must write the DSST Test Center Code for that institution on your answer sheet at the time of testing. DSST Test Center Codes are noted in the DSST Participating Colleges and Universities listing on the Web site.

If you prefer to send a score report to an institution at a later date, there is a transcript fee of $20 for each transcript ordered.

Thomson Prometric
DSST Program
2000 Lenox Drive, Third Floor
Lawrenceville, NJ 08648

Toll-free: 877-471-9860
609-895-5011

E-mail: pnj-dsst@thomson.com

MAKING A COLLEGE DEGREE WITHIN YOUR REACH

Today, there are many educational alternatives to the classroom—you can learn from your job, your reading, your independent study, and special interests you pursue. You may already have learned the subject matter covered by some college-level courses.

The DSST Program is a nationally recognized testing program that gives you the opportunity to receive college credit for learning acquired outside the traditional college classroom. Colleges and universities throughout the United States administer the program, developed by Thomson Prometric, year-round. Annually, over 90,000 DSSTs are administered to individuals who are interested in continuing their education. Take advantage of the DSST testing program; it speeds the educational process and provides the flexibility adults need, making earning a degree more feasible.

Since requirements differ from college to college, please check with the credit-awarding institution before taking a DSST. More than 1,800 colleges and universities currently award credit for DSSTs, and the number is growing every day. You can choose from 37 test titles in the areas of Social Science, Business, Mathematics, Applied Technology, Humanities, and Physical Science. A brief description of each examination is found on the pages that follow.

Reach Your Career Goals Through DSSTs

Use DSSTs to help you earn your degree, get a promotion, or simply demonstrate that you have college-level knowledge in subjects relevant to your work.

Save Time...

You don't have to sit through classes when you have previously acquired the knowledge or experience for most of what is being taught and can learn the rest yourself. You might be able to bypass introductory-level courses in subject areas you already know.

Save Money...

DSSTs save you money because the classes you bypass by earning credit through the DSST Program are classes you won't have to pay for on your way to earning your degree. You can use the money instead to take more advanced courses that can be more challenging and rewarding.

Improve Your Chances for Admission to College

Each college has its own admission policies; however, having passing scores for DSSTs on your transcript can provide strong evidence of how well you can perform at the college level.

Gain Confidence Performing at a College Level

Many adults returning to college find that lack of confidence is often the greatest hurdle to overcome. Passing a DSST demonstrates your ability to perform on a college level.

Make Up for Courses You May Have Missed

You may be ready to graduate from college and find that you are a few credits short of earning your degree. By using semester breaks, vacation time, or leisure time to study independently, you can prepare to take one or more DSSTs, fulfill your academic requirements, and graduate on time.

If You Cannot Attend Regularly Scheduled Classes...

If your lifestyle or responsibilities prevent you from attending regularly scheduled classes, you can earn your college degree from a college offering an external degree program. The DSST Program allows you to earn your degree by study and experience outside the traditional classroom.

Many colleges and universities offer external degree or distance learning programs. For additional information, contact the college you plan to attend or:

Center for Lifelong Learning
American Council on Education
One DuPont Circle NW, Suite 250
Washington, DC 20036
202-939-9475
www.acenet.edu
(Select "Center for Lifelong Learning" under "Programs & Services"
for more information)

Fact Sheets

For each test, there is a Fact Sheet that outlines the topics covered by each test and includes a list of sample questions, a list of recommended references of books that would be useful for review, and the number of credits awarded for a passing score as recommended by the American Council on Education (ACE). *Please note that some schools require scores that are higher than the minimum ACE-recommended passing score.* It is suggested that you check with your college or university to determine what score they require in order to earn credit. You can obtain Fact Sheets by:
- Downloading them from www.getcollegecredit.com
- E-mailing a request to pnj-dsst@thomson.com
- Completing a Candidate Publications Order Form

DSST Online Practice Tests

DSST online practice tests contain items that reflect a *partial range of difficulty* identified in the Content Outline section on each Fact Sheet. There is an online DSST Practice Test in the following categories:
- Mathematics
- Social Science
- Business
- Physical Science
- Applied Technology
- Humanities

Although the online DSST Practice Test questions do not indicate the full range of difficulty you would find in an actual DSST test, they will help you assess your knowledge level. Each online DSST Practice Test can be purchased by visiting www.getcollegecredit.com and clicking on DSST Practice Exams.

TAKING DSST EXAMINATIONS

Earning College Credit for DSST Examinations

To find out if the college of your choice awards credit for passing DSST scores, contact the admissions office or counseling and testing office. The college can also provide information on the scores required for awarding credit, the number of credit hours awarded, and any courses that can be bypassed with satisfactory scores.

It is important that you contact the institution of your choice as early as possible since credit-awarding policies differ among colleges and universities.

Where to Take DSSTs

DSSTs are administered at colleges and universities nationwide. Each location determines the frequency and scheduling of test administrations. To obtain the most current list of participating DSST colleges and universities:
- Visit and download the information from www.getcollegecredit.com
- E-mail pnj-dsst@thomson.com

Scheduling Your Examination

Please be aware that some colleges and universities provide DSST testing services to enrolled students only. After you have selected a college or university that administers DSSTs, you will need to contact them to schedule your test date.

The fee to take a DSST is $60 per test. This fee entitles you to two score reports after the test is scored. One will be sent directly to you and the other will be sent to the college or university that you designate on your answer sheet. You may pay the test fee with a certified check or U.S. money order made payable to Thomson Prometric or you may charge the test fee to your Visa, MasterCard or American Express credit card. Note: The credit card statement will reflect a charge from Thomson Prometric for all DSST examinations. *(Declined credit card charges will be assessed an additional $25 processing fee.)*

In addition, the test site may also require a test administration fee for each examination, to be paid directly to the institution. Contact the test site to determine its administration fee and payment policy.

Other Testing Arrangements

If you are unable to find a participating DSST college or university in your area, you may want to contact the testing office of a local accredited college or university to determine whether a representative from that office will agree to administer the test(s) for you.

The school's representative should then contact the DSST Program at 866-794-3497 to arrange for this administration. If you are unable to locate a test site, contact Thomson Prometric for assistance at pnj-dsst@thomson.com or 866-794-3497.

Testing Accommodations for Students with Disabilities

Thomson Prometric is committed to serving test takers with disabilities by providing services and reasonable testing accommodations as set forth in the provisions of the *Americans with Disabilities Act* (ADA). If you have a disability, as prescribed by the ADA, and require special testing services or arrangements, please contact the test administrator at the test site. You will be asked to submit to the test administrator documentation of your disability and your request for special accommodations. The test administrator will then forward your documentation along with your request for testing accommodations to Thomson Prometric for approval.

Please submit your request as far in advance of your test date as possible so that the necessary accommodations can be made. Only test takers with documented disabilities are eligible for special accommodations.

On the Day of the Examination

It is important to review this information and to have the correct identification present on the day of the examination:
- Arrive on time as a courtesy to the test administrator.
- Bring a valid form of government-issued identification that includes a current photo and your signature (acceptable documents include a driver's license, passport, state-issued identification card or military identification). *Anyone who fails to present valid identification will not be allowed to test.*
- Bring several No. 2 (soft-lead) sharpened pencils with good erasers, a watch, and a black pen if you will be writing an essay.
- Do not bring books or papers.
- Do not bring an alarm watch that beeps, a telephone, or a phone beeper into the testing room.
- The use of nonprogrammable calculators, slide rules, scratch paper and/or other materials is permitted for some of the tests.

DSST SCORING POLICIES

Your DSST examination scores are reported only to you, unless you request that they be sent elsewhere. If you want your scores sent to your college, you must provide the correct DSST code number of the school on your answer sheet at the time you take the test. See the *DSST Directory of Colleges and Universities* on the Web site www.getcollegecredit.com.

If your institution is not listed, contact Thomson Prometric at 866-794-3497 to establish a code number. (Some schools may require a student to be enrolled prior to receiving a score report.)

Receiving Your Score Report

Allow approximately four weeks after testing to receive your score report.

Calling DSST Customer Service before the required four-week score processing time has elapsed will not expedite the processing of your scores. Due to privacy and security requirements, scores will not be reported to students over the telephone under any circumstance.

Scoring of Principles of Public Speaking Speeches

The speech portion of the *Principles of Public Speaking* examination will be sent to speech raters who are faculty members at accredited colleges that currently teach or have previously taught the course. Scores for the *Principles of Public Speaking* examination are available six to eight weeks from receipt by Thomson Prometric. If you take the *Principles of Public Speaking* examination and fail (either the objective, speech portion, or both), you must follow the retesting policy waiting period of six months (180 days) before retaking the entire exam.

Essays

The essays for *Ethics in America* and *Technical Writing* are optional and thus are not scored by raters. The essays are forwarded to the college or university that you designate, along with your score report, for their use in determining the award of credit. Before taking the *Ethics in America* or *Technical Writing* examinations, check with your college or university to determine whether the essay is required.

NOTE: *Principles of Public Speaking* speech topic cassette tapes and essays are kept on file at Thomson Prometric for one year from the date of administration.

How to Get Transcripts

There is a $20 fee for each transcript you request. Payment must be in the form of a certified check, U.S. money order payable to Thomson Prometric, or credit card. Personal checks and debit cards are NOT an acceptable method of payment. One transcript may include scores for one or more examinations taken. To request a transcript, download the Transcript Order Form from www.getcollegecredit.com.

DESCRIPTION OF THE DSST EXAMINATIONS

Mathematics

• **Fundamentals of College Algebra** covers mathematical concepts such as fundamental algebraic operations; linear, absolute value; quadratic equations, inequalities, radials, exponents and logarithms, factoring polynomials and graphing. The use of a nonprogrammable, handheld calculator is permitted.

• **Principles of Statistics** tests the understanding of the various topics of statistics, both qualitatively and quantitatively, and the ability to apply statistical methods to solve a variety of problems. The topics included in this test are descriptive statistics; correlation and regression; probability; chance models and sampling and tests of significance. The use of a nonprogrammable, handheld calculator is permitted.

Social Science

• **Art of the Western World** deals with the history of art during the following periods: classical; Romanesque and Gothic; early Renaissance; high Renaissance, Baroque; rococo; neoclassicism and romanticism; realism, impressionism and post-impressionism; early twentieth century; and post-World War II.

• **Western Europe Since 1945** tests the knowledge of basic facts and terms and the understanding of concepts and principles related to the areas of the historical background of the aftermath of the Second World War and rebuilding of Europe; national political systems; issues and policies in Western European societies; European institutions and processes; and Europe's relations with the rest of the world.

• **An Introduction to the Modern Middle East** emphasizes core knowledge (including geography, Judaism, Christianity, Islam, ethnicity); nineteenth-century European impact; twentieth-century Western influences; World Wars I and II; new nations; social and cultural changes (1900-1960) and the Middle East from 1960 to present.

• **Human/Cultural Geography** includes the Earth and basic facts (coordinate systems, maps, physiography, atmosphere, soils and vegetation, water); culture and environment, spatial processes (social processes, modern economic systems, settlement patterns, political geography); and regional geography.

- **Rise and Fall of the Soviet Union** covers Russia under the Old Regime; the Revolutionary Period; New Economic Policy; Pre-war Stalinism; The Second World War; Post-war Stalinism; The Khrushchev Years; The Brezhnev Era; and reform and collapse.

- **A History of the Vietnam War** covers the history of the roots of the Vietnam War; the First Vietnam War (1946-1954); pre-war developments (1954-1963); American involvement in the Vietnam War; Tet (1968); Vietnamizing the War (1968-1973); Cambodia and Laos; peace; legacies and lessons.

- **The Civil War and Reconstruction** covers the Civil War from presecession (1861) through Reconstruction. It includes causes of the war; secession; Fort Sumter; the war in the east and in the west; major battles; the political situation; assassination of Lincoln; end of the Confederacy; and Reconstruction.

- **Foundations of Education** includes topics such as contemporary issues in education; past and current influences on education (philosophies, democratic ideals, social/economic influences); and the interrelationships between contemporary issues and influences.

- **Life-span Developmental Psychology** covers models and theories; methods of study; ethical issues; biological development; perception, learning and memory; cognition and language; social, emotional, and personality development; social behaviors, family life cycle, extrafamilial settings; singlehood and cohabitation; occupational development and retirement; adjustment to life stresses; and bereavement and loss.

- **Drug and Alcohol Abuse** includes such topics as drug use in society; classification of drugs; pharmacological principles; alcohol (types, effects of, alcoholism); general principles and use of sedative hypnotics, narcotic analgesics, stimulants, and hallucinogens; other drugs (inhalants, steroids); and prevention/treatment.

- **General Anthropology** deals with anthropology as a discipline; theoretical perspectives; physical anthropology; archaeology; social organization; economic organization; political organization; religion; and modernization and application of anthropology.

- **Introduction to Law Enforcement** includes topics such as history and professional movement of law enforcement; overview of the U.S. criminal justice system; police systems in the U.S.; police organization, management, and issues; and U.S. law and precedents.

- **Criminal Justice** deals with criminal behavior (crime in the U.S., theories of crime, types of crime); the criminal justice system (historical origins, legal foundations, due process); police; the court system (history and organization, adult court system, juvenile court, pre-trial and post-trial processes); and corrections.

- **Fundamentals of Counseling** covers historical development (significant influences and people); counselor roles and functions; the counseling relationship; and theoretical approaches to counseling.

Business
- **Principles of Finance** deals with financial statements and planning; time value of money; working capital management; valuation and characteristics; capital budgeting; cost of capital; risk and return; and international financial management. The use of a nonprogrammable, handheld calculator is permitted.

- **Principles of Financial Accounting** includes topics such as general concepts and principles, accounting cycle and classification; transaction analysis; accruals and deferrals; cash and internal control; current accounts; long- and short-term liabilities; capital stock; and financial statements. The use of a nonprogrammable, handheld calculator is permitted.

- **Human Resource Management** covers general employment issues; job analysis; training and development; performance appraisals; compensation issues; security issues; personnel legislation and regulation; labor relations and current issues; an overview of the Human Resource Management Field; Human Resource Planning; Staffing; training and development; compensation issues; safety and health; employee rights and discipline; employment law; labor relations and current issues and trends.

- **Organizational Behavior** deals with the study of organizational behavior (scientific approaches, research designs, data collection methods); individual processes and characteristics; interpersonal and group processes and characteristics; organizational processes and characteristics; and change and development processes.

- **Principles of Supervision** deals with the roles and responsibilities of the supervisor; management functions (planning, organization and staffing, directing at the supervisory level); and other topics (legal issues, stress management, union environments, quality concerns).

- **Business Law II** covers topics such as sales of goods; debtor and creditor relations; business organizations; property; and commercial paper.

- **Introduction to Computing** includes topics such as history and technological generations; hardware/software; applications to information technology; program development; data management; communications and connectivity; and computing and society. The use of a nonprogrammable, handheld calculator is permitted.

- **Management Information Systems** covers systems theory, analysis and design of systems, hardware and software; database management; telecommunications; management of the MIS functional area and informational support.

- **Introduction to Business** deals with economic issues affecting business; international business; government and business; forms of business ownership; small business, entrepreneurship and franchise; management process; human resource management; production and operations; marketing management; financial management; risk management and insurance; and management and information systems.

- **Money and Banking** covers the role and kinds of money; commercial banks and other financial intermediaries; central banking and the Federal Reserve system; money and macroeconomics activity; monetary policy in the U.S.; and the international monetary system.

- **Personal Finance** includes topics such as financial goals and values; budgeting; credit and debt; major purchases; taxes; insurance; investments; and retirement and estate planning. The use of auxiliary materials, such as calculators and slide rules, is NOT permitted.

- **Business Mathematics** deals with basic operations with integers, fractions, and decimals; round numbers; ratios; averages; business graphs; simple interest; compound interest and annuities; net pay and deductions; discounts and markups; depreciation and net worth; corporate securities; distribution of ownership; and stock and asset turnover.

Physical Science
• **Astronomy** covers the history of astronomy, celestial mechanics; celestial systems; astronomical instruments; the solar system; nature and evolution; the galaxy; the universe; determining astronomical distances; and life in the universe.

• **Here's to Your Health** covers mental health and behavior; human development and relationships; substance abuse; fitness and nutrition; risk factors, disease, and disease prevention; and safety, consumer awareness, and environmental concerns.

• **Environment and Humanity** deals with topics such as ecological concepts (ecosystems, global ecology, food chains and webs); environmental impacts; environmental management and conservation; and political processes and the future.

• **Principles of Physical Science I** includes physics: Newton's Laws of Motion; energy and momentum; thermodynamics; wave and optics; electricity and magnetism; chemistry: properties of matter; atomic theory and structure; and chemical reactions.

• **Physical Geology** covers Earth materials; igneous, sedimentary, and metamorphic rocks; surface processes (weathering, groundwater, glaciers, oceanic systems, deserts and winds, hydrologic cycle); internal Earth processes; and applications (mineral and energy resources, environmental geology).

Applied Technology
• **Technical Writing** covers topics such as theory and practice of technical writing; purpose, content, and organizational patterns of common types of technical documents; elements of various technical reports; and technical editing. Students have the option to write a short essay on one of the technical topics provided. Thomson Prometric will not score the essay; however, for determining the award of credit, a copy of the essay will be forwarded to the college or university you've designated along with the score report or transcript.

Humanities
• **Ethics in America** deals with ethical traditions (Greek views, Biblical traditions, moral law, consequential ethics, feminist ethics); ethical analysis of issues arising in interpersonal and personal-societal relationships and in professional and occupational roles; and relationships between ethical traditions and the ethical analysis of situations. Students have the option to write an essay to analyze a morally problematic situation in terms of issues relevant to a decision and arguments for alternative positions. Thomson Prometric will not score the essay; however, for determining the award of credit, a copy of the essay will be forwarded to the college or university you've designated along with the score report or transcript.

• **Introduction to World Religions** covers topics such as dimensions and approaches to religion; primal religions; Hinduism; Buddhism; Confucianism; Taoism; Judaism; Christianity; and Islam.

• **Principles of Public Speaking** consists of two parts: Part One consists of multiple-choice questions covering considerations of Principles of Public Speaking; audience analysis; purposes of speeches; structure/organization; content/supporting materials; research; language and style; delivery; communication apprehension; listening and feedback; and criticism and evaluation. Part Two requires the student to record an impromptu persuasive speech that will be scored.

FREQUENTLY ASKED QUESTIONS ABOUT DSSTs

In order to pass the test, must I study from one of the recommended references?

The recommended references are a listing of books that were being used as textbooks in college courses of the same or similar title at the time the test was developed. Appropriate textbooks for study are not limited to those listed in the fact sheet. If you wish to obtain study resources to prepare for the examination, you may reference either the current edition of the listed titles or textbooks currently used at a local college or university for the same class title. It is recommended that you reference more than one textbook on the topics outlined in the fact sheet. You should begin by checking textbook content against the content outline included on the front page of the DSST fact sheet before selecting textbooks that cover the text content from which to study. Textbooks may be found at the campus bookstore of a local college or university offering a course on the subject.

Is there a penalty for guessing on the tests?

There is no penalty for guessing on DSSTs, so you should mark an answer for each question.

How much time will I have to complete the test?

Many DSSTs can be completed within 90 minutes; however, additional time can be allowed if necessary.

What should I do if I find a test question irregularity?

Continue testing and then report the irregularity to the test administrator after the test. This may be done by asking that the test administrator note the irregularity on the Supervisor's Irregularity Report or you can write to Thomson Prometric, DSST Program, 2000 Lenox Drive, Third Floor, Lawrenceville, NJ 08648, and indicate the form and question number(s) or circumstances as well as your name and address.

When will I receive my score report?

Allow approximately four weeks from the date of testing to receive your score report. Allow six to eight weeks to receive a score report for the *Principles of Public Speaking* examination.

Will my test scores be released without my permission?

Your test score will not be released to anyone other than the school you designate on your answer sheet unless you write to us and ask us to send a transcript elsewhere. Instructions about how to do this can be found on your score report. Your scores may be used for research purposes, but individual scores are never made public nor are individuals identified if research findings are made public.

If I do not achieve a passing score on the test, how long must I wait until I can take the test again?

If you do not receive a score on the test that will enable you to obtain credit for the course, you may take the test again after six months (180 days). Please do not attempt to take the test before six months (180 days) have passed because you will receive a score report marked *invalid* and your test fee will not be refunded.

Can my test scores be canceled?

The test administrator is required to report any irregularities to Thomson Prometric. <u>The consequence of bringing unauthorized materials into the testing room, or giving or receiving help, will be the forfeiture of your test fee and the invalidation of test scores.</u> The DSST Program reserves the right to cancel scores and not issue score reports in such situations.

What can I do if I feel that my test scores were not accurately reported?

Thomson Prometric recognizes the extreme importance of test results to candidates and has a multi-step quality-control procedure to help ensure that reported scores are accurate. If you have reason to believe that your score(s) were not accurately reported, you may request to have your answer sheet reviewed and hand scored.

The fees for this service are:
- $20 fee if requested within six months of the test date
- $30 fee if requested more than six months from the test date
- $30 fee if a re-evaluation of the *Principles of Public Speaking* speech is requested

The fee for this service can be paid by credit card or by certified check or U.S. money order payable to Thomson Prometric. Submit your request for score verification along with the appropriate fee or credit card information (credit card number and expiration date) to Thomson Prometric, DSST Program, 2000 Lenox Drive, Third Floor, Lawrenceville, NJ 08648. Include your full name, the test title, the date you took the test, and your Social Security number. Candidates will be notified if a scoring discrepancy is discovered within four weeks of receipt of the request.

What does ACE recommendation mean?

The ACE recommendation is the minimum passing score recommended by the American Council on Education for any given test. It is equivalent to the average score of students in the DSST norming sample who received a grade of C for the course. Some schools require a score higher than the ACE recommendation.

Who is NLC?

National Learning Corporation (NLC) has been successfully preparing candidates for 40 years for over 5,000 exams. NLC publishes Passbook® study guides to help candidates prepare for all DANTES and CLEP exams and almost every other type of exam from high school through adult career.

Go to our website — www.passbooks.com — or call (800) 632-8888 for information about ordering our Passbooks.

To get detailed information on the DSST program and DSST preparation materials, visit www.getcollegecredit.com.

If you are interested in taking the DSST exams, call 877-471-9860 or e-mail pnj-dsst@thomson.com.

DANTES Subject Standardized Tests

Fact Sheet

PRINCIPLES OF STATISTICS

TEST INFORMATION

This test was developed to enable schools to award credit to students for knowledge equivalent to that which is learned by students taking the course. The school may choose to award college credit to the student based on the achievement of a passing score. The passing score for each examination is determined by the school based on recommendations from the American Council on Education (ACE). This minimum credit-awarding score is equal to the mean score of students in the norming sample who received a grade of C in the course. Some schools set their own standards for awarding credit and may require a higher score than the ACE recommendation. Students should obtain this information from the institution where they expect to receive credit.

CONTENT

The test will cover all of the material that is usually taught in an introductory statistics course. The mathematical prerequisite for the test is high school algebra. Of particular importance are such topics as the algebraic and geometric aspects of linear equations, interpretations of certain curves and areas bounded by them, and simple inequalities. The questions in the examination will test the students' understanding of the various topics of statistics, both qualitatively and quantitatively, and the ability to apply statistical methods to solve a variety of problems of a statistical nature.

The following topics commonly taught in courses on this subject are covered by this examination:

	Approximate Percent
1. Descriptive Statistics	**20-30%**

   Histograms, averages, standard deviation, normal approximation for data, standard units, areas under the normal curve, quartiles, and percentiles

2. Correlation and Regression	**15-20%**

   Scatter diagrams, correlation coefficient, estimation and the line of best fit

3. Probability	**20-25%**

   Basic concepts, dependent and independent events, compatible and incompatible events, binomial formula, combinations and permutations

4. Chance Models and Sampling	**15-20%**

   The law of averages, expected values, standard error, normal approximation, confidence intervals, sample size, sample average and estimating accuracy of sample average

5. Tests of Significance	**15-20%**

   Null hypothesis, significance levels, comparing two samples, t-test and x2 test

NOTE: A number of test questions could be cross listed, that is, fall into several categories.

from the official announcement for instructional purposes

SAMPLE QUESTIONS

Certain words, concepts, and symbols on this test are defined as follows:

$$\text{average} = \text{arithmetic mean}$$
$$\text{correlation} = \text{linear correlation}$$
$$\text{SD} = \text{standard deviation}$$
$$\text{Rms} = \text{root-mean-square} = \sqrt{\frac{\sum x^2}{n}}$$

area of a rectangle with adjacent edges a and b = $a.b$
area of a triangle with base b and corresponding altitude h = $\frac{1}{2}b.h$

---

1. A 100 question multiple-choice test has 4 choices for each question. If a student selects all choices randomly, how many correct answers could the student expect?

   (A) 4
   (B) 8
   (C) 25
   (D) 40

2. Each of the following statements is true for all probability curves for random variable x EXCEPT:

   (A) The area under the curve is 1.
   (B) The highest point on the curve occurs at the average.
   (C) The curve does not cross the x-axis.
   (D) The probability that x is between a and b is equal to the area of the region bounded by the curve, the x-axis, and the lines $x = a$ and $x = b$.

3. Which of the following could NOT be the value of a correlation coefficient?

   (A) -1
   (B) 0
   (C) 1
   (D) 2

4. The average and SD of a set of 50 scores are 30 and 7, respectively. If each of these scores is increased by 10, then which of the following is true for the new set of scores?

   (A) The average is 60.
   (B) The average is 40.
   (C) The SD is 17.
   (D) The SD is 7.2.

5. A bag contains 15 marbles, of which 8 are red, 5 are blue, and 2 are white. Two marbles are drawn randomly from the bag one after the other, without replacement. What is the probability that both marbles are red?

   (A) 4/15
   (B) 64/225
   (C) 32/105
   (D) 8/15

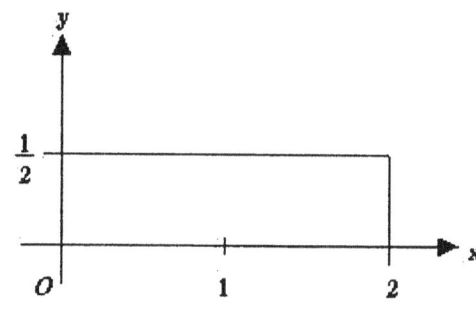

6. If the figure above is a probability histogram, what is the probability that $x \geq 1/2$?

   (A) 1/4
   (B) 1/2
   (C) 5/8
   (D) 3/4

7. Which of the following pairs of parameters is sufficient to define a specific normal curve?

   (A) The average and the standard deviation
   (B) The range and the standard deviation
   (C) The average and the Chi-Square (x^2)-value
   (D) The standard deviation and the Chi-Square (x^2)-value

8. A random sample of 100 values of x is taken from a distribution whose SD is k. What will be the approximate value of the standard error of the average of x?

   (A) $0.01k$
   (B) $0.1k$
   (C) $0.5k$
   (D) k

9. If H_0 is the null hypothesis and P is the observed (computed) significance level, then

   (A) "small" values of P are evidence for H_0
   (B) "small" values of P are evidence against H_0
   (C) "small" values of P give no information for or against H_0
   (D) a rejected H_0 " corresponds to a negative value of P"

10. A balanced die is rolled 4 times. What is the probability that a six will NOT appear on any roll?

    (A) $(5/6)^4$
    (B) $6(5/6)^4$
    (C) $5/6$
    (D) $1-(1/6)^4$

STUDYING FOR THE EXAMINATION

The following is a list of reference publications that were being used as textbooks in college courses of the same or similar title at the time the test was developed. Appropriate textbooks for study are not limited to those listed below. If you wish to obtain study resources to prepare for the examination, you may reference either the current edition of the following titles **or** textbooks currently used at a local college or university for the same class title. It is recommended that you reference **more than one textbook** on the topics outlined in this fact sheet. You should **begin by checking textbook content against the content outline** included on the front page of this Fact Sheet **before** selecting textbooks that cover the test content from which to study. Textbooks may be found at the campus bookstore of a local college or university offering a course on the subject.

Sources for study material suggested but not limited to the following:

Freedman, David, Pisani, Robert and Purves, Roger. *Statistics*. Nortan and Company, current edition.

McCabe, George P. and Moore, David S. *Introduction to the Practice of Satistics*. W.H. Freeman, current edition.

Moore, David S. *Against All Odds Study Guide*. W.H. Freeman, current edition.

Adler, Henry L. and Roessler, Edward R. *Introduction to Probability and Statistics*. W.H. Freeman, current edition.

Bain and Englehardt. *Introduction to Probability and Mathematical Statistics*. Duxbury Press, PWS Kent Publishers, current edition.

Berensen, Mark L. and Levine, David M. *Basic Business Statistics: Concepts and Applications*. Prentice-Hall, current edition.

Hoel, Paul G. *Elementary Statistics*. Wiley, current edition.

Mendenhall, William. *Introduction to Probability and Statistics*. Duxbery Press, PWS Kent Publishers, current edition.

Mendenhall, William and Sinchich, Terry. *Statistics for Engineering and Computer Science*. Dellere Publishers, current edition.

Neter, John, Wasserman, William and Whitmore, G.A. *Applied Statistics*. Allyn, Bacon, current edition.

Smith, G. *Statistical Reasoning*. Allyn, Bacon, current edition.

Strait, Peggy T. *A First Course in Probability and Statistics with Applications*. Harcourt, current edition.

Current textbook used by a local college or university for a course on the subject.

CREDIT RECOMMENDATIONS

The Center for Adult Learning and Educational Credentials for the American Council on Education (ACE) has reviewed and evaluated the DSST examination development process. The American Council on Education has made the following recommendations:

Area or Course
  Equivalent: Principles of Statistics
Level: Lower level baccalaureate
Amount of Credit: Three (3) semester hours
Source: ACE Commission on Educational Credit and Credentials

Colleges and universities that would like additional information about the national norming, or assistance in local norming or score validation studies should write to: DSST Program, Mail Stop 11-P, The Chauncey Group International, 664 Rosedale Road, Princeton, New Jersey 08540.

It is advisable that schools develop a consistent policy about awarding credit based on scores from this test and that the policy be reviewed periodically. The Chauncey Group will be happy to help schools in this effort.

Correct Responses to sample questions: 1.C; 2.B; 3.D; 4.B; 5.A; 6.D; 7.A; 8.B; 9.B; 10.A

I.N. D204313

HOW TO TAKE A TEST

You have studied long, hard and conscientiously.

With your official admission card in hand, and your heart pounding, you have been admitted to the examination room.

You note that there are several hundred other applicants in the examination room waiting to take the same test.

They all appear to be equally well prepared.

You know that nothing but your best effort will suffice. The "moment of truth" is at hand: you now have to demonstrate objectively, in writing, your knowledge of content and your understanding of subject matter.

You are fighting the most important battle of your life—to pass and/or score high on an examination which will determine your career and provide the economic basis for your livelihood.

What extra, special things should you know and should you do in taking the examination?

I. YOU MUST PASS AN EXAMINATION

A. WHAT EVERY CANDIDATE SHOULD KNOW
Examination applicants often ask us for help in preparing for the written test. What can I study in advance? What kinds of questions will be asked? How will the test be given? How will the papers be graded?

B. HOW ARE EXAMS DEVELOPED?
Examinations are carefully written by trained technicians who are specialists in the field known as "psychological measurement," in consultation with recognized authorities in the field of work that the test will cover. These experts recommend the subject matter areas or skills to be tested; only those knowledges or skills important to your success on the job are included. The most reliable books and source materials available are used as references. Together, the experts and technicians judge the difficulty level of the questions.
Test technicians know how to phrase questions so that the problem is clearly stated. Their ethics do not permit "trick" or "catch" questions. Questions may have been tried out on sample groups, or subjected to statistical analysis, to determine their usefulness.
Written tests are often used in combination with performance tests, ratings of training and experience, and oral interviews. All of these measures combine to form the best-known means of finding the right person for the right job.

II. HOW TO PASS THE WRITTEN TEST

A. BASIC STEPS

1) Study the announcement

How, then, can you know what subjects to study? Our best answer is: "Learn as much as possible about the class of positions for which you've applied." The exam will test the knowledge, skills and abilities needed to do the work.

Your most valuable source of information about the position you want is the official exam announcement. This announcement lists the training and experience qualifications. Check these standards and apply only if you come reasonably close to meeting them. Many jurisdictions preview the written test in the exam announcement by including a section called "Knowledge and Abilities Required," "Scope of the Examination," or some similar heading. Here you will find out specifically what fields will be tested.

2) Choose appropriate study materials

If the position for which you are applying is technical or advanced, you will read more advanced, specialized material. If you are already familiar with the basic principles of your field, elementary textbooks would waste your time. Concentrate on advanced textbooks and technical periodicals. Think through the concepts and review difficult problems in your field.

These are all general sources. You can get more ideas on your own initiative, following these leads. For example, training manuals and publications of the government agency which employs workers in your field can be useful, particularly for technical and professional positions. A letter or visit to the government department involved may result in more specific study suggestions, and certainly will provide you with a more definite idea of the exact nature of the position you are seeking.

3) Study this book!

III. KINDS OF TESTS

Tests are used for purposes other than measuring knowledge and ability to perform specified duties. For some positions, it is equally important to test ability to make adjustments to new situations or to profit from training. In others, basic mental abilities not dependent on information are essential. Questions which test these things may not appear as pertinent to the duties of the position as those which test for knowledge and information. Yet they are often highly important parts of a fair examination. For very general questions, it is almost impossible to help you direct your study efforts. What we can do is to point out some of the more common of these general abilities needed in public service positions and describe some typical questions.

1) General information

Broad, general information has been found useful for predicting job success in some kinds of work. This is tested in a variety of ways, from vocabulary lists to questions about current events. Basic background in some field of work, such as sociology or economics, may be sampled in a group of questions. Often these are principles which have become familiar to most persons through exposure rather than through formal training. It is difficult to advise you how to study for these questions; being alert to the world around you is our best suggestion.

2) Verbal ability

An example of an ability needed in many positions is verbal or language ability. Verbal ability is, in brief, the ability to use and understand words. Vocabulary and grammar tests are typical measures of this ability. Reading comprehension or paragraph interpretation questions are common in many kinds of civil service tests. You are given a paragraph of written material and asked to find its central meaning.

IV. KINDS OF QUESTIONS

1. Multiple-choice Questions

Most popular of the short-answer questions is the "multiple choice" or "best answer" question. It can be used, for example, to test for factual knowledge, ability to solve problems or judgment in meeting situations found at work.

A multiple-choice question is normally one of three types:
- It can begin with an incomplete statement followed by several possible endings. You are to find the one ending which best completes the statement, although some of the others may not be entirely wrong.
- It can also be a complete statement in the form of a question which is answered by choosing one of the statements listed.
- It can be in the form of a problem – again you select the best answer.

Here is an example of a multiple-choice question with a discussion which should give you some clues as to the method for choosing the right answer:

When an employee has a complaint about his assignment, the action which will best help him overcome his difficulty is to
- A. discuss his difficulty with his coworkers
- B. take the problem to the head of the organization
- C. take the problem to the person who gave him the assignment
- D. say nothing to anyone about his complaint

In answering this question, you should study each of the choices to find which is best. Consider choice "A" – Certainly an employee may discuss his complaint with fellow employees, but no change or improvement can result, and the complaint remains unresolved. Choice "B" is a poor choice since the head of the organization probably does not know what assignment you have been given, and taking your problem to him is known as "going over the head" of the supervisor. The supervisor, or person who made the assignment, is the person who can clarify it or correct any injustice. Choice "C" is, therefore, correct. To say nothing, as in choice "D," is unwise. Supervisors have and interest in knowing the problems employees are facing, and the employee is seeking a solution to his problem.

2. True/False

3. Matching Questions

Matching an answer from a column of choices within another column.

V. RECORDING YOUR ANSWERS

Computer terminals are used more and more today for many different kinds of exams.

For an examination with very few applicants, you may be told to record your answers in the test booklet itself. Separate answer sheets are much more common. If this separate answer sheet is to be scored by machine – and this is often the case – it is highly important that you mark your answers correctly in order to get credit.

VI. BEFORE THE TEST

YOUR PHYSICAL CONDITION IS IMPORTANT

If you are not well, you can't do your best work on tests. If you are half asleep, you can't do your best either. Here are some tips:

1) Get about the same amount of sleep you usually get. Don't stay up all night before the test, either partying or worrying—DON'T DO IT!
2) If you wear glasses, be sure to wear them when you go to take the test. This goes for hearing aids, too.
3) If you have any physical problems that may keep you from doing your best, be sure to tell the person giving the test. If you are sick or in poor health, you relay cannot do your best on any test. You can always come back and take the test some other time.

Common sense will help you find procedures to follow to get ready for an examination. Too many of us, however, overlook these sensible measures. Indeed, nervousness and fatigue have been found to be the most serious reasons why applicants fail to do their best on civil service tests. Here is a list of reminders:

- Begin your preparation early – Don't wait until the last minute to go scurrying around for books and materials or to find out what the position is all about.
- Prepare continuously – An hour a night for a week is better than an all-night cram session. This has been definitely established. What is more, a night a week for a month will return better dividends than crowding your study into a shorter period of time.
- Locate the place of the exam – You have been sent a notice telling you when and where to report for the examination. If the location is in a different town or otherwise unfamiliar to you, it would be well to inquire the best route and learn something about the building.
- Relax the night before the test – Allow your mind to rest. Do not study at all that night. Plan some mild recreation or diversion; then go to bed early and get a good night's sleep.
- Get up early enough to make a leisurely trip to the place for the test – This way unforeseen events, traffic snarls, unfamiliar buildings, etc. will not upset you.
- Dress comfortably – A written test is not a fashion show. You will be known by number and not by name, so wear something comfortable.
- Leave excess paraphernalia at home – Shopping bags and odd bundles will get in your way. You need bring only the items mentioned in the official notice you received; usually everything you need is provided. Do not bring reference books to the exam. They will only confuse those last minutes and be taken away from you when in the test room.

- Arrive somewhat ahead of time – If because of transportation schedules you must get there very early, bring a newspaper or magazine to take your mind off yourself while waiting.
- Locate the examination room – When you have found the proper room, you will be directed to the seat or part of the room where you will sit. Sometimes you are given a sheet of instructions to read while you are waiting. Do not fill out any forms until you are told to do so; just read them and be prepared.
- Relax and prepare to listen to the instructions
- If you have any physical problem that may keep you from doing your best, be sure to tell the test administrator. If you are sick or in poor health, you really cannot do your best on the exam. You can come back and take the test some other time.

VII. AT THE TEST

The day of the test is here and you have the test booklet in your hand. The temptation to get going is very strong. Caution! There is more to success than knowing the right answers. You must know how to identify your papers and understand variations in the type of short-answer question used in this particular examination. Follow these suggestions for maximum results from your efforts:

1) Cooperate with the monitor

The test administrator has a duty to create a situation in which you can be as much at ease as possible. He will give instructions, tell you when to begin, check to see that you are marking your answer sheet correctly, and so on. He is not there to guard you, although he will see that your competitors do not take unfair advantage. He wants to help you do your best.

2) Listen to all instructions

Don't jump the gun! Wait until you understand all directions. In most civil service tests you get more time than you need to answer the questions. So don't be in a hurry. Read each word of instructions until you clearly understand the meaning. Study the examples, listen to all announcements and follow directions. Ask questions if you do not understand what to do.

3) Identify your papers

Civil service exams are usually identified by number only. You will be assigned a number; you must not put your name on your test papers. Be sure to copy your number correctly. Since more than one exam may be given, copy your exact examination title.

4) Plan your time

Unless you are told that a test is a "speed" or "rate of work" test, speed itself is usually not important. Time enough to answer all the questions will be provided, but this does not mean that you have all day. An overall time limit has been set. Divide the total time (in minutes) by the number of questions to determine the approximate time you have for each question.

5) Do not linger over difficult questions

If you come across a difficult question, mark it with a paper clip (useful to have along) and come back to it when you have been through the booklet. One caution if you do this – be sure to skip a number on your answer sheet as well. Check often to be sure that you have not lost your place and that you are marking in the row numbered the same as the question you are answering.

6) Read the questions

Be sure you know what the question asks! Many capable people are unsuccessful because they failed to read the questions correctly.

7) Answer all questions

Unless you have been instructed that a penalty will be deducted for incorrect answers, it is better to guess than to omit a question.

8) Speed tests

It is often better NOT to guess on speed tests. It has been found that on timed tests people are tempted to spend the last few seconds before time is called in marking answers at random – without even reading them – in the hope of picking up a few extra points. To discourage this practice, the instructions may warn you that your score will be "corrected" for guessing. That is, a penalty will be applied. The incorrect answers will be deducted from the correct ones, or some other penalty formula will be used.

9) Review your answers

If you finish before time is called, go back to the questions you guessed or omitted to give them further thought. Review other answers if you have time.

10) Return your test materials

If you are ready to leave before others have finished or time is called, take ALL your materials to the monitor and leave quietly. Never take any test material with you. The monitor can discover whose papers are not complete, and taking a test booklet may be grounds for disqualification.

VIII. EXAMINATION TECHNIQUES

1) Read the general instructions carefully. These are usually printed on the first page of the exam booklet. As a rule, these instructions refer to the timing of the examination; the fact that you should not start work until the signal and must stop work at a signal, etc. If there are any special instructions, such as a choice of questions to be answered, make sure that you note this instruction carefully.

2) When you are ready to start work on the examination, that is as soon as the signal has been given, read the instructions to each question booklet, underline any key words or phrases, such as least, best, outline, describe and the like. In this way you will tend to answer as requested rather than discover on reviewing your paper that you listed without describing, that you selected the worst choice rather than the best choice, etc.

3) If the examination is of the objective or multiple-choice type – that is, each question will also give a series of possible answers: A, B, C or D, and you are called upon to select the best answer and write the letter next to that answer on your answer paper – it is advisable to start answering each question in turn. There may be anywhere from 50 to 100 such questions in the three or four hours allotted and you can see how much time would be taken if you read through all the questions before beginning to answer any. Furthermore, if you

come across a question or group of questions which you know would be difficult to answer, it would undoubtedly affect your handling of all the other questions.

4) If the examination is of the essay type and contains but a few questions, it is a moot point as to whether you should read all the questions before starting to answer any one. Of course, if you are given a choice – say five out of seven and the like – then it is essential to read all the questions so you can eliminate the two that are most difficult. If, however, you are asked to answer all the questions, there may be danger in trying to answer the easiest one first because you may find that you will spend too much time on it. The best technique is to answer the first question, then proceed to the second, etc.

5) Time your answers. Before the exam begins, write down the time it started, then add the time allowed for the examination and write down the time it must be completed, then divide the time available somewhat as follows:
    - If 3-1/2 hours are allowed, that would be 210 minutes. If you have 80 objective-type questions, that would be an average of 2-1/2 minutes per question. Allow yourself no more than 2 minutes per question, or a total of 160 minutes, which will permit about 50 minutes to review.
    - If for the time allotment of 210 minutes there are 7 essay questions to answer, that would average about 30 minutes a question. Give yourself only 25 minutes per question so that you have about 35 minutes to review.

6) The most important instruction is to read each question and make sure you know what is wanted. The second most important instruction is to time yourself properly so that you answer every question. The third most important instruction is to answer every question. Guess if you have to but include something for each question. Remember that you will receive no credit for a blank and will probably receive some credit if you write something in answer to an essay question. If you guess a letter – say "B" for a multiple-choice question – you may have guessed right. If you leave a blank as an answer to a multiple-choice question, the examiners may respect your feelings but it will not add a point to your score. Some exams may penalize you for wrong answers, so in such cases only, you may not want to guess unless you have some basis for your answer.

7) Suggestions
    a. Objective-type questions
        1. Examine the question booklet for proper sequence of pages and questions
        2. Read all instructions carefully
        3. Skip any question which seems too difficult; return to it after all other questions have been answered
        4. Apportion your time properly; do not spend too much time on any single question or group of questions
        5. Note and underline key words – all, most, fewest, least, best, worst, same, opposite, etc.
        6. Pay particular attention to negatives
        7. Note unusual option, e.g., unduly long, short, complex, different or similar in content to the body of the question
        8. Observe the use of "hedging" words – probably, may, most likely, etc.

9. Make sure that your answer is put next to the same number as the question
10. Do not second-guess unless you have good reason to believe the second answer is definitely more correct
11. Cross out original answer if you decide another answer is more accurate; do not erase until you are ready to hand your paper in
12. Answer all questions; guess unless instructed otherwise
13. Leave time for review

b. Essay questions
1. Read each question carefully
2. Determine exactly what is wanted. Underline key words or phrases.
3. Decide on outline or paragraph answer
4. Include many different points and elements unless asked to develop any one or two points or elements
5. Show impartiality by giving pros and cons unless directed to select one side only
6. Make and write down any assumptions you find necessary to answer the questions
7. Watch your English, grammar, punctuation and choice of words
8. Time your answers; don't crowd material

8) Answering the essay question

Most essay questions can be answered by framing the specific response around several key words or ideas. Here are a few such key words or ideas:

M's: manpower, materials, methods, money, management
P's: purpose, program, policy, plan, procedure, practice, problems, pitfalls, personnel, public relations

a. Six basic steps in handling problems:
1. Preliminary plan and background development
2. Collect information, data and facts
3. Analyze and interpret information, data and facts
4. Analyze and develop solutions as well as make recommendations
5. Prepare report and sell recommendations
6. Install recommendations and follow up effectiveness

b. Pitfalls to avoid
1. Taking things for granted – A statement of the situation does not necessarily imply that each of the elements is necessarily true; for example, a complaint may be invalid and biased so that all that can be taken for granted is that a complaint has been registered
2. Considering only one side of a situation – Wherever possible, indicate several alternatives and then point out the reasons you selected the best one
3. Failing to indicate follow up – Whenever your answer indicates action on your part, make certain that you will take proper follow-up action to see how successful your recommendations, procedures or actions turn out to be
4. Taking too long in answering any single question – Remember to time your answers properly

EXAMINATION SECTION

EXAMINATION SECTION
TEST 1

DIRECTIONS: Each question or incomplete statement is followed by several suggested answers or completions. Select the one that BEST answers the question or completes the statement.

Questions 1-2.

DIRECTIONS: Questions 1 and 2 are based on Table I, which appears immediately below.

Table I

x	u_x	Δ	Δ^2	Δ^3	Δ^4
0	1				
		2			
1	3		4		
		6		-3	
2	9		1		-2
		7		-5	
3	16		-4		
		3			
4	19				

Assume fourth differences are constant.

1. Using Table I, determine the numerical value of $\mu\delta^3 u_1$.
   - A. -8
   - B. -6
   - C. -5
   - D. -4
   - E. -2
   - F. 0
   - G. 7
   - H. Cannot be determined from data given.

2. Using Table I, determine the numerical value of

   $(1-\frac{\Delta}{E})^{-1}_{u_3}$
   - A. 4
   - B. 6
   - C. 8
   - D. 9
   - E. 16
   - F. 19
   - G. 21
   - H. 23

3. Evaluate $\sum_{x=0}^{9} (x+3)(x+4)(x+5)$.

   x = 0
   A. 1360
   B. 5976
   C. 8100
   D. 8160
   E. 8190
   F. 10,830
   G. 32,400
   H. 32,640

4. Which one of the following polynomials has $12x^2 - 6x$ as its second ordinary advancing difference?
   A. $x^4 - 5x^3 + 8x^2 + 1$
   B. $x^4 - 5x^3 + 4x - 1$
   C. $x^4 - x^3 + x$
   D. x^4
   E. 24
   F. $x^4 + 7x^3 + 10x^2 + 2x$
   G. $4x^3 + 3x^2 + 2x - 3$
   H. None of the above

5. If $u_x = x^4 + 2x^3 + 3x^2 + 2x + 1$, then
   $$\Delta^3_{bcd} u_a - \Delta^3_{bce} u_a = (?)$$
   A. 0
   B. e-d
   C. d-e
   D. $\dfrac{d-e}{4}$
   E. $\dfrac{d-e}{4!} \Delta^4_{bcde} u_a$
   F. 4(a-6)
   G. d + e - 2a
   H. $(e-a) + (d-a) \Delta^3_{bce}(u_d - u_a)$

6. If $u_x = 1 + (x-a) + \dfrac{(x-a)(x-b)}{2}$
   $+ \dfrac{(x-a)(x-b)(x-c)}{4} + \dfrac{(x-a)(x-b)(x-c)(x-d)}{8}$, then $\Delta^2_{bc} u_a = (?)$

A. $\frac{1}{8}$

B. $\frac{1}{4}$

C. $\frac{1}{2}$

D. 1

E. $\frac{2a^2}{(a-b)(a-c)(b-c)}$

F. $\frac{2(bc+ac+ab)}{(a-b)(a-c)(b-c)}$

G. $\frac{c-b+2}{2}$

H. $\frac{2(c-a)+c^2-(a+b)c+ab}{2(c-a)}$

7. If $\Delta^4 u_x = 0$ for all values of x, and $u_0 = 16$, $u_1 = 32$, $u_2 = 10$, $u_3 = 22$, and $u_4 = 140$, find $\int_0^4 u_x dx$.

   A. 196/3
   B. 80
   C. 382/3
   D. 392/3
   E. 158
   F. 220
   G. 658
   H. 5576/3

8. If x, y, z are uncorrelated statistical variables with standard deviations 5, 12, 9, respectively, and if $u = x + y$ and $v = y + z$, find the correlation coefficient r between u and v.

   A. 0
   B. 13/270
   C. 4/65
   D. 13/135
   E. 58/441
   F. 48/119
   G. 1/2
   H. 48/65

9. What is the probability of throwing exactly 9 heads exactly twice in 5 throws of 10 true coins?

   A. $\left(\dfrac{50!}{41!\,9!}\right)^2 \left(\dfrac{1}{2}\right)^{100}$

   B. $\dfrac{50!}{18!\,32!}\left(\dfrac{1}{2}\right)^{50}$

   C. $10\left(\dfrac{1}{11}\right)^2 \left(\dfrac{10}{11}\right)^3$

   D. $10\left(\dfrac{1}{2^9}\right)^2 \left(1-\dfrac{1}{2^9}\right)^3$

   E. $10\left(\dfrac{10}{2^{10}}\right)^2 \left(1-\dfrac{10}{2^{10}}\right)^3$

   F. $\dfrac{50!}{9!\,41!}\left(\dfrac{1}{2}\right)^{50}$

   G. $\dfrac{1}{2^9}$

   H. $10\left(\dfrac{10}{2^{10}}\right)^3 \left(1-\dfrac{10}{2^{10}}\right)^2$

10. Two samples of 100 cases each have variances 14 and 18, respectively. The square of the difference between the means of the two samples is 20. If the two samples are pooled to form a single sample of 200 cases, what is the variance of the pooled sample?
    A. 12
    B. 16
    C. 21
    D. 26
    E. 30
    F. 32
    G. 35
    H. 36

11. The means and standard deviations of scores obtained by administering tests T and R to a group of students are as follows:

	Mean	σ
Test T	75	18
Test R	40	6

    The correlation between tests T and R is 0.75. Student K made a score of 103 on test T but did not take test R. What is the best estimate which can be made of the score which student K would have obtained on Test R, if he had taken it?

A. 40
B. 47
C. 49
D. 55
E. 61
F. 63
G. 68
H. 103

12. M throws 3 coins and N rolls 2 dice. If this experiment is repeated 10 times, what is the probability that 3 heads and a pair of sixes appear simultaneously at least once?

    A. $\dfrac{1}{288}$

    B. $\dfrac{5}{144}$

    C. $1 - \left(\dfrac{143}{144}\right)^{10}$

    D. $1 - \left(\dfrac{245}{288}\right)^{10}$

    E. $1 - \left(\dfrac{287}{288}\right)^{10}$

    F. $\dfrac{287}{288}$

    G. $\left(\dfrac{287}{288}\right)^{9}$

    H. $\sum\limits_{i=1}^{9} \left(\dfrac{287}{288}\right)^{i}$

13. Let the proportions of families in a given state having 0, 1, 2, 3, ... children be $p_0, p_1, p_2, p_3,$ ... ($\Sigma\, p_i = 1$). Estimate the proportion of all families having exactly j sons. (Assume that the probability of having sons or daughters is equal.)

    A. $\sum\limits_{i \geq j} \dfrac{\binom{i}{j}}{2^i} p_i$

    B. $\sum\limits_{i \geq j} \dfrac{1}{2^i} p_i$

    C. $\dfrac{1}{2} \sum\limits_{i \geq j} \binom{i}{j} p_i$

    D. $\sum\limits_{i \geq j} \dfrac{\binom{i}{j}}{2^j}$

E. $\sum_{i \geq j} \dfrac{\binom{i}{j}}{2^j} P_i$

F. $\sum_{i \geq j} \dfrac{\binom{i}{j}}{2^i}$

G. $\sum_{i \geq j} \dfrac{P_i}{2^j}$

H. $\sum_{i \geq j} \dfrac{1}{2^i}$

14. A lot contains n articles. If it is known that r of the articles are defective, and the articles are inspected in a random order, one at a time, what is the probability that the kth article inspected will be the last defective one in the lot?

A. $\binom{k}{r}\left(\dfrac{r}{n}\right)^r\left(\dfrac{n-r}{n}\right)^{k-r}$

B. $\dfrac{1}{\binom{n}{r}}$

C. $\dfrac{\binom{n-r}{n-k}\binom{k-1}{r-1}}{n!}$

D. $\dfrac{\binom{k-1}{r-1}}{\binom{n}{r}}$

E. $\dfrac{\binom{k}{r}}{\binom{n}{r}}$

F. $\dfrac{\binom{r}{r-1}\binom{n-r}{n-k}}{\binom{m}{k-1}}$

G. $\dfrac{\binom{r}{r-1}\binom{n-k}{n-r}}{\binom{n}{k-1}}$

H. $\dfrac{1}{n-k+1}$

15. Extensive tests show that 80% of a certain kind of grass seed germinates. If a sample of 900 seeds is taken from a sack of this grass seed, the probability is approximately .9773 that at least how many of the seeds will germinate?

    A. 684
    B. 696
    C. 700
    D. 704
    E. 708
    F. 720
    G. 744
    H. 880

KEY (CORRECT ANSWERS)

1. E
2. F
3. D
4. A
5. C

6. C
7. D
8. H
9. E
10. C

11. B
12. E
13. A
14. D
15. B

EXAMINATION SECTION
TEST 1

DIRECTIONS: Each question or incomplete statement is followed by several suggested answers or completions. Select the one that BEST answers the question or completes the statement.

The reference tables needed for solving the problems and notes concerning definitions and conventions used in the examination are set forth below on pages 1-5.

REFERENCE TABLES AND NOTES (Pages 1-5)

NOTE.- Throughout this examination, $Pr(E)$ is the probability that the event E occurs.

$\binom{n}{r}$ is the number of combinations of n objects taken r at a time.

ln x is the natural logarithm of x.

All problems involving cards refer to an ordinary deck of 52 playing cards consisting of 4 suits of 13 cards each. A bridge hand consists of 13 cards.

Unless otherwise specified, all problems involving dice refer to the ordinary six-sided die.

If A and B are sets, then $A \cup B$ (the union of A and B) is the set of all elements belonging either to A or to B; $A \cap B$ (the intersection of A and B) is the set of all elements belonging both to A and to B.

Normal Distribution

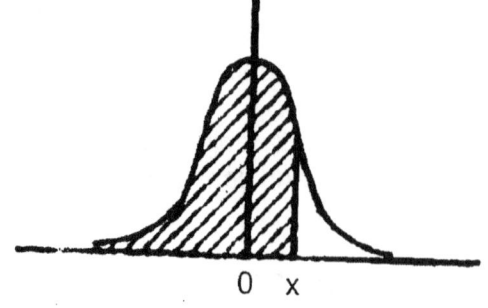

The tables below give the value of dt for certain values of

$$F(x) = \frac{1}{\sqrt{2p}} \int_{-\infty}^{x} e^{-t^{2/2}} \, dt$$ for certain values oe x.

x	.0	.1	.2	3	.4	.5	.6	.7	.8	.9
0	.5000	5398	.5793	.6179	.6554	6915	.7257	.7580	7881	.8159
1	.8413	8643	.88-19	9032	9192	9332	.9452	.9554	.9641	.9713
2	.9772	.9821	.9861	.9893	9918	.9938	.9953	.9965	.9974	.9981
3	.9987	9990	.9993	.9995	.9997					

x	1.282	1 440	1.645	1.960	2.326	2.576	3.090
F(x)	0.900	0.925	0.950	0.975	0.990	0.995	0.999

x^2 Distribution

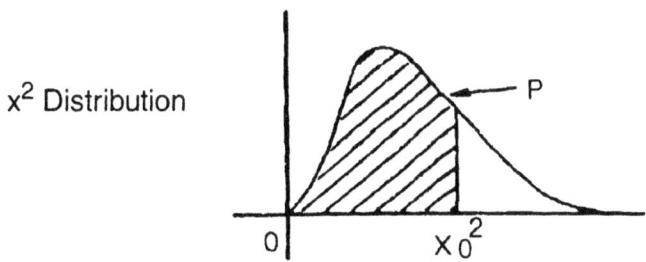

For a given number of degrees of freedom and a given value of P, the table below gives the value X_o^2 for which $Pr(x^2 < X_o^2) = P$

Degrees of freedom	Value of P							
	0.005	0.010	0.025	0.050	0.950	0.975	0.990	0.995
1	0.000	0.000	0.001	0.004	3.84	5.02	6.63	7.88
2	0.010	0.020	0.051	0.103	5.99	7.38	9.21	10.6
3	0.072	0.115	0.216	0.352	7.81	9.35	11.3	12.8
4	0.207	0.297	0.484	0.711	9.49	11.1	13.3	14.9
5	0.412	0.554	0.831	1.15	11.1	12.8	15.1	16.7
6	0.676	0.872	1.24	1.64	12.6	14.4	16.8	18.5
7	0.989	1.24	1.69	2.17	14.1	16.0	18.5	20.3
8	1.34	1.65	2.18	2.73	15.5	17.5	20.1	22.0
9	1.73	2.09	2.70	3.33	16.9	19.0	21.7	23.6
10	2.16	2.56	3.25	3.94	18.3	20.5	23.2	25.2
11	2.60	3.05	3.82	4.57	19.7	21.9	24.7	26.8
12	3.07	3.57	4.40	5.23	21.0	23.3	26.2	28.3
13	3.57	4.11	5.01	5.89	22.4	24.7	27.7	29.8
14	4.07	4.66	5.63	6.57	23.7	26.1	29.1	31.3
15	4.60	5.23	6.26	7.26	25.0	27.5	30.6	32.8
16	5.14	5.81	6.91	7.96	26.3	28.8	32.0	34.3
17	5.70	6.41	7.56	8.67	27.6	30.2	33.4	35.7
18	6.26	7.01	8.23	9.39	28.9	31.5	34.8	37.2
19	6.84	7.63	8.91	10.1	30.1	32.9	36.2	38.6
20	7.43	8.26	9.59	10.9	31.4	34.2	37.6	40.0

4 (#1)

For a given number of degrees of freedom and a given value of P, the table below gives the value t_0 for which $Pr(-\infty < t < t_o) = P$.

Degrees of freedom	Value of P				
	0.900	0.950	0.975	0.990	0.995
1	3.08	6.31	12.7	31.8	63.7
2	1.89	2.92	4.30	6.96	9.92
3	1.64	2.35	3.18	4.54	5.84
4	1.53	2.13	2.78	3.75	4.60
5	1.48	2.02	2.57	3.36	4.03
6	1.44	1.94	2.45	3.14	3.71
7	1.42	1.90	2.36	3.00	3.50
8	1.40	1.86	2.31	2.90	3.36
9	1.38	1.83	2.26	2.82	3.25
10	1.37	1.81	2.23	2.76	3.17
11	1.36	1.80	2.20	2.72	3.11
12	1.36	1.78	2.18	2.68	3.06
13	1.35	1.77	2.16	2.65	3.01
14	1.34	1.76	2.14	2.62	2.98
15	1.34	1.75	2.13	2.60	2.95
20	1.32	1.72	2.09	2.53	2.84
25	1.32	1.71	.2.06	2.48	2.79
30	1.31	1.70	2.04	2.46	2.75
∞	1.28	1.64	1.96	2.33	2.58

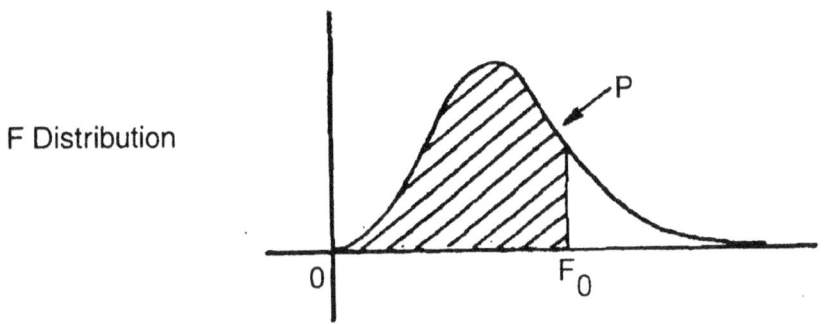

F Distribution

For given numbers of degrees of freedom and a given value of P, the table below gives the value F_0 for which $Pr(F < F_0) = P$.

Value of P	Degrees of freedom for denominator (lesser mean square)	Degrees of freedom for numerator (greater mean square)					
		5	6	7	8	9	10
0.950	5	5.05	4.95	4.88	4.82	4.77	4.74
0.975		7.15	6.98	6.85	6.76	6.68	6.62
0.990		11.0	10.7	10.5	10.3	10.2	10.1
0.995		14.9	14.5	14.2	14.0	13.8	13.6
0.950	6	4.39	4.28	4.21	4.15	4.10	4.06
0.975		5.99	5.82	5.70	5.60	5.52	5.46
0.990		8.75	8.47	8.26	8.10	7.98	7.87
0.995		11.5	11.1	10.8	10.6	10.4	10.2
0.950	7	3.97	3.87	3.79	3.73	3.68	3.64
0.975		5.29	5.12	4.99	4.90	4.82	4.76
0.990		7.46	7.19	6.99	6.84	6.72	6.62
0.995		9.52	9.16	8.89	8.68	8.51	8.38
0.950	8	3.69	3.58	3.50	3.44	3.39	3.35
0.975		4.82	4.65	4.53	4.43	4.36	4.30
0.990		6.63	6.37	6.18	6.03	5.91	5.81
0.995		8.30	7.95	7.69	7.50	7.34	7.21
0.950	9	3.48	3.37	3.29	3.23	3.18	3.14
0.975		4.48	4.32	4.20	4.10	4.03	3.96
0.990		6.06	5.80	5.61	5.47	5.35	5.26
0.995		7.47	7.13	6.88	6.69	6.54	6.42
0.950	10	3.33	3.22	3.14	3.07	3.02	2.98
0.975		4.24	4.07	3.95	3.85	3.78	3.72
0.990		5.64	5.39	5.20	5.06	4.94	4.85
0.995		6.87	6.54	6.30	6.12	5.97	5.85

1. On the average, 2 out of every 1,000 deaths in the United States are among people from 15 to 24 years of age. Use the Poisson distribution to approximate the probability that among a sample of 500 deaths, none is from this age group.

   A. 1/500
   B. e^{-2}
   C. $2e^{-2}$
   D. e^{-1}
   E. $2e^{-1}$

2. If $Pr(E_1) = p_1$, $Pr(E_2) \; p_2$ and if the sample space is $E_1 \cup E_2$, what is $Pr(E_1 \cap E_2)$?

   A. $p_1 p_2$
   B. $p_1 + p_2$
   C. $1 - p_1 - p_2$
   D. $p_1 + p_2 - 1$
   E. $p_1 + p_2 - p_1 p_2$

3. The probability density function of the random variable X is defined by

   $$\begin{cases} f(x) = 3x^2, & 0 \leq x \leq 1, \\ f(x) = 0, & \text{elsewhere.} \end{cases}$$

   What is the probability that neither of two independent observations of X falls in the interval [1/3, 2/3]?

   A. 49/729
   B. 64/729
   C. 329/729
   D. 361/729
   E. 400/729

4. If $Pr(S) = p_s$, $Pr(T) = p_t$ and the events S and T are independent, what is $Pr(S \cap T \backslash S)$?

   A. p_t
   B. $p_s p_t$
   C. $1 - p_s p_t$
   D. $1 - p_t + \dfrac{p_t}{p_s}$
   E. 1

5. A company annually uses many thousands of electric lamps which burn continuously day and night. Assume that under such conditions the life of a lamp may be regarded as a variable normally distributed about a mean of 50 days with a standard deviation of 19 days. On January 1, the company put 5,000 new lamps into service. How many (to the nearest 5) would be expected to need replacement by February 1?

   A. 270
   B. 395
   C. 795
   D. 855
   E. 1,705

6. The probability function of the discrete random variable X is defined by $f(x) = 2^{-x}$, $x = 1, 2, 3, \ldots$; $f(x) = 0$, elsewhere. What is the nth moment of X about the origin?

A. $\sum_{x=1}^{\infty} 2^{-x}$

B. $\sum_{x=1}^{\infty} 2^{-nx}$

C. $2^{-n} \sum_{x=1}^{\infty} x^n$

D. $\sum_{x=1}^{\infty} x^n 2^{-x}$

E. $\sum_{x=1}^{\infty} n^x 2^{-x}$

Questions 7-8 refer to the random variable X whose probability density function is defined by

$$\begin{cases} f(x) = \frac{3}{x^4}, & x \geq 1; \\ f(x) = 0, & \text{elsewhere.} \end{cases}$$

7. What is the median of X?

   A. $\frac{1}{\sqrt[3]{2}}$

   B. $\sqrt{\frac{3}{2}}$

   C. $\sqrt[3]{2}$

   D. $\frac{3}{2}$

   E. 3

8. What is the mean of X?

   A. $\frac{3}{4}$

   B. $\sqrt{\frac{3}{2}}$

   C. $\sqrt[3]{2}$

   D. $\frac{3}{2}$

   E. 3

9. Given a bivariate distribution with $\mu_x = \mu_y = 0$, $\sigma_x = 2$, $\sigma_y = 1$ and a coefficient of correlation between x and y of 0.5, what is the coefficient of correlation between x - y and y?

   A. -0.5
   B. -0.25
   C. 0
   D. 0.25
   E. 1.0

10. One hundred cards numbered from 1 to 100 are shuffled and 2 cards are drawn without replacement. What is the probability that the greater of the 2 numbers drawn exceeds 50?

A. $\dfrac{137}{198}$ B. $\dfrac{3}{4}$

C. $\dfrac{149}{198}$ D. $\dfrac{7.599}{10.000}$

E. $\dfrac{629}{825}$

11. The x^2 test (without a correction for continuity) is to be applied to the contingency table

	$\overline{R}$	R	Total
$\overline{S}$	n	$100-n$	100
S	$100-n$	n	100
Total	100	100	200

    to test the hypothesis that the two variables of classification are independent. If the test is conducted at the 5 per cent level of significance, the hypothesis will be accepted if and only if

    A. $48 < n < 52$ B. $47 < n < 53$
    C. $43 < n < 57$ D. $41 < n < 59$
    E. $40 < n < 60$

12. Let X be the number of dots obtained when an unbiased die is thrown. For what number a is $E[X(a - X)]$ zero?

    A. 0   B. 1
    C. 3   D. 7/2
    E. 13/3

13. The specific gravities of samples of a solution produced by a certain process are approximately normally distributed with mean 1.200 and standard deviation 0.010. Let the specific gravity of a sample selected at random be denoted by X. What is the order of relative magnitude of the probabilities defined below?

    $$p_1 = pr(X \leq 1.196)$$
    $$p_2 = pr(1.196 \leq X \leq 1.205)$$
    $$p_3 = pr(1.205 \leq X)$$

    A. $p_1 > p_3 > p_2$ B. $p_2 > p_1 > p_3$
    C. $p_2 > p_3 > p_1$ D. $p_3 > p_1 > p_2$
    E. $p_3 > p_2 > p_1$

14. For a set of n observed points (x_i, y_i) the following sums are known:

    $\frac{1}{n}\sum x_i = 2, \frac{1}{n}\sum y_i = 8; \frac{1}{n}\sum x_i y_i = 36; \frac{1}{n}\sum x_i^2 = 29;$ and $\frac{1}{n}\sum y_i^2 = 100$ A line of the form $y = x + k$ is to be fitted to the n points by means of the method of least squares. What value of k should be used?

    A. 4/5
    B. 4
    C. 6
    D. 10
    E. 6n

15. If an ordinary deck of 52 cards is dealt to four bridge players, what is the probability that the player who gets the ace of spades will also get the ace of hearts?

    A. $\frac{1}{26}$
    B. $\frac{1}{17}$
    C. $\frac{4}{17}$
    D. $\frac{1}{4}$
    E. $\frac{13}{51}$

16. Each of three urns contains nine slips of paper numbered consecutively from 1 through 9. If one slip of paper is drawn at random from each urn, what is the probability that the sum of the numbers on the three slips will be odd?

    A. $\frac{125}{729}$
    B. $\frac{205}{729}$
    C. $\frac{1}{2}$
    D. $\frac{365}{729}$
    E. $\frac{125}{243}$

17. What is the probability of finding the ace of hearts adjacent to the ace of diamonds in a well-shuffled deck of cards?

    A. $\frac{1}{2,652}$
    B. $\frac{1}{52}$
    C. $\frac{1}{51}$
    D. $\frac{1}{26}$
    E. $\frac{2}{51}$

18. The only possible values of the random variable X are 1, 2, 3, ... , 13. The probability of each is 1/13. The frequencies of occurrence of these values in a random sample of $13n$ observations are denoted by f_i (i = 1, 2, 3, ..., 13). If the value of the statistic $\frac{1}{n}\sum_{i=1}^{13}(f_i - n)^2$ is computed for each of 1,000 such samples, what is the expected number of samples for which this statistic will exceed 3.57?

   A. 10
   B. 50
   C. 975
   D. 990
   E. 995

19. Approximately how many times must a true coin be tossed before the probability of getting 53 per cent or more heads will be 1 per cent or less?

   A. 40
   B. 380
   C. 730
   D. 1,090
   E. 1,510

20. Each of the independent random variables $X_1, X_2, \ldots, X_n$ is distributed with mean μ and variance σ^2. If n is n large, for what value of c is $Pr(n\mu - c \leq \sum_{i=1}^{n} X_i \leq n\mu + c)$ approximately 0.99?

   A. $2.326\sigma\sqrt{n}$
   B. $2.576\sigma\sqrt{n}$
   C. 2.576σ
   D. $2.326\frac{\sigma}{\sqrt{n}}$
   E. $2.576\frac{\sigma}{\sqrt{n}}$

21. What is the probability that it will be necessary to throw an unbiased die exactly n times in order to obtain exactly 2 fours?

   A. $\frac{(n-1)(n-2)}{2}\left(\frac{1}{6}\right)^2\left(\frac{5}{6}\right)^{n-2}$
   B. $(n-1)\left(\frac{1}{6}\right)^2\left(\frac{5}{6}\right)^{n-2}$
   C. $n\left(\frac{1}{6}\right)^2\left(\frac{5}{6}\right)^{n-2}$
   D. $\frac{n(n-1)}{2}\left(\frac{1}{6}\right)^2\left(\frac{5}{6}\right)^{n-2}$
   E. $\frac{n(n-1)}{2}\left(\frac{1}{6}\right)^2\left(\frac{5}{6}\right)^{n-2}$

22. The random variables $X_1, X_2, \ldots, X_n$ are identically and independently distributed with mean μ and variance σ^2. What is the variance of the random variable
$$\frac{\sum_{i=1}^{n} a_i X_i}{\sum_{i=1}^{n} a_i}, \text{ where } a_1, a_2, \ldots, a_n \text{ are constants?}$$

A. σ^2

B. $\left(\sum_i a_i^2\right)\sigma^2$

C. $\left(\sum_i a_i\right)^2 \sigma^2$

D. $\dfrac{\sum_i a_i^2}{\left(\sum_i a_i\right)^2}\sigma^2$

E. $\dfrac{\left(\sum_i a_i\right)^2}{\sum_i a_i^2}\sigma^2$

23. The moment generating function of the random variable X is defined by $M(t) = (1 - 2t)^{-n}$ (n a positive integer). What is the kth moment of X about the origin?

A. $2^k n(n+1)\ldots(n+k-1)$

B. $(-1)^k n(n+1)\ldots(n+k-1)$

C. $2^k \dfrac{(n+k-1)!}{(k-1)!}$

D. $2^k \dfrac{n!}{k!}$

E. $(1-2k)^{-n}$

24. The probability is p that there will be at least one accident in a certain factory in any given week. If the number of weekly accidents in this factory is Poisson-distributed, what is the mean number of weekly accidents?

A. $\dfrac{1}{P}$

B. $\dfrac{1}{1-P}$

C. $e^1 - P$

D. $-\ln$

E. $-\ln(1-p)$

25. A bag contains 2 unbiased coins and 1 two-headed coin. One of these 3 coins is chosen at random and tossed 4 times. Without examining both sides of the coin, it is noted that all 4 tosses are heads. What is the probability that the next toss will be a head?

A. $\dfrac{17}{32}$

B. $\dfrac{2}{3}$

C. $\dfrac{8}{9}$ D. $\dfrac{15}{16}$

E. $\dfrac{17}{18}$

26. The probability density function of the random variable X is given by

$$\begin{cases} f(x)=1, \ 0 \leq x \leq 1; \\ f(x)=0, \text{ elsewhere.} \end{cases}$$

Let $Y = \sin X$. How is the probability density function of Y defined for $0 \leq y \leq \sin 1$?

A. $\dfrac{1}{\sin 1}$ B. $\sin y$

C. $\sin^{-1} y$ D. $\dfrac{1}{\sqrt{1-y^2}}$

E. $\sqrt{1-y^2}$

27. The random variables X, Y, U, V, have independent X2 distributions with nx, ny, nu, nv degrees of freedom, respectively. Which of the following describes the distribution of the random variable

$$\dfrac{(X+Y)/(n_x+n_y)}{(U+V)/(n_u+n_v)} ?$$

A. X^2 with $(n_X + n_Y + n_U + n_V - 4)$ degrees of freedom
B. X^2 with $(n_X + n_Y - n_U - n_V - 4)$ degrees of freedom
C. F with the pair of degrees of freedom $(n_X + n_Y, n_U + n_V)$
D. F with the pair of degrees of freedom $(n_X + n_Y - 1, n_U + n_V - 1)$
E. F with the pair of degrees of freedom $(n_X + n_Y - 2, n_U + n_V - 2)$

28. A man alternately tosses an unbiased coin and throws an unbiased die, beginning with the coin. What is the probability that he will get a 3 or a 4 before he gets a head?

A. $\dfrac{1}{6}$ B. $\dfrac{1}{4}$

C. $\dfrac{1}{3}$ D. $\dfrac{2}{5}$

E. $\dfrac{1}{2}$

29. The probability density function of the random variable X is defined by

$$\begin{cases} f(x)=(\ln \theta)\theta^{-x}, \ 0 \leq x, \ 1<\theta; \\ f(x)=0, \text{ elsewhere.} \end{cases}$$

What is the maximum likelihood estimator of the parameter θ based on n independent observations..... $X_1, X_2, , X_n$?

A. $e^{n/\Sigma x_i}$

B. $e^{-\Sigma x_i/n}$

C. $e^{-n/\Sigma x_i}$

D. $\dfrac{\Sigma x_i}{n}$

E. $\dfrac{n}{\Sigma x_i}$

30. The probability density function of the random variable X is defined by

$$\begin{cases} f(x;\theta)=(\theta+1)x^\theta, \ 0 \leq x, \leq 1, \\ f(x;\theta)=0, \text{ elsewhere.} \end{cases}$$

where θ is an unknown nonnegative integer. A single random observation of X is to be used to test the hypothesis $H_0: \theta = n$ against the alternative hypothesis $H_1: \theta\ n + 1$. Which of the following defines the best critical region of size 0.05 for this test?

A. $x \leq 1 - \sqrt[n+1]{0.95}$

B. $x \leq \sqrt[n+1]{0.05}$

C. $x \geq 1 - \sqrt[n+1]{0.05}$

D. $x \geq 1 - \sqrt[n+1]{0.95}$

E. $\sqrt[n+1]{0.05} \leq x \leq \sqrt[n+1]{0.95}$

31. The random variables X and Y are independently distributed. The random variable X is normally distributed with mean μ. The random variable Y^2 has the χ^2 distribution with n degrees of freedom. If the random variable has Student's t distribution with n degrees of freedom, what is the variance of X?

A. $\dfrac{1}{\sqrt{n}}$

B. 1

C. $\sqrt{n-1}$

D. $\sqrt{n}$

E. n

32. A certain industrial process yields a large number of steel cylinders whose lengths are approximately normally distributed with mean 3.25 inches and variance 0.0008 square inch. If two cylinders are chosen at random and placed end to end, what is the probability (to the nearest 0.01) that their combined length is less than 6.55 inches?

A. 0.84   B. 0.89   C. 0.95   D. 0.98   E. 0.99

33. A curve of the form $y = \lambda(x + \dfrac{1}{x})$ is to be fitted to the n observed points $(x_1, y_1), (x_2, y_2), \ldots, (x_n, y_n)$ by the method of least squares. What value of λ should be used?

A. $$\dfrac{\sum_i y_i}{\sum_i (x_i + \tfrac{1}{x_i})}$$

B. $$\dfrac{\sum_i y_i^2}{\sum_i (x_i + \tfrac{1}{x_i})}$$

C. $$\dfrac{\sum_i y_i (x_i + \tfrac{1}{x_i})}{\sum_i (x_i + \tfrac{1}{x_i})}$$

D. $$\dfrac{\sum_i y_i (x_i + \tfrac{1}{x_i})}{\sum_i (x_i^2 + \tfrac{1}{x_i^2})}$$

E. $$\dfrac{\sum_i y_i (x_i + \tfrac{1}{x_i})}{\sum_i (x_i + \tfrac{1}{x_i})^2}$$

34. The random variable X is such that $\Pr(a \le X \le b) = \dfrac{1}{a} - \dfrac{1}{b}$ for $b \ge a \ge 1$. How is the probability density function of X denned for $x \ge 1$?

A. $\dfrac{1}{x}$
B. $\dfrac{1}{x^2}$
C. $1 - \dfrac{1}{x}$
D. $1 - \dfrac{1}{x^2}$
E. $\ln x$

35. If X is a binomially distributed random variable with parameters n 162 and $p = 1/3$ and if ϕ is the cumulative normal distribution function with mean 0 and variance 1, what is the normal approximation to $\Pr(X = 54)$?

A. $\phi(0)$

B. $\phi(\dfrac{1}{9\sqrt{2}}) - \phi(-\dfrac{1}{9\sqrt{2}})$

C. $\phi(\dfrac{1}{12}) - \phi(-\dfrac{1}{12})$

D. $\phi(\dfrac{1}{6}) - \phi(-\dfrac{1}{6})$

E. $\phi(\dfrac{1}{2}) - \phi(-\dfrac{1}{2})$

36. A random sample $(x_1, x_2, x_3, x_4, x_5)$ from a normal population gives $\bar{x} = 2500$ and $\sum_{i=1}^{5}(x_i - \bar{x})^2 = 80.00$. $(-\infty, \beta)$ is a 95 per cent confidence interval for the mean of the population, what is the value of β?

A. 29.26
B. 30.14
C. 30.56
D. 34.08
E. 41.24

Questions 37-38 refer to the random variables X and Y whose joint probability density function is defined by

$$\begin{cases} f(x,y) = \frac{1+xy \cdot y}{4}, & -1 \le y \le 1; \\ f(x,y) = 0, & \text{elsewhere.} \end{cases}$$

37. What is $pr(X \ge \frac{1}{2} | Y \le -\frac{1}{2}) - pr(Y \ge \frac{1}{2} | X \le -\frac{1}{2})$?

    A. 0

    B. $\frac{1}{64}$

    C. $\frac{1}{28}$

    D. $\frac{7}{16}$

    E. 1

38. What is the equation of the curve of regression of X on Y9

    A. $x - 1 = 0$
    B. $3x + 1 = 0$
    C. $6x - y + 1 = 0$
    D. $3y + 1 = 0$
    E. $6y - x + 1 = 0$

39. If the random variables X_1 and X_2 are independent and have equal variances, what is the coefficient of correlation between the random variables X_1 and $aX_1 + X_2$, where a is a constant?

    A. 0

    B. $\frac{1}{a}$

    C. a

    D. $\frac{1}{\sqrt{a^2+1}}$

    E. $\frac{a}{\sqrt{a^2+1}}$

40. Random samples of size 10 and 6 are drawn from normal populations P and Q, respectively. Unbiased estimates of the population variances are computed from the samples and denoted by $\hat{\sigma}P^2$ and $\hat{\sigma}Q^2$ ($\hat{\sigma}p^2 > \hat{\sigma}Q^2$). If the variances of the populations are equal, what is the probability that $\hat{\sigma}p^2 > 10.2\hat{\sigma}Q^2$?

    A. .005   B. .010   C. .050   D. .950   E. .995

41. The probability density function of the random variable X is defined by
$$\begin{cases} f(x) = 2x, & 0 \le x \le 1; \\ f(x) = 0, & \text{elsewhere.} \end{cases}$$
What is the moment generating function of X for $t \ne 0$?

A. $2te^t$

B. $\dfrac{e^t - 1}{t}$

C. $\dfrac{2}{t^2}(te^t - te^t)$

D. $\dfrac{te^t + e^t}{t^2}$

E. $\dfrac{2}{t^2}(1 - e^t + te^t)$

42. If $E(X) = 0$, $E(X^2) = \sigma^2$, $E(X^3) = 0$ and $E(X-1)^4 = 3\sigma^4 + 6\sigma^2 + 1$, what is $E(X^4)$?

A. $3\sigma^4$

B. $3\sigma^4 - 6\sigma^2 - 1$

C. $3\sigma^4 - 6\sigma^2$

D. $6\sigma^2 + 1$

E. $3\sigma^4 + 6\sigma^2 + 1$

43. If X is a binomially distributed random variable with parameters n and 1/2, what is $E(X^2)$?

A. $\dfrac{n}{4}$

B. $\dfrac{n}{2}$

C. $\dfrac{n(n-1)}{4}$

D. $\dfrac{n^2}{4}$

E. $\dfrac{n(n+1)}{4}$

Questions 44-45 refer to the random variable X whose probability density function is defined by
$$\begin{cases} f(x;\theta) = 1 + 2\theta - 3\theta x^2, & 0 \le x \le 1; \\ f(x;\theta) = 0, & \text{elsewhere.} \end{cases}$$

44. What is the maximum likelihood estimate of θ based on two independent observations, 1/2 and 1?

A. $-\dfrac{3}{2}$

B. $-\dfrac{3}{4}$

C. $\dfrac{3}{4}$

D. 1

E. $3/2$

45. What is the power function of θ with respect to the critical region defined by $x < x_0 (0 < x_0 < 1)$?

   A. $1 + x_0(2 - 3x_0)\theta$
   B. $x_0 + (x_0^2 - x_0^2)\theta$
   C. $(1 - x_0)(1 - x_0^2 \theta)$
   D. $(x_0^2 - x_0^2)\theta$
   E. $x_0 + x_0^2 \theta - x_0^3 \theta^2$

46. A random sample $(x_1, x_2,..., x_{10})$ from a normal population gives $\sum_{i=1}^{10} x_i = 10\bar{x}$ and $\sum_{i=1}^{10}(x_i - \bar{x})^2 = 1{,}000$. Which of the following is a 99 per cent confidence interval for the mean of the population?

   A. $(\bar{x}-9.40, \bar{x}+9.40)$
   B. $(\bar{x} - 10.83, \bar{x} + 10.83)$
   C. $(\bar{x} - 27.64, \bar{x} + 27.64)$
   D. $(\bar{x} - 28.21, \bar{x} + 28.21)$
   E. $(\bar{x} - 32.50, \bar{x} + 32.50)$

Questions 47-49 refer to the pair of random variables (X, Y) which is uniformly distributed over the parallelogram with vertices $(0, 0)$, $(1, 0)$, $(1, 1)$, $(2, 1)$.

47. What is $\Pr(Y \leq \frac{1}{2} \mid X \leq 1)$?

   A. $\frac{1}{8}$
   B. $\frac{1}{4}$
   C. $\frac{3}{8}$
   D. $\frac{1}{2}$
   E. $\frac{3}{4}$

48. How is the marginal probability density function of X defined for $0 \leq x \leq 2$

   A. $\frac{1}{2}, 0 \leq x \leq 2$
   B. $\frac{1}{2}x, 0 \leq x \leq 2$
   C. $1 - \frac{1}{2}, 0 \leq x \leq 2$
   D. $x, 0 \leq x \leq 1; 2-x, 1 < x \leq 2$
   E. $\frac{1}{2}x^2, 0 \leq x \leq 1; 2 - \frac{1}{2}x^2 - 1, 1 < x \leq 2$

49. Let Z be the random variable $X + Y$. What is for $(Z \leq z)$

   A. $1/4z$
   B. $1/2z$
   C. $1/8z^2$
   D. $1/4z^2$
   E. $1/2z^2$

50. The random variables $X_1, X_2, \ldots, X_n$ are independently distributed, each with moment generating function defined by $M(t) = e^{at^2}$ $(a \geq 0)$. How is the moment generating function of $\frac{1}{n}\sum_{i=1}^{n} X_i$ defined?

   A. e^{at^2}
   B. $\frac{1}{n} e^{at^2}$
   C. $e^{(1/\sqrt{n})at^2}$
   D. $e^{(1/n)at^2}$
   E. e^{nat^2}

51. In controlling the quality of a manufactured product, care is taken to keep the mean of a certain variable at $\mu = 0$ and the standard deviation at $\sigma = \frac{1}{10}$. A random sample of 12 measurements $(x_1, x_2, \ldots, x_{12})$ is taken. Assume that the population mean, μ, has not changed and denote the sample mean by $\bar{x}$. What value must $\sum_{i=1}^{12}(x_i - \bar{x})^2$ exceed in order to reject at the 5 per cent significance level the hypothesis $\sigma = \frac{1}{10}$ in favor of the alternative hypothesis $\sigma > \frac{1}{10}$?

   A. 0.046
   B. 0.052
   C. 0.197
   D. 0.210
   E. 0.219

52. If from a batch of 1,000 available questionnaires 80 random samples of 10 questionnaires each are drawn, each sample being replaced in the batch immediately after it has been drawn, what is the probability that no questionnaire will be drawn more than once in the entire sampling procedure?

   A. $\dfrac{(990!)^{80}}{200!(1{,}000!)^{79}}$
   B. $\dfrac{(990!)^{80}(10!)^{80}}{(1{,}000!)^{80}}$
   C. $\dfrac{(10!)^{80}(990!)^{80}}{200!800!(1{,}000!)^{79}}$
   D. $\dfrac{(990!)^{80}}{200!800!(1{,}000!)^{78}}$
   E. $1 - \dfrac{800}{(10)^{80}}$

53. The probability density function of the random variable X is defined by
$$\begin{cases} f(x) = e^{-x}, & x \geq 0, \\ f(x) = 0, & \text{elsewhere.} \end{cases}$$

Let Y be the second greatest observation in random samples of size 4 drawn from the distribution of X. Which of the following defines the probability density function of Y?

A. $4(1-e^{-y})^3 e^{-y}$
B. $12(1-e^{-y})^2 e^{-2y} - 4(1-e^{-y})^3 e^{-y}$
C. $12(1-e^{-y})^2 e^{-2y}$
D. $4(1-e^{-y})^3 e^{-y} + (1-e^{-y})^4$
E. $12(1-e^{-y}) e^{-3y}$

54. The final examination scores of 100 students have mean 50 and standard deviation 15. The term scores of these students have mean 60 and standard deviation 10. The coefficient of correlation between the two sets of scores is 0.8. Use a least-squares regression line to predict the final examination score for a student whose term score is 70.

    A. 44.7
    B. 55.3
    C. 58
    D. 62
    E. 65

55. The random variables $X_1, X_2, \ldots, X_n$ are uniformly and independently distributed on [0, 1]. Let Y be the random variable max $\{X_1, X_2, \ldots, X_n\}$. What is the variance of Y?

    A. $\dfrac{1}{12}$
    B. $\dfrac{1}{12n}$
    C. $\dfrac{1}{(n+1)(n+2)}$
    D. $\dfrac{n}{(n+1)(n+2)}$
    E. $\dfrac{n}{(n+1)^2(n+2)}$

KEY (CORRECT ANSWERS)

1. D	11. C	21. B	31. E	41. E	51. C
2. D	12. E	22. D	32. B	42. A	52. A
3. E	13. B	23. A	33. E	43. E	53. C
4. A	14. C	24. E	34. B	44. A	54. D
5. C	15. C	25. E	35. C	45. B	55. E
6. D	16. D	26. D	36. A	46. B	
7. C	17. D	27. C	37. A	47. E	
8. D	18. D	28. B	38. B	48. D	
9. C	19. E	29. A	39. E	49. D	
10. C	20. B	30. D	40. B	50. D	

EXAMINATION SECTION
TEST 1

DIRECTIONS: Each question or incomplete statement is followed by several suggested answers or completions. Select the one that BEST answers the question or completes the statement. *PRINT THE LETTER OF THE CORRECT ANSWER IN THE SPACE AT THE RIGHT.*

1. If the median of a set of 45 marks is 82.5 and if the marks 100, 95, 40, and 15 are added to the set, the new median is

    A. 72.5　　B. 77.0　　C. 80.0　　D. 82.5

    1._____

2. The standard deviation of the set of scores 2, 5, 8 is equal to the standard deviation of which one of the following sets of scores?

    A. 4, 5, 6　　B. 4, 25, 64　　C. 4, 10, 16　　D. 4, 7, 10

    2._____

3. Assume that a jury panel contains 70 names, and among these are the names of Mr. C and Mr. D.
    If 12 jury men are to be selected by lot, the probability that BOTH Mr. C and Mr. D will be selected is

    A. 1/66　　B. 22/805　　C. 36/1225　　D. 1/6

    3._____

4. The odds in favor of getting a seven or an eleven on a single throw of a pair of dice are

    A. 1:9　　B. 1:8　　C. 2:9　　D. 2:7

    4._____

5. If the arithmetic mean of 40 marks is 72.5 and if four additional marks of 55, 65, 85, and 96 are added to the first 40, the new arithmetic mean is

    A. 72.00　　B. 72.50　　C. 72.70　　D. 72.75

    5._____

6. The statistic which is obtained from a set of N numbers x_i, (i = 1, 2...N) by the computation

    $$\frac{\sum_{i=1}^{N} x_i}{N}$$

    is the set's

    A. median　　　　　　　　B. arithmetic mean
    C. mode　　　　　　　　　D. standard deviation

    6._____

7. A coin which may fall either heads or tails is tossed four times.
    The probability of getting at least one head is

    A. 3/4　　B. 13/16　　C. 7/8　　D. 15/16

    7._____

8. There are four test scores of which three are known to be 83, 82, and 72.
    If, using an assumed arithmetic mean of 80, the mean deviation of the four scores from the assumed mean is -2.25, the fourth score is

    8._____

A. the smallest of the four B. 74
C. 76 D. 79

9. The mean of a set of n numbers is equal to m, and the standard deviation is s. If each number of the set is tripled and then increased by 5, the mean and the standard deviation of the new set of numbers are, respectively,

   A. m+5, 3s B. 3m, 9s
   C. 3m+5, 3s D. 3m+5, 3s+5

10. How many even numbers greater than 40,000 may be formed using the digits 3, 4, 5, 6, and 9 if each digit must be used exactly once in each number?

    A. 36 B. 48 C. 64 D. 96

11. What is the probability of getting 80% or more of the questions correct on a five question true-false exam merely by guessing?

    A. 1/16 B. 5/32 C. 3/16 D. 7/32

12. Bag A contains 5 red and 4 black balls. Bag B contains 4 red and 6 black balls. If a bag is chosen at random and a ball is drawn from this bag, what is the probability that it will be black?

    A. 4/15 B. 10/19 C. 47/90 D. 7/10

13. The standard deviation of the measures -4, 8, 0, -3, 9 is CLOSEST to

    A. 5.5 B. 4.8 C. 7.0 D. 1.0

14. From a group of 5 men and 3 women, a committee of 2 is chosen. What is the probability that the committee will consist of 2 men?

    A. 5/14 B. 1/3 C. 25/64 D. 2/5

15. In how many ways can six people sit in a row if two particular ones are not to sit next to each other?

    A. 240 B. 360 C. 480 D. 720

16. The probability of drawing an ace or a heart from a standard deck of 52 cards, in a single drawing, is

    A. 2/13 B. 4/13 C. 4/52 D. 13/52

17. From among the following sets of scores,
    Set A 7, 2, 6, 7, 3
    Set B 7, 3, 9, 3, 8
    Set C 4, 3, 4, 5, 4
    the one set in which the mode is greater than the median and the median is GREATER than the mean is

    A. Set A B. Set B
    C. Set C D. none of these

18. If a set of obtained measures is 8, 3, 5, 9, 13, 14, 22, 11, 2, 9, 8, 8, 18, which one of the following has the value 9?

    A. Median
    B. Mode
    C. Arithmetic mean
    D. Mean deviation

19. The standard deviation of the measures -6, 5, 0, -2, 8 is

    A. 1.00   B. 4.26   C. 4.98   D. 5.37

20. The probability that X will solve a problem is 1/3 and that Y will solve this problem is 4/5. If both work the problem independently, the probability the problem will be solved is

    A. 2/15   B. 4/15   C. 8/15   D. 13/15

KEY (CORRECT ANSWERS)

1.	D	11.	C
2.	D	12.	C
3.	B	13.	A
4.	D	14.	A
5.	D	15.	C
6.	B	16.	B
7.	D	17.	A
8.	B	18.	A
9.	C	19.	C
10.	A	20.	D

SOLUTIONS TO PROBLEMS

1. 82.5 must be the 23rd score, either counting from the highest to lowest or lowest to highest scores. By adding 100, 95, 40, and 15, 82.5 would still be the median since 24 scores lie below 82.5 and 24 scores lie above it. (Ans. D)

2. Standard deviation = $\sqrt{\dfrac{\sum(x-\bar{x})^2}{N}}$. For 2, 5, 8 standard deviation = $\sqrt{6}$, which is exactly the same for the numbers 4, 7, 10. (Ans. D)

3. The probability that C and D will be chosen first and second in either order is (2/70)(1/69). However, since a total of 12 will be selected, there are $_{12}C_2 = 66$ different combinations of selection numbers for C and D when both are chosen.
Final probability = 66(2/70)(1/69) = 22/805. (Ans. B)

4. There are a total of 8 combinations which will yield 7 or 11. There are a total of 36 combinations for both dice. Odds = probability of success ÷ probability of failure =
$\dfrac{8}{36} \div \dfrac{28}{36} = 2:7$. (Ans. D)

5. The total sum of all 40 marks = (72.5)(40) = 2900. By adding the four new numbers, the new total = 3201.
Then, 3201 ÷ 44 = 72.75. (Ans. D)

6. The arithmetic mean is denoted by the sum of the numbers divided by the number of numbers. (Ans. B)

7. Probability (at least one head) = 1 - Probability (no heads) = 1 - $(1/2)^4$ = 15/16. (Ans. D)

8. The mean deviation is the average of the absolute values (positive) of the differences between the raw scores and the mean. Assumed mean = 80. Mean deviation = -2.25 = 77.75 Four scores 83, 82, 72 and x must average 77.75. Fourth score is 74. (Ans. B)

9. Each operation on the original numbers will affect the mean of those numbers in the same way. However, the standard deviation is NOT affected by adding a constant to each number. (Ans. C)

10. If the first digit is 4, then the last digit must be 6 and there would be $_3P_3 = 6$ possibilities. Since 6 and 4 could be interchanged, there would be 6 possibilities of 6 _ _ _ 4.
But, if the first (highest) digit is 5 or 9, then the last digit could be 4 or 6, and the number of possibilities is $(2)(_3P_3)(2) = 24$. Total number of possibilities = 6 + 6 + 24 = 36. (Ans. A)

11. Probability of 4 right = $_5C_4(.5)^4(.5)^1 = .15625$
Probability of 5 right = $_5C_5(.5)^5(.5)^0 = .03125$
The sum of these probabilities = .1875 = 3/16. (Ans. C)

12. Let P = probability. P(black ball) = P(black ball from A) P(choosing A) + P(black ball from B). P(choosing B) = $\frac{4}{9} \cdot \frac{1}{2} + \frac{6}{10} \cdot \frac{1}{2} = \frac{47}{90}$. (Ans. C)

13. Standard deviation = $\sqrt{[n\Sigma x^2 - (\Sigma x)^2]/n^2} = \sqrt{[5(170)-100]/25} = \sqrt{30} = 5.5$ (Ans. A)

14. The total number of committees is $_8C_2 = \frac{8 \cdot 7}{2 \cdot 1} = 28$.

    The number of committees which will contain only men is $_5C_2 = \frac{5 \cdot 4}{2 \cdot 1} = 10$. Thus, the required probability = 10/28 or 5/14.
    Note: $_nC_R$ means the number of combinations of R objects from a group of n objects. Of course, n≥R. (Ans. A)

15. We want to eliminate all permutations where the two individuals would be both occupying seats 1 and 2, or seats 2 and 3, or .... or seats 5 and 6. This represents $10(_4P_4) = 240$. The total number of permutations = $_6P_6 = 6.5.4.3.2.4 = 720$. Thus, the number of acceptable arrangements = 480. (Ans. C)

16. There are 16 cards in the deck which are either a heart, an ace, or both. The probability = 16/52 = 4/13. (Ans. B)

17. In Set A, the mode = 7, median = 6, and mean = 5. (Ans. A)

18. When these numbers are arranged in ascending order, they appear as: 2, 3, 5, 8, 8, 8, 9, 9, 11, 13, 14, 18, 22. The median is the seventh number, which is 9. (Ans. A)

19. Standard deviation = $\sqrt{\Sigma(x-\bar{x})^2/n}$. Since $\bar{x}=1$, this becomes $\sqrt{124/5} = 4.98$. (Ans. C)

20. Probability of either event = 1/3 + 4/5 - (1/3)(4/5) = 13/15. (Ans. D)

TEST 2

DIRECTIONS: Each question or incomplete statement is followed by several suggested answers or completions. Select the one that BEST answers the question or completes the statement. *PRINT THE LETTER OF THE CORRECT ANSWER IN THE SPACE AT THE RIGHT.*

1. The number of ways in which 5 women and 1 man can be seated at a rectangular table at which the man may occupy only a position marked with an x is

   A. 60
   B. 120
   C. 240
   D. 360

2. Four men, M, N, R, and S, stand in a row.
   The probability that M and N are next to each other is

   A. 1/6   B. 1/4   C. 1/3   D. 1/2

3. The probability of obtaining 3 heads and 1 tail in a throw of 4 coins is

   A. 3/4   B. 1/2   C. 3/8   D. 1/4

4. Mr. P.Q. Simpson is a football fan and says that there is a 70% probability that he will attend next Sunday's local football game if it does NOT snow, but only a 30% probability if it DOES snow. The weather bureau forecast is that there is a 60% chance that it will snow on Sunday.
   The probability that Mr. Simpson will attend the game on Sunday is

   A. 28%   B. 40%   C. 46%   D. 54%

5. A teacher gave his class the problem of writing five, numbers whose mean, median, and mode are the same. Pupils A, B, C, and D obtained answers of, respectively,
   20,10,20,10,20; 10,2,16,12,10; 5,.05,5,50,5; and $1/2, 5\times10^{-1}, 3/4, .75, .5$.
   The CORRECT answer was that of Pupil

   A. A   B. B   C. C   D. D

6. A box contains only red cards and black cards. If a card is selected at random from the box, the probability that it is red is 3/5.
   Which of the statements below is CORRECT?

   A. The box contains 3 red cards and 2 black cards.
   B. The box contains 3 red cards and 5 black cards.
   C. If a card is selected at random from the box, the probability that it is black is 2/5.
   D. If a card is selected at random from the box, the probability that it is black cannot be determined from the given information.

7. If n and r represent positive integers and n > r, then $\dfrac{n(n-1)(n-2)\ldots(n-r+1)}{1\cdot 2\cdot 3\cdot\ldots\cdot r}$ is an integer

   A. *only* if n is composite
   B. *only* if r divides n
   C. *only* if n is composite and r divides n
   D. for all values of n and r

34

8. In a survey of the population of the village of Great Neck, it was found that 27% of the population needed eyeglasses, 14% of the population were left-handed, and 5% needed eyeglasses and were also left-handed.
What percent of the population of Great Neck neither needed eyeglasses nor were left-handed?

   A. 54   B. 59   C. 64   D. 69

   8.____

9. The odds AGAINST throwing an 8 in a single roll with two dice is

   A. 36 to 5   B. 5 to 1   C. 6 to 1   D. 31 to 5

   9.____

10. A set of students' marks on a quiz worth ten points was as follows: 2, 2, 3, 3, 5, 5, 5, 7, 7, 7, 7, 9, 10. The arithmetic mean, median, and mode of this set of marks, arranged in descending order of magnitude, will be

    A. median, mode, arithmetic mean
    B. mode, arithmetic mean, median
    C. mode, median, arithmetic mean
    D. arithmetic mean, median, mode

    10.____

11. Three *fair* coins are tossed.
What is the probability of getting exactly two heads?

    A. 3/8   B. 1/8   C. 2/3   D. 1/2

    11.____

12. Two *fair* coins are tossed.
The probability that both coins show heads is

    A. 1   B. 3/4   C. 1/2   D. 1/4

    12.____

13. The number of permutations of the elements of the set $\{x_1, x_2, ..., x_n\}$, using all the elements of the set in each permutation, is

    A. 2^n B. n^2 C. $n!$ D. $\sum_{i=1}^{n} x_i$

    13.____

14. A box contains only red cards and black cards. If a card is selected at random from the box, the probability that it is red is 4/7.
Which of the statements below is CORRECT?

    A. The box contains 4 red cards and 7 black cards.
    B. If a card is selected at random from the box, the probability that it is black cannot be determined from the given information.
    C. The box contains 4 red cards and 3 black cards.
    D. If a card is selected at random from the box, the probability that it is black is 3/7.

    14.____

15. A box contains 3 white balls and 2 red balls. If a ball is drawn at random and not replaced and a second ball is drawn at random, what is the probability that both balls are red?

    A. 1/10   B. 2/25   C. 2/5   D. 13/20

    15.____

KEY (CORRECT ANSWERS)

1. C
2. B
3. D
4. C
5. B

6. C
7. D
8. C
9. D
10. B

11. A
12. D
13. C
14. D
15. A

SOLUTIONS TO PROBLEMS

1. The number of ways of seating the man = $_2P_1$ = 2.
   The number of ways of seating the 5 women = $_5P_5$ = 120.
   The total number of arrangements of all people = (2)(120) = 240. (Ans. C)

2. There are $_4P_4$ = 24 ways in which M, N, R, and S can be arranged in a row. There are 6 ways in which M and N are next to each other. The required probability is 6/24 = 1/4. (Ans. B)

3. Probability of any 3 heads and 1 tail out of 4 coins = $_4C_3$ $(1/2)^3(1/2)$ = (4)(1/16) = 1/4. (Ans. D)

4. Probability = (.70)(.40) + (.30)(.60) = .46 = 46%. (Ans. C)

5. Pupil B's example has a mean, median, and mode = 10. (Ans. B)

6. Probability of a black card = 1 - 3/5 = 2/5 . (Ans. C)

7. Recognize that $\frac{n(n-1)(...)(n-r+1)}{(1)(2)(...)(r)} = {_nC_R}$ which is the number of combinations of n items taken r at a time. $_nC_R$ must always be an integer. (Ans. D)

8. Let A = event that a person needs glasses, B = event that a person is left-handed. Then, P(A) = .27, P(B) = .14, and $P(A \cap B)$ = .05. Then, $P(A \cup B)$ = .27 + .14 - .05 = .36.
   This means that 36% of the people either need glasses or are left-handed or both. Thus, 64% fall into neither category. (Ans. C)

9. Probability of rolling an 8 = 5/36 , so probability of NOT rolling an 8 = 31/36 . This translates to odds of 31 to 5. (Ans. D)

10. Mean = 72/13 = 5.54. Mode = 7 Median = 5
    The descending order is mode, mean, median. (Ans. B)

11. Probability (exactly 2 heads) = (3)(probability of getting heads on 2 specific coins) = (3)(1/8) = 3/8. (Ans. A)

12. Probability = $(1/2)^2$ = 1/4. (Ans. D)

13. The number of permutations of n elements (using all elements) = n(n-1)(n-2)(...)(1) = n! (Ans. C)

14. Probability of selecting a red card + probability of selecting a black card = 1. Thus, the required probability = 1 - 4/7 = 3/7. (Ans. D)

15. Probability (2 red balls) = (2/5) (1/4) = 1/10.(Ans. A)

EXAMINATION SECTION
TEST 1

DIRECTIONS: Each question or incomplete statement is followed by several suggested answers or completions. Select the one that BEST answers the question or completes the statement. *PRINT THE LETTER OF THE CORRECT ANSWER IN THE SPACE AT THE RIGHT.*

1. An unbiased coin is tossed 10 times and 7 heads appear. It is MOST likely that the number of heads appearing in the next ten tosses of the coin will be

   A. 1 B. 2 C. 5 D. 6

2. The one of the following which is NOT a measure of the spread or variability of a distribution is the

   A. range
   B. mean deviation
   C. standard deviation
   D. fiducial deviation

3. If $x_1 = X_1 - \overline{X}$
   $x_2 = X_2 - \overline{X}$
   ....
   $x_N = X_N - \overline{X}$

   where $\overline{X} = \dfrac{\sum_{i=1}^{N} X_i}{N}$, then $\sum_{i=1}^{N} x_i = \sum_{i=1}^{N} (X_i - \overline{X}) = \sum_{i=1}^{N} X_i - N\overline{X}$.

   Therefore, $\sum_{i=1}^{N} x_i$ is equal to

   A. 0 B. $2N\overline{X}$ C. $\dfrac{2\sum_{i=1}^{N} x_i}{N}$ D. $N\sum_{i=1}^{N} x_i$

4. An urn contains 10 balls numbered from 1 to 10. The mean plus the variance of this population is MOST NEARLY

   A. 20 B. 17 C. 14 D. 11

5. In a sample of 600 cases taken from a large population, the mean is 65 and the standard deviation is 5. The standard error of the mean is MOST NEARLY

   A. .10 B. .20 C. .35 D. .40

6. If an unbiased coin is thrown 4 times, the probability of getting exactly 3 heads is

   A. 1/16 B. 1/4 C. 5/16 D. 3/32

7. The correlation ratio, eta(n) is used in _____ correlation.

   A. rank
   B. serial
   C. regressive
   D. non-linear

8. A study of the hourly earnings of workers in four firms showed the following:

	Firm I	Firm II	Firm III	Firm IV
Mean hourly earnings	$9.20	$10.20	$8.25	$11.10
Standard deviation of hourly earnings	.46	.56	.55	.61

   Using the coefficient of variation, the firm with the greatest internal wage differentials is Firm

   A. I
   B. II
   C. III
   D. IV

9. If the size of a sample is tripled, the variance of the mean computed from the sample is multiplied by

   A. $\sqrt{5}$
   B. 4
   C. 2/9
   D. 1/3

10. A random sample of 100 cases shows that 50 percent of the persons in the sample have a certain characteristic.
    The 95 percent confidence interval for this percentage is MOST NEARLY from

    A. .35 to .61
    B. .40 to .60
    C. .41 to .57
    D. .43 to .59

11. Five units of each of four identically priced different brands of a certain electrical appliance were tested for length of service with the following results (in hundreds of hours):

	Mean	Median	Mode	Range
Brand A	36.0	37.0	33.0	33-39
Brand B	35.6	38.0	38.0	30-38
Brand C	35.2	37.0	37.0	30-40
Brand D	34.8	35.0	39.0	30-39

    Assume that the above results are similar to those which would be obtained from very large samples. If large quantities of this electrical appliance are to be purchased for a large housing development and minimum cost per hour of service is the selection criterion, it would be BEST to purchase Brand

    A. A
    B. B
    C. C
    D. D

12. An urn contains 2 white and 3 black balls, while a second urn contains 4 white balls and 1 black ball.
    If an urn is selected at random and a single ball is drawn, the probability that it will be white is

    A. 7/10
    B. 1/5
    C. 5/8
    D. 3/5

13. In cluster sampling, it is desirable that each cluster, within itself, should be

    A. heterogeneous
    B. homogeneous
    C. homoscedastic
    D. normally distributed

14. When it is necessary to compare the variability of distributions described in different units, it is MOST desirable to use

   A. rank correlation
   B. analysis of variance
   C. the coefficient of variation
   D. the normal distribution

15. The heights of all the men in the American Army were measured and found to be normally distributed with the mean equal to 68 inches and the standard deviation equal to 3 inches.
   The percentage of this population with heights from 65 inches to 74 inches is MOST NEARLY _____ percent.

   A. 82   B. 76   C. 75   D. 64

16. If an urn contains 95 white and 5 black balls, the probability that a random sample of 5 balls, drawn one at a time with replacement, will contain exactly one black ball is MOST NEARLY

   A. .28   B. .20   C. .12   D. .04

17. A stationary time series is one which has no

   A. autocorrelation
   B. cyclical movement
   C. correlative integration
   D. trend

18. Given the following data:

   $\bar{x} = 3, \sigma_x = 2$
   $\bar{y} = 3, \sigma_y = 2 \quad r_{xy} = .6$

   The equation of the regression line of y on x is y =
   A. .6x+1.2
   B. 2x +3
   C. .4x +.8
   D. 5x +.3

19. The Doolittle method is used in

   A. testing hypotheses
   B. computing x^2
   C. sequential sampling
   D. solving normal equations

20. Seven persons are tested on their knowledge of mathematics before and after taking a refresher course by being given Form A of a certain test before the course begins and an equivalent Form B of this test after the course has ended. The scores are:

Person	Score On Form A	Form B
I	54	60
II	59	73
III	60	75
IV	62	80
V	66	90
VI	68	95
VII	72	91

   The rank correlation coefficient of their scores on these two tests is
   A. .99   B. .96   C. .93   D. .90

21. If the value of a statistic approaches more and more closely the value of the population parameter as the sample size is indefinitely increased, the statistic is called

   A. consistent
   B. valid
   C. sufficient
   D. reliable

22. Ten persons are scored on two tests x and y with the following results:

Individual	1	2	3	4	5	6	7	8	9	10
X	4	4	2	1	0	-1	-2	-2	-3	-3
y	4	2	1	3	-1	-2	-2	0	-2	-3

   The product-moment correlation between x and y is approximately
   A. .87   B. .79   C. .67   D. .54

23. The hypothesis that a sample whose mean value is x could have come from a population whose mean value is X and whose standard deviation is a may be tested by using

   A. Snedecor's F
   B. Goldbart's y
   C. Student's t
   D. Neyman's λ

24. The scores of a large group of high school seniors on three tests were correlated and the following correlation coefficients were obtained:

   General intelligence test and arithmetic ability $r = .7$
   General intelligence test and knowledge of $r = .5$
   English literature Arithmetic ability and knowledge of English literature $r = .4$

   The partial correlation coefficient between intelligence and arithmetic ability for this group, when knowledge of English literature is held constant, is MOST NEARLY

   A. .57   B. .60   C. .63   D. .66

25. In fitting a curve to the data on the population in a large city for each decade between 1790 and 1980, it would be MOST appropriate for a statistician to use a

   A. straight line
   B. parabola
   C. parameter
   D. logistic

26. Given the following data on unemployment in the United States:

Year (X)		Unemployment in Millions (Y)
1988	-3	10.4
1989	-2	9.5
1990	-1	8.1
1991	0	5.6
1992	1	2.7
1993	2	1.1
1994	3	0.7

   The equation of the least square trend line $(Y = a + bX)$ is Y =
   A. 5.4-1.8X   B. 4.3-2.3X   C. 6.7-3.5X   D. 6.2-2.9X

27. In using the chi-square technique for testing independence, if the data are tabulated in r rows and c columns, the number of degrees of freedom is equal to

   A. $\dfrac{r+c}{c-1}$ B. $(r-1)(c-1)$ C. $\dfrac{rc-1}{1-rc}$ D. $re + 1$

28. The U.S. Census Bureau uses the following seasonal index of unemployment:

January	- 114.3	July	- 105.5
February	- 113.2	August	- 89.6
March	- 108.3	September	- 83.1
April	- 99.0	October	- 78.5
May	- 98.5	November	- 95.5
June	- 116.0	December	- 98.6

    The Census Bureau reported that unemployment in December of one year was 4,100,000. Assuming that unemployment follows the seasonal pattern next year, it may be estimated that, in the high month, unemployment will be MOST NEARLY

    A. 4,300,000   B. 4,500,000   C. 4,750,000   D. 4,800,000

29. Of the following statistical processes that one which does NOT involve an underlying assumption of the normality of population distribution is

    A. analysis of variance
    B. produce-moment correlation
    C. rank correlation
    D. tetrachoric correlation

30. The use of moving averages will

    A. provide a mathematical expression for the curve
    B. reveal the general trend more clearly
    C. make possible predictions of values beyond the range of the original data
    D. eliminate bias

31. The U.S. Bureau of Labor Statistics issues each month a Consumer Price Index which may be described as a(n) _____ type index.

    A. modified Laspeyres
    B. Michele Ideal
    C. moving average
    D. adjusted Paasche

32. The daily rents of four families are listed in Stratum I as follows:
    Stratum I: $16, $28, $34, $36.
    Similarly, the monthly rents of four other families are listed in Stratum II as follows:
    Stratum II: $42, $48, $58, $90.
    If a simple random sample of size two is taken from Stratum I, and a simple random sample of size two is taken from Stratum II, the number of possible samples of size four that can be drawn is

    A. 15   B. 26   C. 36   D. 44

33. Use the data and sampling method given in Question 32. The variance of the rents in Stratum I is 81, and the variance of the rents in Stratum II is 457. The variance of the weighted sample mean X_s is given by the formula:

    $$V(\bar{X}_s) = W_1^2 \left(1 - \frac{n_1}{N_1}\right) \frac{\sqrt{1^2}}{n_1} + W_2^2 \left(1 - \frac{n_2}{N_2}\right) \frac{\sqrt{2^2}}{n_2} \text{ where}$$

    W_i is the fraction of the population in Stratum i,
    n_i is the size of the sample drawn from Stratum i,
    N_i is the number of elements in Stratum i, and
    $\sqrt{i^2}$ is the variance of the rents in Stratum i.
    Using this formula on the above data, $V(\bar{X}_S)$ is approximately

    A. 29   B. 34   C. 39   D. 44

34. Three of the four groups of forces which may be regarded as influencing an economic time series are seasonal variation, cyclical variation, and residual variation. The fourth is _____ variation.

   A. reticular
   B. serial
   C. systematic
   D. secular

35. An index of industrial production is issued by the

   A. Bureau of Labor Statistics
   B. Bureau of the Census
   C. Federal Reserve Board
   D. Federal Trade Commission

36. Orthogonal polynomials have been used by R.A. Fisher for

   A. time series analysis
   B. projection of experiments
   C. discriminant function analysis
   D. chi-square tests

37. The following data show the correlations among three nornally distributed variables x, y, and z based on a large number of observations:

   $$r_{xy} = .7, \; r_{xz} = .3, \; r_{yz} = -.1$$

   The multiple correlation coefficient $R_{x.yz}$ is MOST NEARLY
   A. .71   B. .74   C. .78   D. .79

38. Because of the extreme non-normality of the sampling distribution of r, the correlation coefficient, when testing the significance of an observed correlation coefficient, it is desirable to use

   A. Fisher's z
   B. Hotelling's T^2
   C. Pearson's Type III
   D. Poling's correction

39. Data are available on the financial returns from each of a large sample of motion pictures which can be divided into two groups, those rated *above average* by movie critics, and those rated *below average*. A useful method, in this instance, for determining the correlation between excellence in dramatic art and financial success is _____ correlation.

   A. rank
   B. peripatetic
   C. biserial
   D. canonical

40. A least squares line has been fitted to certain annual data and the following equation has been obtained:
   $$Y = 10.6 + 0.7X, \; (1973=0, \text{ and the X variable is in units of 1 year})$$
   If the origin is shifted three years forward so that 1976 = 0, the resulting equation is Y =

   A. 29.5 + 0.6X
   B. 12.7 + 0.7X
   C. 30.5 + 2.2X
   D. 12.7 + 1.7X

41. The Latin Square is used in

   A. curve fitting
   B. space series analysis
   C. experimental design
   D. biserial correlation

42. Given the following data on the number of retirees in three city departments who chose each of three possible options for receiving retirement allowances:

Option	Department I	Department II	Department III	Row Totals
A	30	25	44	99
B	39	30	30	99
C	30	44	25	99
Column Totals	99	99	99	

   Chi-square analysis can be used in determining whether there is a significant relationship between the department where the retiree worked and the option selected. The closeness of the relationship can be measured by computing the contingency coefficient, C, which for the data above is MOST NEARLY

   A. .10   B. .20   C. .30   D. .40

43. Sequential analysis is associated with the work of

   A. R.A. Fisher
   B. S.U. Wilks
   C. J.P. Neyman
   D. A. Wald

44. In recent years, the mathematical problem of maximizing or minimizing a linear function of many non-negative variables which, in addition, must satisfy certain linear restrictions, has received considerable attention.
   Such a problem has become known as a(n) _____ problem.

   A. linear programming
   B. vertical hypothesis
   C. input-output
   D. statistical decision

45. The MOST correct inference which can be drawn from Chebyshev's inequality is that the proportion of an unknown distribution which lies within two standard deviations of the mean is MOST NEARLY _____ percent.

   A. 90   B. 88   C. 80   D. 75

46. Neyrian and Pearson have published important papers on

   A. quantity control
   B. testing hypotheses
   C. periodic correlation
   D. time series analysis

47. In making certain studies of work experience over a period of years, the Bureau of Old Age and Survivors Insurance has used a sample of persons whose Social Security account numbers end in certain selected digits.
   This type of sample is known as a _____ sample.

   A. systematic
   B. residential
   C. purposive
   D. cluster

48. The fraction of a finite population included in a sample affects the standard error of the mean computed from the sample as is apparent from the formula:

$$\sigma_{\bar{x}} = \sqrt{\frac{N-n}{N-1}} \cdot \frac{\sigma}{\sqrt{n}}$$

where N is the number of members of the population and n is the number of members in the sample.
Thus, for a certain size sample, the percent by which the standard error of the mean, obtained from the formula under the assumption that the population is infinite, would be reduced if that same sample constituted 20 percent of a finite population is
   A. 25%   B. 18%   C. 12%   D. 10%

49. When sample sizes are small and assumptions of normality become untenable, or when the underlying distribution of the population is unknown, it is frequently possible to use methods of estimating parameters and testing hypotheses which are known as _____ methods.

   A. nonputative   B. nonparametic
   C. noniterative   D. nonlinear

50. The error committed in accepting a false null hypothesis is called a _____ error.

   A. Chi-square   B. Grumann
   C. Type II   D. Pearson Type III

51. When the statistician does not fix the sample size in advance, but proceeds to take one observation at a time until a decision can be made, subject to the desired risks of error, he is using a procedure called _____ sampling.

   A. conservative   B. sequential
   C. purposive   D. precision

52. A sample statistic which summarizes all of the relevant information which the observations contain concerning the population parameter is called a(n) _____ statistic.

   A. consistent   B. resistant
   C. efficient   D. sufficient

53. Suppose that drawings are made from an urn containing black and white balls in a known proportion, and that each ball drawn is returned to the urn, but only after the next drawing has been made. The probability that the (n+1) st ball drawn will be white is known if we know the color of the nth ball drawn and this probability is independent of what happened at the (n-1) st or earlier drawing.
Such trials are said to constitute a

   A. spurious sample   B. systematic sample
   C. Markov chain   D. Bernoullian series

54. In statistical quality control theory, the possibility that a batch of goods of acceptable quality will be rejected by the sampling scheme as a result of a pessimistic-looking sample is called the

   A. Producer's Risk   B. Consumer's Risk
   C. Corrective Function   D. Error Function

55. If T is distributed between -1/2 and +1/2 in a rectangular distribution, the cube root $Z = T^{1/3}$ is distributed in a _____ distribution.

    A. Vichy
    B. u-shaped
    C. Type I
    D. rectangular

56. If $\sigma(\overline{X}_j)$ is defined as the probability that a variable X takes a particular value X_j, and G(T), the generating function, is defined as $G(T) = \sum_j \sigma(X_j) T^{X_J}$, then the j generating function for an asymmetrical coin for which the probability of heads (Value = 1) is p, and of tails (Value = 0) is q, is

    A. 1/3 (T+1)
    B. pT+q
    C. 1/4 (pT+q)
    D. 1/5(1-T)

57. In order to test the hypothesis that a coin is not biased, it is decided to toss it five times and to reject the hypothesis if either five heads or five tails occur. If p, the true probability of getting a head in one toss, is actzally 1/2, the probability of rejecting the hypothesis can be calculated. Similarly, if p is really 2/3 or any other value, the probability of rejecting the hypothesis can be computed.
    The probability of rejecting the hypothesis of no bias, considered as a function of p, is called the

    A. error of Type III
    B. power series of Type II
    C. power function of the test
    D. axillary limit of the function

58. An axiomatic foundation for the theory of probability has been published by

    A. Siegall
    B. Pearson
    C. Pushkin
    D. Kolmogorov

59. Given an urn with four balls in it, either white or black, let Hu be the hypothesis that there are two white balls in the urn. The following experiment is designed to test whether Hu is to be accepted as the true hypothesis:
    A ball is drawn from the urn and its color is noted as 0 if it is white and 1 if it is black. This first ball is replaced in the urn and a second ball is drawn and the color noted.
    Assuming that Hu is true, the possible results are (0,0) or two white balls; (0,1) a white ball and then a black ball; (.1,0) a black ball and then a white ball; and (1,1) or two black balls; and each of these four possible results has a probability equal to 1/4. We may select any one of these four sample results as a CRITICAL REGION of size 1/4 and decide to reject Hu if the experiment produces this particular result. Otherwise, we do not reject Hu.
    If actually there is only one white ball in the urn, i.e., Hu is not true, the critical region which is best, in the sense that it gives us the greatest probability of correctly rejecting Hu, is

    A. (0,0)   B. (0,1)   C. (1,0)   D. (1,1)

60. Four high jumpers tie for first place in a track meet. Since there are three medals, the four draw by lot for the gold medal. Then the three losers draw for the silver medal. Then the two remaining draw for the bronze medal. Jones, one of the four, reasons that he has one chance in four of getting the gold medal, plus one chance in three of getting the silver medal, plus one chance in two of getting the bronze medal and, therefore, he is certain that he will get a medal.

    The one of the following which is an accurate statement of the probabilities associated with the distribution of the medals is that Jones has one chance in

    A. three of getting the bronze medal
    B. four of getting the gold medal
    C. four of getting the silver medal
    D. two of not getting a medal

60____

KEY (CORRECT ANSWERS)

1.	C	16.	B	31.	A	46.	B
2.	D	17.	D	32.	C	47.	A
3.	A	18.	A	33.	B	48.	D
4.	C	19.	D	34.	D	49.	B
5.	B	20.	B	35.	C	50.	C
6.	B	21.	A	36.	A	51.	B
7.	D	22.	A	37.	D	52.	D
8.	C	23.	C	38.	A	53.	C
9.	D	24.	C	39.	C	54.	A
10.	B	25.	D	40.	B	55.	D
11.	A	26.	A	41.	C	56.	B
12.	D	27.	B	42.	B	57.	C
13.	A	28.	D	43.	D	58.	D
14.	C	29.	C	44.	A	59.	D
15.	A	30.	B	45.	D	60.	C

SOLUTIONS TO PROBLEMS

1. **CORRECT ANSWER: C**

   Previous tosses of a coin are not relevant. Regardless of the number of heads which <u>had already</u> appeared, the most likely number of heads for the next 10 tosses is 5. Probability of heads on each toss = 1/2.

2. **CORRECT ANSWER: D**

   Fiducial means *based on trust,* which is not a mathematical measurement.

3. **CORRECT ANSWER: A**

   $$\sum_{i=1}^{n} x_i = x_1 + x_2 + x_3 + \ldots + x_n$$

   $$= \sum_{i=1}^{n} X_i - N\bar{X} = \sum_{i=1}^{n} X_i - (N)\left(\frac{\sum_{i}^{n} X_i}{N}\right)$$

   $$= \sum_{i=1}^{n} X_i - \sum_{i=1}^{n} X_i = 0$$

4. **CORRECT ANSWER: C**

   Mean = (1+2+3+...+10)/10 = 55/10 = 5.5
   Variance = $\sum(x_i-\bar{x})^2/10$ = $(1-5.5)^2/10 + (2-5.5)^2/10 + \ldots (10-5.5)^2/10$ = 8.25
   Mean + Variance = 5.5 + 8.25 = 13.75 ≈ 14

5. **CORRECT ANSWER: B**

   Standard error of the mean = standard deviation divided by the square root of the number of cases = $5/\sqrt{600}$ ≈ .20

6. **CORRECT ANSWER: B**

   $$\text{Probability of 3 heads} = (_4C_3)\left(\frac{1}{2}\right)^3\left(\frac{1}{2}\right)$$

   $$= \left(\frac{4 \cdot 3 \cdot 2}{1 \cdot 2 \cdot 3}\right)(.125)(.5) = 1/4$$

7. **CORRECT ANSWER: D**

   Correlation ratio (n) measures a quantitative dependent factor against a qualitative independent factor.

8. **CORRECT ANSWER: C**

   The coefficient of variation = standard deviation divided by the mean. For Form III, this value = .55/8.25 = .0$\overline{6}$. This value is higher than the figures for Firms I, II, and IV.

9. **CORRECT ANSWER: D**

The variance of the mean $\sigma_{\bar{x}}^2 = \sigma^2/n$, when n = size of sample.

If the new sample size is $\sigma_{\bar{x}}^2$ becomes $\sigma^2/(3n)$.

10. CORRECT ANSWER: B

The 95% confidence interval is given by $.50 \pm 1.96 \frac{\sqrt{(.50)(.50)}}{100}$
= .50 ± .098 = .402 to .598 or approx. .40 to .60.

11. CORRECT ANSWER: A

The best brand would have the highest mean and a range consisting of a relatively high low point and high point. Brand A seems to fit best.

12. CORRECT ANSWER: D

Probability of white ball = (Prob. of white) x (Prob of urn 1) + (Prob of white) x (Prob of urn 2) = (2/5)(l/2) + (4/5X1/2) = 3/5

13. CORRECT ANSWER: A

Each cluster should be a mixed representation of the original population.

14. CORRECT ANSWER: C

The coefficient of variation equals the standard deviation divided by the mean, expressed as a percent. Thus, it is not associated with specific units.

15. CORRECT ANSWER: A

The standard score for 65 is (65-68) ÷ 3 = -1 and the standard score for 74 is (74-68) ÷ 3 = 2. Using the Standard Normal Distribution table, the percent of data lying between -1 and 2 = 34.13% + 47.72% ≈ 82%.

16. CORRECT ANSWER: B

The probability that exactly one drawn ball is black = $(5)(.05)(.95)^4 \approx .20$

17. CORRECT ANSWER: D

A trend is a pattern which shows growth or a decrease over time, which stationary series don't have.

18. CORRECT ANSWER: A

The equation of the regression line is y = mx+b, where m = $(r_{xy})(5y)/5_x$ and $b = \bar{y} - m\bar{x}$. Use 5y in place of σ_y; 5x in place of σ_x. Then, m = (.6)(2)/2 = .6 and b = 3 - (.6)(3) = 1.2

19. CORRECT ANSWER: D

The Doolittle Method basically solves 2 linear equations in 2 variables by multiplying and adding to eliminate 1 variable.

20. CORRECT ANSWER: B

The rank correlation coefficient $r_s = 1 - \dfrac{6\Sigma d^2}{n(n^2-1)}$ where d = difference between ranks within each pair of data, and n = number of pairs. The ranks for persons I through VII on Form A are 1, 2, 3, 4, 5, 6, 7. On Form B, they are 1, 2, 3, 4, 5, 7, 6. Σd^2 =0+0+0+0+0+1+1=2

$r_s = 1 - \dfrac{(6)(2)}{(7)(48)} \approx .96$

21. CORRECT ANSWER: A

A statistic is consistent if, as the sample size is increased, the statistic approaches the parameter (of the population).

22. CORRECT ANSWER: A

The product-moment correlation between x and y,

$r = \dfrac{\Sigma(x-\bar{x})(y-\bar{y})^2}{(n-1)(s_x)(sy)}$. For this example, $\bar{x} = \bar{y} = 0$, n = 10,

$s_x = \dfrac{\sqrt{\Sigma(x-\bar{x})^2}}{n-1} \approx 2.67$ and $sy = \dfrac{\sqrt{\Sigma(y-\bar{y})^2}}{n-1} \approx 2.4$

So, $r = 50/[(19)(2.67)(2.4)] \approx .87$

23. CORRECT ANSWER: C

This distribution is used on small samples to test if the sample whose mean = m could have come from a population with mean x. A small sample has size less than 30.

24. CORRECT ANSWER: C

Let X_1 = Intelligence, X_2 = Arithmetic, X_3 = English Literature.

The partial correlation coefficient, $r_{12 \cdot 3} = (r_{12} - r_{13} r_{23})/\sqrt{(1-r_{13}^2)(1-r_{23}^2)}$

$= [.7 - (.5)(.4)] / \sqrt{(1-.5^2)(1-.4^2)} \approx .63$

25. CORRECT ANSWER: D

The logistic equation used is $y = S/[1+Ce^{-skt}]$, where y = population, S = maximum possible population, C = (S-yo)/yo with yo being initial population, t = time for population y, and k = constant.

26. CORRECT ANSWER: A

We solve $\Sigma Y = na + b\Sigma x$ and $\Sigma xy = a\Sigma x + b\Sigma x^2$. Since n = 7, we get 38.1 = 7a + 0b and -51.3 = 0a + 28b. Solving, a = 5.4 and b = -1.8.

27. CORRECT ANSWER: B

    Using X^2 (chi-square) for independence, the number of degrees of freedom = (r-1)(c-1).

28. CORRECT ANSWER: D

    Since unemployment is highest in June, its values = (116.0/98.6)(4,100,000) ≈ 4,800,000.

29. CORRECT ANSWER: C

    This is called the Spearman rank correlation test, and it is a non-parametric method designed to measure the degree of association between two sets of ranked data. The population from which the data is extracted need not be normal.

30. CORRECT ANSWER: B

    Moving averages tend to *smoothen* the data. With time series, the effects of seasonality and irregularity will be reduced. Thus, a general trend can be more easily viewed.

31. CORRECT ANSWER: A

    As with the Consumer Price Index, the modified Lespeyres Price Index uses the base year as the denominator of the formula,

    which is $\dfrac{\sum_{i=1}^{n} P_{ti} Q_{ot}}{\sum_{i=1}^{n} P_{oi} Q_{oi}} \times 100$, where P_{ti} = price in year t, P_{oi} = price in base year, and Q_{oi} = quantity in base year.

32. CORRECT ANSWER: C

    The number of samples of size four = $(_4C_2)(_4C_2) = 6^2 = 36$

33. CORRECT ANSWER: B

    $$V(\bar{x}_s) = \left(\frac{1}{2}\right)^2 \left(1 - \frac{1}{2}\right)\left(\frac{81}{2}\right) + \left(\frac{1}{2}\right)^2 \left(1 - \frac{1}{2}\right)\left(\frac{457}{2}\right)$$
    $$= 5.0625 + 28.5625 \approx 34$$

34. CORRECT ANSWER: D

    This type of variation is also called a trend. This refers to a smooth upward or downward movement over a long (at least 15 years) time.

35. CORRECT ANSWER: C

    This index will measure changes in the physical amount of output of manufacturing, mining, and utilities.

36. CORRECT ANSWER: A

Orthogonal polynomials are a computational method in determining curves to fit trend data in time series problems.

37. CORRECT ANSWER: D

$$R^2_{x.yz} = \frac{.7^2 + .3 - (2)(.7)(.3)(-.1)}{1-(-.1)^2} = .62\overline{8}, \text{ so } R_{x.yz} \approx .79$$

38. CORRECT ANSWER: A

This is a transformation for an observed correlation coefficient, r, to a quantity, h, defined as

$$h = \frac{1}{2}|\text{Log}_e\left(\frac{1+r}{1-r}\right)| \text{ and also } s_h^2 = \frac{1}{n-3}, \text{ n= number of pairs of data.}$$

39. CORRECT ANSWER: C

In this type of correlation, values which are similar seem to follow earlier values, especially true in trends related to time series.

40. CORRECT ANSWER: B

Since the new line will be parallel to the original line, the slope (.7) must be the same. The initial y value for the new line will be 10.6 + (.7)(3) = 12.7.

41. CORRECT ANSWER: C

This type of arrangement (Latin Square) permits each treatment to be applied exactly once under each level of the blocking variables.

42. CORRECT ANSWER: B

Each expected cell entry would be (99)(99)/297 = 33. The contingency coefficient, C, is first computed with $\sum_{i=1}^{9} (O_i - E_i)^{2/E_i}$

= [36 + 128 + 242 + 36] ÷ 33 ≈ 13.4

Then, C = $\sqrt{13.4/(13.4+297)}$ ≈ .2078 ≈ .20

43. CORRECT ANSWER: D

Abraham Wald suggested the use of the maximum criterion in sequential analysis. This involves maximizing a payoff under pessimistic assumptions.

44. CORRECT ANSWER: A

This branch of mathematics involves linear inequalities identified by certain restrictions on the variables. The objective is then to either minimize or maximize a function of the variables.

45. CORRECT ANSWER: D

By Chebyshev's Theorem, at least $(1-1/k^2) \times 100$ percent of the given data must lie within k standard deviations of the mean. When $k = 2$, $(1-1/2^2) \times 100 = 75\%$

46. **CORRECT ANSWER: B**

In particular, the Neyman-Pearson Theorem is used to find the best critical region in conjunction with a likelihood ratio test.

47. **CORRECT ANSWER: A**

A particular restriction is being applied in order to reduce the actual population from which the sample will be drawn randomly.

48. **CORRECT ANSWER: D**

Let n be replaced by .20N. Then, $\frac{\sqrt{N-n}}{N-1} = \frac{\sqrt{.80N}}{N-1} \approx .894$. The percent reduction is $(1-.894) \times 100 \approx 10\%$

49. **CORRECT ANSWER: B**

These tests are also called distribution-free, since they do not assume a normally distributed population.

50. **CORRECT ANSWER: C**

This error is committed when a false null hypothesis is accepted. Type I error means rejecting a true null hypothesis.

51. **CORRECT ANSWER: B**

In sequential sampling, each observation is taken in sequence until a sound decision can be made.

52. **CORRECT ANSWER: D**

A sufficient statistic utilizes all the relevant information which a sample contains about the parameter to be estimated in the population.

53. **CORRECT ANSWER: C**

With respect to a discrete random variable (color of each ball), a Markov chain explains future values based on a present event and only dependent on an immediately preceding event.

54. **CORRECT ANSWER: A**

This probability is also called a Type I error. It represents the probability that a batch of goods which meets the acceptable quality level will actually be rejected, based on sampling.

55. **CORRECT ANSWER: D**

17 (#1)

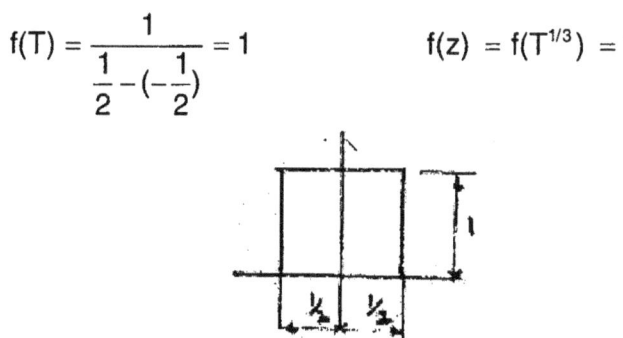

$$f(T) = \frac{1}{\frac{1}{2}-(-\frac{1}{2})} = 1 \qquad f(z) = f(T^{1/3}) = 1$$

The ordinate must be 1 because the area under a probability distribution is $1 \cdot \sqrt[3]{1} = 1$. The probability distribution is unchanged.

56. **CORRECT ANSWER: B**

$$6(T) = \phi(0)T^0 + \phi(1)T^1 = (q)(1) + (p)(T)$$
$$= pT + q$$

57. **CORRECT ANSWER: C**

The power function equals 1-3, where g is the probability of a Type II error.

58. **CORRECT ANSWER: D**

He constructed the foundation in set theory which was directly applied to probability in 1933.

59. **CORRECT ANSWER: D**

This represents the event of drawing 2 black balls, with replacement, one at a time.
If there is only 1 white ball, this probability is $(3/4)^2 = 9/16$.
The probabilities associated with (0,0), (0,1), and (1,0) are 1/16, 3/16, and 3/16, respectively. Thus, (1,1) has the highest probability.

60. **CORRECT ANSWER: C**

The probability that Jones will get a silver medal is equivalent to the probability of not getting the gold medal, then getting the silver medal.
Mathematically, this means $(3/4)(1/3) = 1/4$

EXAMINATION SECTION
TEST 1

DIRECTIONS: Each question or incomplete statement is followed by several suggested answers or completions. Select the one that BEST answers the question or completes the statement. *PRINT THE LETTER OF THE CORRECT ANSWER IN THE SPACE AT THE RIGHT.*

1. The one of the following which is NOT a measure of the spread or variability of a distribution is the _____ deviation.

    A. mean   B. orthogonal   C. quartile   D. standard

2. The one of the following which is NOT a probability or frequency distribution is a _____ distribution.

    A. rectangular   B. binomial   C. hypergeometric   D. circular

3. The mean is always equal to the variance in a _____ distribution.

    A. Poisson   B. rectangular   C. Lexian   D. Cauchy

4. In a certain large office, 40 percent of the employees are women. If a sample of five employees is selected at random, the probability that exactly two of the five are women is MOST NEARLY

    A. .45   B. .35   C. .20   D. .15

5. The coefficient of variation is a useful measure of relative variability when

    A. two variables with different units of measure are to be compared
    B. two variables are correlated
    C. two variables are normally distributed
    D. a qualitative variable is compared with a measurable variable

6. A stationary time series is a series which has no

    A. autocorrelation   B. cyclical movement
    C. variance   D. trend

7. A hundred observations on a certain variable X are obtained and found to have variance equal to 2. Suppose that every observation is multiplied by 2. The hundred observations on the new variable Y = 2X have variance equal to

    A. 3   B. 5   C. 7   D. 8

Questions 8-9.

DIRECTIONS: Questions 8 and 9 are to be answered on the basis of the following data.

The following distribution of workers in a certain country by annual income class was obtained:

Annual Income Class	Fraction of All Workers
1 (lowest income group)	.35
2	.40
3	.13
4	.09
5 (highest income group)	.03
Total	1.00

8. If two workers are selected at random, the probability that one will belong to class 2 and the other will belong to class 4 is MOST NEARLY

   A. 30.6   B. 3.6   C. .36   D. .036

9. If a single worker is selected at random, the probability that he will belong to either class 1 or class 5 is MOST NEARLY

   A. .57   B. .38   C. .234   D. .0212

10. If the value of a statistic approaches more and more closely the estimated parameter as the sample size is indefinitely increased, it is called

    A. consistent   B. valid
    C. sufficient   D. reliable

11. The limiting form of the binomial distribution as P becomes very small is the _____ distribution.

    A. anomalous   B. Cauchy
    C. Poisson   D. Chi-square

12. The distribution of means of samples from any population, as the size of the sample is increased, tends toward the _____ distribution.

    A. reticular   B. Poisson
    C. normal   D. binomial

Questions 13-15.

DIRECTIONS: Questions 13 through 15 are to be answered on the basis of the following data.

100 trials of an experiment are conducted in which the proba-bility of a *success* on any single trial is .2. Let X be the number of successes obtained in the 100 trials.

13. The average (expected) value of X in repeated sets of 100 trials is

    A. 15   B. 20   C. 25   D. 35

14. The variance of X in repeated sets of 100 trials is

    A. 2   B. 6   C. 16   D. 32

15. The variance of X/100 in repeated sets of 100 trials is

Questions 16-18.

DIRECTIONS: Questions 16 through 18 are to be answered on the basis of the following table.

95 Percent Confidence Interval for Binomial Distribution

Fraction of successes observed x/n	Size of Sample					
	100		250		1,000	
.15	.09	.24	.10	.20	.13	.17
.25	.17	.35	.20	.31	.22	.28
.35	.26	.45	.29	.41	.32	.38

16. In a sample of 100 cases, the fraction of successes observed, x/n, is .25.
    Using the above table, the one of the following hypotheses which should be accepted is that P

    A. is less than .14
    B. is more than .34
    C. is less than .38
    D. = .35

17. If the sample totaled 250 cases and x/n = .15, the one of the following hypotheses which should be rejected is that P is

    A. .13
    B. .15
    C. .19
    D. .22

18. A random sample of individuals is checked for an attribute, and 95 percent confidence limits for the fraction of individuals in the population having the attribute are obtained from tables like the one above.
    The limits obtained are such that

    A. 95 percent of the individuals lie within the limits
    B. 95 percent of future sample fractions will lie within these limits
    C. the probability that the population fraction lies within these limits is .95
    D. if we always obtain our limits in this way, then they will include the population fraction 95 percent of the time

19. The hypothesis that no true difference exists between two samples, that in fact these samples were randomly drawn from the same population and differ only by accidents of sampling, is called the _____ hypothesis.

    A. null
    B. collateral
    C. Tchebycheff
    D. Neyman-Pearson

20. If H_0 is the given hypothesis and H_1 is the alternative hypothesis, an error of Type I is made when

    A. H_1 is rejected although it is in fact the correct hypothesis
    B. H_0 is accepted although it is in fact the incorrect hypothesis
    C. H_0 is rejected although it is in fact the correct hypothesis
    D. H_0 is accepted as not being significantly different from H_1 although it is in fact different

21. If H_0 is the given hypothesis and H_1 is the alternative hypothesis, the power of the critical region R with respect to the alternative hypothesis H_1 is equal to

    A. 1 minus the probability of making an error of Type II
    B. the probability of making an error of Type I
    C. 1 minus the probability of making an error of Type III
    D. the probability of making an error of Type II

22. In testing the significance of differences between percentages, the distribution to be used is the _____ distribution.

    A. normal
    B. hypergeometric
    C. rectangular
    D. Lorian

23. In using the chi-square formula for testing agreement between observed and expected results, if the data are tabulated in r rows and c columns, the number of degrees of freedom is equal to

    A. rc + 1r
    B. (r-1)(c-1)
    C. (r+c)(r-c)
    D. rc - 1c

24. In testing whether a regression coefficient is signifi-cantly different from zero, the distribution to be used is the _____ distribution.

    A. Cauchy
    B. catastrophic
    C. Poisson
    D. t-

25. *In 176 years, the Lower Mississippi River has shortened itself 242 miles. Therefore, a million years ago, the Lower Mississippi River was 1,300,000 miles long.*
    This is an example of an unwarranted use of

    A. correlative regression
    B. linear regression
    C. extrapolation
    D. curvilinear interpolation

26. The correlation coefficient is usually spoken of as a measure of the strength of the linear relationship between two

    A. means
    B. modes
    C. parameters
    D. variables

27. No assumption about the normality of the population distribution is necessary when one uses

    A. analysis of compatibility
    B. multiple correlation
    C. partial correlation
    D. rank correlationRT

28. The linear function of the observations which will dis-tinguish better than any other linear function between the two groups on which common measurements are available is called a _____ function.

    A. regression
    B. discriminant
    C. least squares
    D. concentric

29. A statistical association between two variables may be evidence of a real association according to various tests and measurements of the regression analysis, but statis-tical association can in no way imply

    A. variation
    B. causation
    C. correlation
    D. integration

30. A fairly regular oscillation in a time series within each year which occurs regardless of the general trend or the position of the cyclical movement is called a(n)

    A. autocorrelation
    B. slant correlation
    C. seasonal variation
    D. variate difference

31. Given a least squares regression line of y on x: y = .4 + .12x, where x is the yearly income (in thousands of dollars) and y is the monthly food bill (in hundreds of dollars). If a family has a yearly income of $7,000, the predicted monthly expenditure for food is MOST NEARLY

    A. $96   B. $124   C. $184   D. $216

32. For a certain group of persons, the correlation between average grades in college and earnings ten years after graduation is found to be .64.
    The percentage of the variability in earnings which is explainable by differences in college grades is MOST NEARLY _____ percent.

    A. 72   B. 68   C. 41   D. 32

33. The regression equation for y on x may be written as: $y - \bar{y} = r(\frac{\sigma y}{\sigma x})(x - \bar{x})$ The regression equation for x on y when $\bar{x} = 3$, $\bar{y} = 6$, $\sigma x = 2$, $\sigma y = 3$ and r = .6 is

    A. 5x = 2y + 3
    B. 5x = 3y - 16
    C. x = 2y - 12
    D. x = y - 16

34. The number of different samples of three elements that can be drawn from a finite population of six elements is equal to

    A. 16   B. 19   C. 20   D. 23

35. As far as possible, in cluster sampling, each cluster, within itself, should be

    A. normally distributed
    B. consistent
    C. heterogeneous
    D. homogeneous

36. In sample surveys, failure to reach all respondents, poor reliability and validity of responses, and faulty interpretation of data are regarded as

    A. part of the random sampling variance
    B. part of the non-sampling errors
    C. part of the systematic variances
    D. nugatory since they tend to cancel each other.

37. Systematic sampling is LEAST likely to be similar to _____ sampling.

    A. simple random
    B. cluster
    C. stratified random
    D. quota

38. In stratified random sampling,

    A. a sample of selected strata is used
    B. a sample is selected from each stratum
    C. every K-th item is selected for the sample
    D. each stratum should be heterogeneous

39. If the sample size is doubled, the variance of the sampling distribution of the mean is multiplied by

   A. 3   B. 1   C. /3   D. 1/2

40. If random samples of size n are drawn from a specified population in order to estimate the proportion, P, of individuals possessing a certain characteristic, the sample proportion, P, of individuals possessing this characteristic can be used as an estimate of P.

   The variance of P' is $\dfrac{(N-n)}{(n-1)} \cdot \dfrac{P(1-P)}{n}$, where N is the total size of the population.

   The quantity $\dfrac{N-n}{N-1}$ is frequently referred to as

   A. Sheppard's correction
   B. correction factor for finite population
   C. correction factor for degrees of freedom
   D. correction factor for elasticity

KEY (CORRECT ANSWERS)

1.	B	11.	C	21.	A	31.	B
2.	D	12.	C	22.	A	32.	C
3.	A	13.	B	23.	B	33.	A
4.	B	14.	C	24.	D	34.	C
5.	A	15.	A	25.	C	35.	C
6.	D	16.	C	26.	D	36.	B
7.	D	17.	D	27.	D	37.	D
8.	D	18.	D	28.	B	38.	B
9.	B	19.	A	29.	B	39.	D
10.	A	20.	C	30.	C	40.	B

SOLUTIONS TO PROBLEMS

1. **CORRECT ANSWER: B**
   Orthogonal deviations are fictitious. Deviations can be mean, quartile, or standard.

2. **CORRECT ANSWER: D**
   No distribution can be described as circular. Rectangular, binomial, and hypergeometric can be used to describe a frequency distribution.

3. **CORRECT ANSWER: A**
   The formula can be written as $P(X-x) = e^{-\lambda} \cdot \lambda^x / x!$ for $x = 0,1,2,..., \lambda > 0$. The mean = the variance = λ.

4. **CORRECT ANSWER: B**
   The probability = $_5C_2(.40)^2(.60)^3 = .3456 \approx .35$

5. **CORRECT ANSWER: A**
   The coefficient of variation = $(\sigma/\mu) \cdot 100$ where σ = standard deviation and μ = mean.

6. **CORRECT ANSWER: D**
   A trend is a pattern which shows growth or a decrease over time, which stationary series lack.

7. **CORRECT ANSWER: D**
   If each observation is multiplied by 2, the original variance is multiplied by $2^2 = 4$. Since the original variance was 2, the new variance = $(2)(4) = 8$

8. **CORRECT ANSWER: D**
   The required probability = $(.40)(.09) = .036$.

9. **CORRECT ANSWER: B**
   The probability = $.35 + .03 = .38$

10. **CORRECT ANSWER: A**
    A statistic is consistent if: as the sample size is increased, the statistic approaches the population parameter.

11. **CORRECT ANSWER: C**
    If, in a binomial distribution, the number of trials (n) exceeds 30 and $p < .05$, the Poisson distribution can be used as a good approximation. In this case, replace λ by np as the mean.

12. **CORRECT ANSWER: C**
    The distribution of sample means approaches a normal distribution as the sample size increases. The mean of this distribution = the mean of the original population.

13. **CORRECT ANSWER: B**
    The expected value of $x = (.2)(100) = 20$

14. **CORRECT ANSWER: C**
    The variance of $x = (.2)(.8)(100) = 16$

15. **CORRECT ANSWER: A**

    The variance of $\frac{1}{100}x =$ (variance of x)$(\frac{1}{100})^2 = (16)(\frac{1}{10,000}) = .0016$

16. **CORRECT ANSWER: C**

    The chart shows a 95% probability that the value of p lies between .17 and .35.

17. **CORRECT ANSWER: D**

    The chart shows a 95% probability that the value of p lies between .10 and .20. Thus, reject p = .22

18. **CORRECT ANSWER: D**

    By selecting different samples of the same size from the population, we obtain different intervals to capture the value of y. Then 95% of these intervals will actually contain the value of y.

19. **CORRECT ANSWER: A**

    A null hypothesis would assume no actual statistical difference exists between two given samples.

20. **CORRECT ANSWER: C**

    By definition, this is an error of Type I.

21. **CORRECT ANSWER: A**

    The power is 1 - β, where β is the probability of accepting the alternative hypothesis (H_1) when it is false.

22. **CORRECT ANSWER: A**

    In testing the differences between percentages, the normal distribution is applied by converting to a $z = \dfrac{p_1 - p_2}{\sqrt{\bar{p}\,\bar{q}(\frac{1}{n_1} + \frac{1}{n_2})}}$ Here, p_1 and p_2 represent the sample percents (or proportions), n_1, n_2 are the sample sizes, $\bar{p}$ is the pooled percent and $\bar{q} = 1 - \bar{p}$

23. **CORRECT ANSWER: B**

    In chi-square tests for observed and expected values, the degrees of freedom = (r-1)(c-1), where r = number of rows, c = number of columns.

24. **CORRECT ANSWER: D**

    To test the significance of a regression coefficient, β, we would use $t_{n-k-1} = \dfrac{b}{s_b}$, where b = sample statistic used to sb measure β, n-k-1 = degrees of freedom, sb = standard error

25. **CORRECT ANSWER: C**

    Predictive data should only be used for reasonably-sized data values.

26. **CORRECT ANSWER: D**

    A correlation coefficient measures the linear relationship between 2 variables.

27. **CORRECT ANSWER: D**
Rank correlation tests concerning populations are non-parametric. They don't depend on a normal population.

28. **CORRECT ANSWER: B**
By definition.

29. **CORRECT ANSWER: B**
A statistical association indicates the strength of the relation-ship between the two variables. However, we cannot say that one variable's change causes the other variable's change.

30. **CORRECT ANSWER: C**
For each year, the same oscillation occurs at the same time of the time series.

31. **CORRECT ANSWER: B**
Substitute so that y = .4 + (.12)(7) = 1.24 hundreds of dollars = $124.

32. **CORRECT ANSWER: C**
The percentage of variability = (correlation)^2 = (.64)^2 = .41

33. **CORRECT ANSWER: A**
The equation will be $x - \bar{x} = (t)(\frac{\sigma x}{\sigma y})(y - \bar{y})$. Then, $x - 3 = (.6)(\frac{2}{3})(y - 6)$. This simplifies to $x - 3 = \frac{2}{5}(y - 6)$. Finally, 5x - 15 = 2y - 12 or 5x = 2y + 3

34. **CORRECT ANSWER: C**
The number of samples = $_6C_3$ = [(6)(5)(4)]/[(3)(2)(1)] = 120/6 = 20

35. **CORRECT ANSWER: C**
The original population is subdivided into clusters. Each cluster sampled should represent a *mix* of values.

36. **CORRECT ANSWER: B**
These are errors arising from external factors unrelated to the actual sampling process.

37. **CORRECT ANSWER: D**
In systemic sampling, a particular entity (e.g., a name in a phone book) would be selected. Then, every 10th name after this name would be chosen. Quota sampling would seek repre-sentative names of different origins.

38. **CORRECT ANSWER: B**
This is the definition of stratified random sampling.

39. **CORRECT ANSWER: D**
If n = original sample size, the variance of the sampling distribution of the mean = σ^2/n. By increasing the size to 2n, the new variance = $\sigma^2/2n = \frac{1}{2}\sigma^2/n$.

40. CORRECT ANSWER: B
The population correction factor is often used if n > .05N, that is n is a significant part of N in terms of size.

EXAMINATION SECTION
TEST 1

DIRECTIONS: Each question or incomplete statement is followed by several suggested answers or completions. Select the one that BEST answers the question or completes the statement. *PRINT THE LETTER OF THE CORRECT ANSWER IN THE SPACE AT THE RIGHT.*

Questions 1-8.

DIRECTIONS: Questions 1 through 8 are to be answered SOLELY on the basis of the following table.

CONSUMERS' PRICE INDEX FOR MODERATE INCOME FAMILIES IN LARGE CITIES

All Items and Groups

Year	All Items	Food	Clothing	Rent	House furnishings	Fuel, Electricity and Ice	Miscellaneous
1999	122.5	132.5	115.5	141.5	111.5	112.5	104.5
2000	119.5	126.0	112.5	137.5	109.0	111.5	105.0
2001	108.5	104.0	102.5	130.5	98.0	109.0	104.0
2002	97.5	86.5	91.0	117.5	85.5	103.5	101.5
2003	92.5	84.0	88.0	100.5	84.0	100.0	98.5
2004	95.5	93.5	96.0	94.5	93.0	101.5	98.0
2005	98.0	100.5	97.0	94.0	95.0	100.5	98.0
2006	99.0	101.5	97.5	96.5	96.5	100.0	98.5
2007	102.5	105.5	103.0	101.0	104.5	100.0	101.0
2008	101.0	98.0	102.0	104.0	103.5	100.0	101.5
2009	99.5	95.0	100.5	104.5	101.5	99.0	100.5
2010	100.0	96.5	101.5	104.5	100.5	99.5	101.0
2011	105.0	105.5	106.5	106.0	107.5	102.0	104.0
2012	116.5	124.0	124.0	108.5	122.0	105.5	110.0
2013	123.5	138.0	129.5	108.0	125.5	107.5	116.0
2014	125.5	136.0	139.0	108.0	136.5	110.0	121.5
2015	128.5	139.0	146.0	108.5	146.0	110.5	124.0
2016	139.5	159.5	160.0	108.5	159.0	112.5	129.0

1. On the basis of the data given, the base of the index numbers was MOST NEARLY 1.____
   - A. 2002-2008
   - B. 2005-2009
   - C. 2006-2008
   - D. 2007
   - E. 2010

2. In the above table, the price index of all items has apparently been obtained by 2.____
   - A. computing a straight average of the indices of the six items
   - B. giving heavier weight to food than to any of the other items
   - C. giving heavier weight to rent than to any of the other items
   - D. giving heavier weight to clothing than to any of the other items
   - E. none of the methods mentioned

67

3. The item for which the standard deviation is the lowest is

   A. clothing
   B. rent
   C. miscellaneous
   D. house furnishings
   E. fuel, electricity, and ice

4. Suppose that, using 2002 as the base year, it is desired to obtain an index number for 2005 which will be the straight average of the indices of three of the six items listed. This new index number for 2005 would be the highest if the three indices to be averaged were those for

   A. clothing, house furnishings, and miscellaneous
   B. food, clothing, and house furnishings
   C. food, clothing, and miscellaneous
   D. house furnishings, fuel, and miscellaneous
   E. food, rent, and fuel

5. The President's Committee on the Cost of Living, which collected the data given in the above table, felt that the consumers' price index did not fully reflect quality deterioration of commodities. Had it been possible to make an adjustment for these years on account of this factor, the effect would probably have been a

   A. rise in some of the six component indices and no change in the others
   B. fall in some of the six component indices and no change in the others
   C. rise in all of the six component indices
   D. fall in all of the six component indices
   E. fall in some and a rise in the rest of the component indices

6. If it were desired to compute a 7-year moving average for food, the averages centered on 2002, 2003, and 2004 would be MOST NEARLY _____ , respectively.

   A. 103.0, 99.5, 96.5
   B. 103.5, 98.5, 96.5
   C. 103.5, 99.5, 96.5
   D. 104.0, 99.5, 96.5
   E. 104.0, 99.5, 97.0

7. Taking only those values in the column marked *All Items* which are less than 100, the standard deviation of this series is MOST NEARLY

   A. 1.5   B. 2.5   C. 3.5   D. 4.5   E. 5.5

8. If the values in the column marked *Food* were to be arranged in the form of a frequency distribution with class intervals of five beginning with multiples of five, the median of this distribution would be MOST NEARLY

   A. 97.5   B. 100   C. 102.5   D. 105   E. 107.5

Questions 9-10.

DIRECTIONS: Questions 9 and 10 are to be answered on the basis of the following data.

Among the children in school X,
- 8% have defective eyes
- 4% have defective hearing
- 14% have defective teeth
- 1% have defective eyes and hearing
- 1.5% have defective eyes and teeth
- .75% have defective hearing and teeth
- .25% have defective eyes, hearing, and teeth

Each category mentioned includes children who may or may not have other defects also; e.g., of the 8% having defective eyes, some have no other defects, some have defective teeth as well, and some have all three defects.

9. The percentage of children who have neither defective eyes nor defective teeth nor defective hearing is

   A. 99.75   B. 78   C. 77   D. 75.75
   E. not determinable from the data given

10. The percentage of children who have defective eyes only is

    A. 8   B. 7   C. 5.75   D. 5.5
    E. not determinable from the data given

11. Graphic representation of the total population in the United States and of the proportion of the population in each specified age group for a series of years would be MOST properly shown by a

    A. pie chart   B. pictograph
    C. bar chart   D. histogram
    E. frequency curve

12. Quality control charts are an essential part of a statistical procedure which is widely used in industry to answer the question:
    What

    A. statistical factors determine the quality of a product?
    B. is the optimum relationship between quality and quantity?
    C. quality will yield the maximum return on a fixed investment?
    D. is an *excessively high* or an *excessively low* value of a measurement?
    E. is the most efficient method of production, assuming constant quality?

13. Although a particular base for price relatives may be satisfactory for a number of years, that base becomes less meaningful as time passes, and it eventually becomes desirable to shift to a more recent period. The one of the following which is the best reason for such a shift is that

A. the increasingly large variations which will occur in price relatives which are computed on a base of many years' standing will make the computations of aggregate price indices too time-consuming
B. the public to whom price indices are presented prefer to be referred to a base period with which they are familiar
C. if a base of many years' standing is used, only those commodities where the rate of change in the quantity consumed from year to year is constant can be included in computing aggregates
D. comparison of price aggregates of different years is facilitated if the aggregates remain fairly close in value
E. the pattern of consumption usually changes to such an extent that no aggregate of commodities can be found which includes the major expenditures common to both the current and base periods

14. The personnel division of a large organization wishes to include the following chart in its annual report:

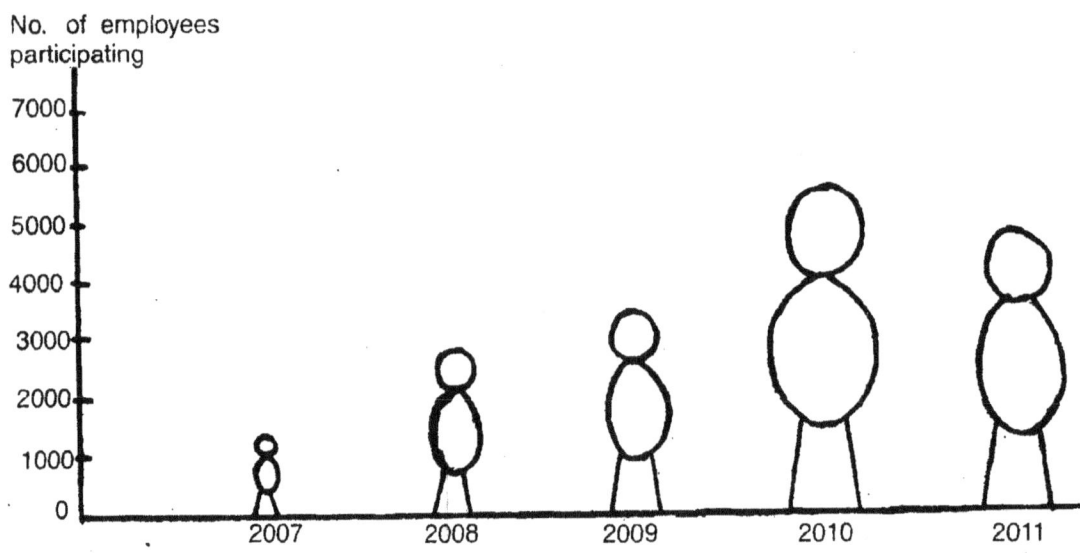

The one of the following evaluations which should influence most the decision as to the usability of the symbols in the above chart is that their use is

A. *improper;* a linear change in the numbers of participating employees is represented by an area change in the picture
B. *proper;* the relative heights of the symbols give the reader at a glance the trend in training activities
C. *improper;* a bar chart in this case is more appropriate than the use of any pictorial symbols
D. *proper;* the pictures vary in both dimensions in proportion to the change in the number of employees participating
E. *improper;* the pictures do not vary in both dimensions in proportion to the change in the number of employees participating

15. The following chart is suggested for publication:

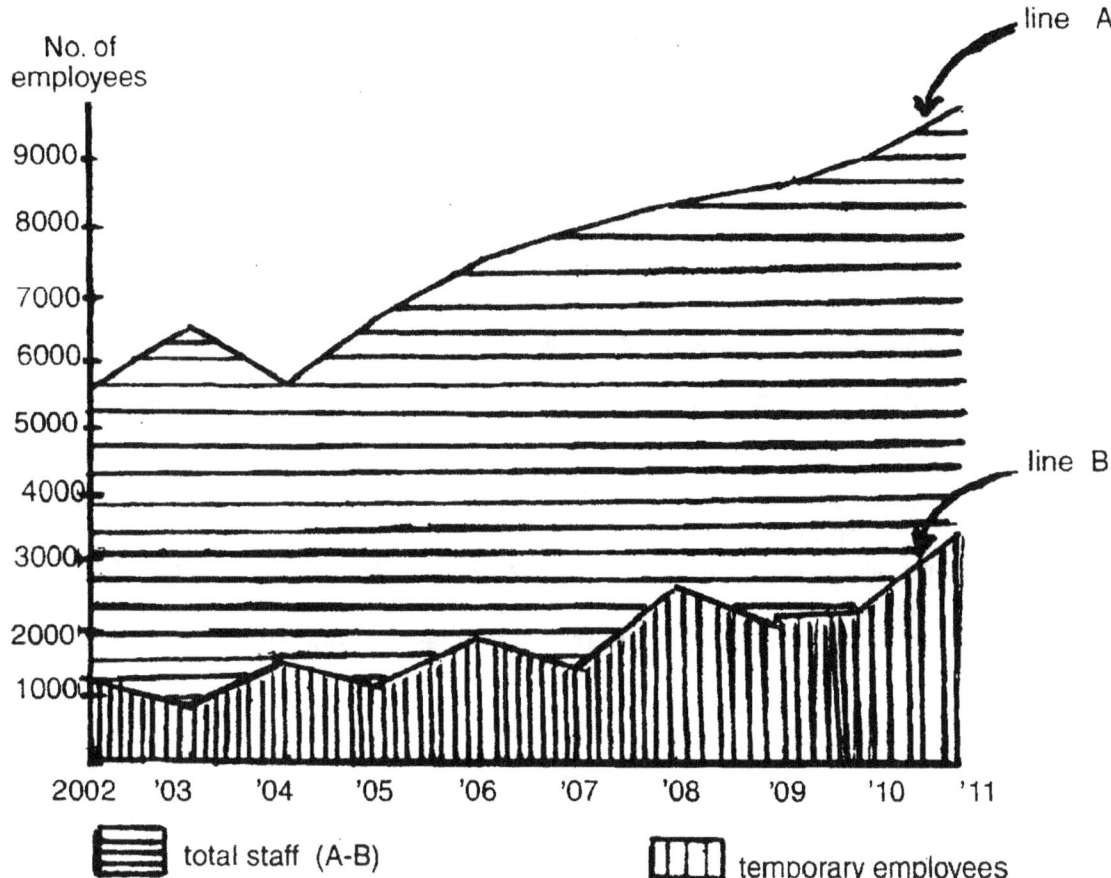

SIZE OF STAFF: 2002-2011

The one of the following estimates of the above chart which should be most influential in determining its usability in the given form is that it is

- A. *bad;* a third field, *permanent employees* should have been included in addition to the two fields shown
- B. *good;* the chart gives at a glance a picture of the ratio of temporary employees to total staff
- C. *bad;* the two items represented should have been *temporary employees* and *permanent employees* with the upper boundary of the graph representing the total staff
- D. *good;* the upper boundary of the chart represents the total of the two items shown
- E. *bad;* the two fields shown should have been *permanent employees* and *total staff*

16. In a health survey of families in a large city, enumerators are given forms, one of which is to be used for entering information dealing with health factors relative to a family. Data on the questionnaires are to be compiled into tables which describe the health status of families in this city. Each questionnaire contains space in which the enumerator is required to enter his name. Of the following, the LEAST important reason for requiring the enumerator to enter his name on the questionnaire is that

- A. the enumerator may be paid on a piece work basis
- B. data may have been omitted on the questionnaire
- C. an error may be made in tabulating data appearing on the questionnaire

D. in the course of tabulating the data some information appearing on the questionnaire may seem unreasonable
E. the tabulation of data may reveal unusual circumstances in some neighborhoods

17. In many experiments it seems obvious that the different conditions must have produced some difference, however small, in effect. Thus, the hypothesis that there is NO difference is unrealistic; the real problem is to obtain estimates of the sizes of the differences. In such types of experiments, in general,

   A. tests of significance are more frequently useful than confidence limits
   B. confidence limits are more frequently useful than tests of significance
   C. tests of significance and confidence limits are of equal value
   D. confidence limits are of no value
   E. tests of significance are of no value

17.____

18. The use of the coefficient of correlation has been found to be of greatest value in the case of

   A. observational data, when we can observe the occurrence of various causes of a phenomenon but cannot control them
   B. controlled experimental conditions where the causes of a phenomenon can be controlled
   C. exact mathematical data where the variates are functionally related
   D. qualitative data which escapes formulation in terms of quantities
   E. the concluding stages of scientific inquiry in order to express our conclusions in the form of a coefficient

18.____

19. In order to compare the attitudes of children with those of adults, in the field of art, a psychologist chooses twelve paintings, four of which have great merit, four of which are ordinary and four of which have little merit in the judgment of adults. He attaches a score of 2 to a picture of great merit, 1 to an ordinary picture, and 0 to a picture of little merit. The children are asked to rate the pictures using this scale. A composite score on the twelve pictures for each child, which will compare his attitude with that of the adults, is best obtained by

   A. subtracting the child's rating for each picture from the adult rating and adding the differences
   B. dividing the child's rating for each picture by the adult rating and adding the ratios
   C. subtracting the child's rating for each picture from the adult rating and adding the absolute values of the differences
   D. adding the child's ratings for the 12 pictures and dividing by 12
   E. multiplying the child's rating for each picture by the adult rating, adding the products and dividing by the coefficient of correlation

19.____

20. An experiment is useless if

   A. no possible result with respect to the probability of the correctness of the hypothesis would satisfy the experimenter sufficiently to cause him to admit that his observations have demonstrated a positive result
   B. it is necessary to forecast all possible results of the experiment and to decide without ambiguity what interpretation shall be placed upon each of them in order to determine the appropriateness of the experimental design
   C. in order to derive any knowledge from it, an inductive inference must be made

20.____

D. in order to derive any knowledge from it, a deductive inference must be made
E. the logical implications of the results of the arithmetical processes employed are not completely determined in advance

21. Of the following, one reason why the range, in spite of its simplicity, convenience, and importance, is used only in restricted situations is that it

   A. is of little value for samples of greater than about 25
   B. is of little value for samples of less than about 25
   C. is not a very sensitive measure of variation among samples
   D. does not give even relatively stable information concerning samples
   E. is difficult to compare a range for one sample size with that for a different sample size

22. In a study of the interrelations existing among four variates X_x, X_2, X_3, and X_4, it is necessary to test the significance of the partial correlation $r_{12.34}$. In making the test, the number of degrees of freedom that a sample of 30 sets or readings is considered to have is

   A. 29   B. 28   C. 27   D. 26   E. 25

23. If the regression coefficient of X_1 on X_2 is b_{12} and if the regression coefficient of X_2 is b_{21}, then the product b

   A. is equal to one
   B. can have any value greater than zero
   C. can have any value between zero and one
   D. can have any value between minus one and one
   E. is equal to $\sqrt{b_{12}^2 - b_{12}}$

24. The values of a particular variate are confined to integral values with by far the most values being even. Class intervals are chosen to extend from 0 to but not including 2, from 2 to but not including 4, etc. This choice of class intervals is

   A. *bad;* it will lead to a systematic error of almost one in computation of the mean value of the variate
   B. *good;* it takes cognizance of the properties of the particular variate in selection of terminal points
   C. no better and not inferior to any other choice of class intervals of length 2
   D. *good;* it takes cognizance of the properties of the particular variate in selecting 2 as the interval length
   E. *bad;* it will lead to a systematic error of almost one in computation of the standard deviation

25. Samples of 100 are drawn from an almost normally distributed infinite population. If the population mean and standard deviation are 25 and 10, respectively, the sample standard deviation is MOST NEARLY

   A. .1   B. 1   C. 2.5   D. 5   E. 10

26. The mean of a sample ($\bar{X}_1$) exceeds the mean of another sample ($\bar{X}_2$) by +1.04, and the standard error of the difference is 2.63. In a normal probability curve with the mean at 0 and a σ of 2.63, .1536 of the total area under the curve lies between the ordinates erected at the mean and at a point +1.04 from the mean. Then, if the true difference between the means of the two samples is zero, the probability that $\bar{X}_1$ might exceed $\bar{X}_2$ by 1.04 or more because of chance variations is MOST NEARLY _____ chances out of 100.

   A. 15   B. 30   C. 35   D. 70   E. 85

27. A difference between samples used for estimating a regression coefficient and those used for estimating a correlation coefficient is that

   A. in the former both variates are selected at random while in the latter one variate is selected and the second chosen at random
   B. the former is stratified with respect to both variates while the latter is stratified with respect to one only
   C. the former is a random sample while the latter is stratified with respect to one variate
   D. the former is stratified with respect to one variate while the latter is with respect to both
   E. in the former one variate is selected and the second chosen at random, while in the latter both variates are selected at random

28. If a random sample of 100 marbles is drawn from a large assortment of black and white marbles in which the proportion of white marbles is known to be 60% of the total, the standard error of the proportion of white marbles is MOST NEARLY

   A. .01   B. .05   C. .1   D. .5   E. 1

29. In a regression function of height on age, where age is the independent variate and height the dependent variate, the regression of height on age will not be influenced by errors occurring in the

   A. ages, if the positive and negative errors at all heights are equally frequent, balancing in the averages
   B. heights, if the positive and negative errors at all ages are equally frequent, balancing in the averages
   C. heights, if the error always has the same sign as the corresponding error in age
   D. ages, if the error always has the same sign as the corresponding error in height
   E. ages, provided the standard deviation of errors in height is equal to the standard deviation of errors in age

30. The result of an experiment with 25 patients on the effect of each of two supposedly sleep-producing drugs X and Y in producing additional hours of sleep was that when drug X was used, patients gained on the average two hours more sleep than when drug Y was used. The variance of the difference for each patient is 2. In order to determine if the difference between results is significantly different from zero, the table for t should be entered with t MOST NEARLY equal to

   A. 1   B. 3   C. 5   D. 7   E. 9

KEY (CORRECT ANSWERS)

1.	B	16.	C
2.	E	17.	B
3.	E	18.	A
4.	B	19.	C
5.	A	20.	A
6.	D	21.	E
7.	B	22.	D
8.	D	23.	C
9.	C	24.	A
10.	C	25.	B
11.	C	26.	C
12.	D	27.	E
13.	E	28.	B
14.	A	29.	B
15.	C	30.	D

SOLUTIONS TO PROBLEMS

1. **CORRECT ANSWER: B**
   In almost every category, the numbers closest to 100.0 lie between the years 2005 to 2009.

2. **CORRECT ANSWER: E**
   The column for all items is not a straight average of any year's indices of the 6 items and gives no special weight to any item.

3. **CORRECT ANSWER: E**
   In this category, the indices range from 99.0 to 112.5, which is smaller than any other category. Thus, its standard deviation must be the lowest.

4. **CORRECT ANSWER: B**

	Food	Clothing	Furnishings Rent	etc.	Fuel etc.	Miscellaneous
2002	86.5	91.0	117.5	85.5	103.5	101.5
2005	100.5	97.0	94.0	95.0	100.5	98.0
	+14.0	+6.0	-23.5	+9.5	-3.0	-3.5

   Food, Clothing, and Furnishings, etc. represent the greatest increases.
   For each of these 3 categories, the index for 2005 is higher than the index for 2002.
   Thus, if 2002 is the base year, the new index for 2005 would be the highest possible.
   The actual value would be:
   $100.5/86.5 + 97.0/91.0 + 95.9/85.5 \div 3 = 111.5$

5. **CORRECT ANSWER: A**
   By increasing some components, the consumer price index would better reflect the deterioration.

6. **CORRECT ANSWER: D**
   For 1999-2005, the 7-yr. average = $727 \div 7 = 103.86$
   For 2000-2006, the 7-yr. average = $696 \div 7 \sim 99.43$
   For 2001-2007, the 7-yr. average = $675.5 \div 7 = 96.5$

7. **CORRECT ANSWER: B**
   The standard deviation of 97.5, 92.5, 95.5, 98.0, 99.0, and 99.5 is found by finding the mean which is $582 * 6 = 97$.
   Then, the standard deviation =

   $$\sqrt{\frac{(97.5-97)^2 + (92.5-97)^2 + (95.5-97)^2 + ... + (99.5-97)^2}{6-1}}$$

   $= \sqrt{6.8} \approx 2.6$, so 2.5 is closest

8. **CORRECT ANSWER: D**
   Since there are 18 values, the median would lie halfway between the 9th and 10th values after arranging all 18 in order. Thus, the median = $(104.0 + 105.5) \div 2 = 104.75 = 105$

9. CORRECT ANSWER: C
The Venn Diagram would be as follows:

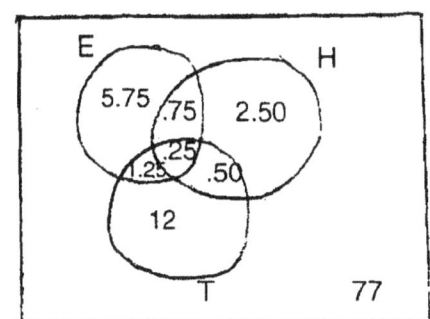

E = defective gears
H = defective hearing
T = defective teeth
All numbers given are percents.

100 - 5.75 - .75 - .25 - 1.25 - 2.50 - .50 - 12 = 77

10. CORRECT ANSWER: C Same diagram as in #9.
8 - 1.25 - .75 - .25 = 5.75

11. CORRECT ANSWER: C
Bar charts are best used to illustrate the ratio of some category to a sum of categories, especially over a period of time. Incidentally, although a pie chart can also demonstrate ratio, it cannot illustrate a change of ratio over time.

12. CORRECT ANSWER: D
In these charts, the mean is obtained, along with the standard deviation. Each data is plotted and horizontal lines are drawn to represent a distance of 1, 2, and 3 standard deviations. Data which fall below or above a distance of 3 standard deviations (from the mean) are identified.

13. CORRECT ANSWER: E
The current and base periods become too far apart for a meaningful comparison.

14. CORRECT ANSWER: A
The width of each picture must be the same, even though the height changes.

15. CORRECT ANSWER: C
Line A would represent the total.
Line B would represent one type of employee.
Area between A and B would represent the other type of employee.

16. CORRECT ANSWER: C
Any error involving the tabulation of data is irrelevant to the enumerator's identity.

17. CORRECT ANSWER: B
Confidence limits will reveal the probability that the interval of data obtained will contain the specified population parameter.

18. CORRECT ANSWER: A
In this way, we test the strength of the dependency of one variable upon another. We don't expect an exact dependency.

19. **CORRECT ANSWER: C**
The lower the sum of these absolute values, the closer are the children's and adults' attitudes of the paintings. Mathematically,

$$\sum_{i=1}^{12} |x_i - y_i|$$ is evaluated x_i = adult, y_i = child.

20. **CORRECT ANSWER: A**
If no probability can be assigned to accuracy, the experiment has no value.

21. **CORRECT ANSWER: E**
For example, one sample of size 100 may have a range of 10, but another sample of size 200 may have a range of 15. Con-clusions would be difficult, absent any other information.

22. **CORRECT ANSWER: D**
Degrees of freedom = number of readings minus number of variates = 30 - 4 = 26.

23. **CORRECT ANSWER: C**

24. **CORRECT ANSWER: A**
For any interval, the class mark will be used to compute the overall mean. However, most values are even, so this is not a true representation.

25. **CORRECT ANSWER: B**
The sample standard deviation is nearly $10 / \sqrt{100} = 1$

26. **CORRECT ANSWER: C**
The probability that $\bar{X}_1$ exceeds $\bar{X}_2$ at all is .50. Thus, the probability that $\bar{X}_1 - \bar{X}_2 \geq 1.04$ is $.50 - .1536 \approx 35\%$.

27. **CORRECT ANSWER: E**

28. **CORRECT ANSWER: B**
The standard error of the proportion is

29. **CORRECT ANSWER: B**
The value of height based on age will be the same predicted value due to the regression equation since all errors will add up to zero.

30. **CORRECT ANSWER: D**

$$t = \frac{2-0}{\sqrt{2}/\sqrt{25}} = \frac{2}{.28} \approx 7$$

TEST 2

DIRECTIONS: Each question or incomplete statement is followed by several suggested answers or completions. Select the one that BEST answers the question or completes the statement. *PRINT THE LETTER OF THE CORRECT ANSWER IN THE SPACE AT THE RIGHT.*

1. If all the points in a scatter diagram for which X is less than C are eliminated, the value of the coefficient of correlation will, in general,

   A. be raised
   B. be lowered
   C. be unaffected
   D. become meaningless
   E. be lowered if r > 1/2 and raised if r < 1/2

   1.____

2. If x is a chance quantity with mean m and standard deviation σ, and if $z = x-m/\sigma$, the mean of z is

   A. -m   B. $-m/\sigma$ C. 0   D. m/σ E. m

   2.____

3. The standard deviation of z, defined in Question 2 above is

   A. 0   B. σ/m C. m/σ D. 1   E. σ

   3.____

4. If the coefficient of correlation between the sets (X_1) and (X_2) is 0, the coefficient of correlation between the sets (X_1) and $(X_1 + X_2)$

   A. is one
   B. is positive, the exact value depending upon other information
   C. may be either positive or negative, depending upon other information
   D. is negative, the exact value depending upon other information
   E. is 0

   4.____

5. If S_X^2 is the variance of the set of measurements $(X_1, X_2, X_3, ...X_n)$, then S_y^2, the variance of the set of measure-ments $(Y_1, Y_2, Y_3, ...Y_n)$, where $Y_i = X_i + a$, is equal to

   A. $S_X^2 + a$ B. $S_X^2 + a^2$ C. $(SX + a)^2$ D. S_X^2
   E. a function of $Y_1, Y_2,....Y_n$, which is independent of S_X

   5.____

6. A bag contains 9 white balls and one black ball; another contains 3 white balls and three black balls. If a bag is chosen at random and a ball drawn from it, the probability that a black ball will be drawn is

   A. 1/10   B. 2/10   C. 3/10   D. 4/10   E. 5/10

   6.____

7. Flowers blossoming from a sample of 1,000 seeds have the following characteristics:

ATTRIBUTE	RED	WHITE	TOTAL
TALL	350	250	600
SHORT	250	150	400
TOTAL	600	400	1000

   If size and color are independent characteristics in this sample, the theoretical number of plants that should have been tall and red is MOST NEARLY

   A. 300   B. 330   C. 360   D. 390   E. 420

   7.____

8. A bowl contains 5 discs numbered 1, 2, 3, 4, 5, respectively. Two are withdrawn, their numbers noted and then the discs are replaced. The procedure is repeated many times. If X is the average value of the two numbers noted each time, the mean of the theoretical sampling distribution of X is

   A. 2.5 B. 3 C. 3.5 D. 4
   E. not determinable from the data given

Questions 9-13.

DIRECTIONS: For Questions 9 through 13, Column I contains 5 problems and Column II lists 5 distributions. For each problem in Column I, select the distribution from Column II which would be of greatest value in solving that problem. Place the letter next to the distribution in the space at the right. (A distribution given in Column II may relate to none, one, or more than one problem.)

9. COLUMN I
   A random sample of 11 elements from a normal bivariate population yields r = .5. Is p significantly different from zero at the 95% level?

   COLUMN II
   A. Binomial distribution
   B. Normal distribution
   C. Poisson distribution
   D. Student's t-distribution
   E. Chi-square distribution

10. The distribution of weights of 1000 infants at birth has a mean of 6.8 lbs. and a standard deviation of 1.4 lbs. If a sample of 100 infants is picked at random from this population, what is the probability that the weight will exceed 7 lbs.?

11. In an experiment, measurements are made in a control group of white mice and an experimental group.
    The data are:

Sample	Sample Size	Sample Mean	Sample σ
Control	20	2.61	.34
Experimental	17	2.92	.31

    Establish 95% confidence limits of the difference of the means of the populations

12. Assume that the city buys a large shipment of electric lightbulbs with the assurance that on the average only one bulb in a thousand (the size of a standard shipment) is defective. On the basis of this information, what percentage of shipments would you estimate to have no defective bulbs?

13. Assume that on the average one telephone number out of ten called between ten and eleven A.M. on weekdays in city offices is busy. What is the probability that if 20 randomly selected telephone numbers are called not more than two will be busy?

14. The difference between two proportions based on two samples is found to be statistically not significant. From this, we may conclude that

    A. continued sampling will show the two populations to be identical
    B. the populations have not been shown to be different
    C. if larger samples are chosen they will show a more significant difference
    D. if larger and larger samples are drawn the differences between them will get smaller and smaller
    E. there is no reason for continuing the study

    14.____

15. As the number of cases increases, the **Student's** t-distribution approaches a _____ distribution with _____ .

    A. normal; mean 0 and variance 1
    B. Poisson; a mean m
    C. binomial; $p = q = 1/2$
    D. Poisson; mean 1
    E. normal; mean 1 and variance 1

    15.____

Questions 16-19.

DIRECTIONS: For Questions 16 through 19, Column I gives description of four statistical distributions. Column II lists seven mathematical functions. For each distribution in Column I, select the function from Column II which represents that distribution and place the letter of the function in the space at the right.

COLUMN I

16. A binomial distribution with probability of success equal to n

17. A chi-square distribution with n degrees of freedom

18. A Poisson distribution with mean n

19. A normal distribution with mean equal to zero and standard deviation equal to n

COLUMN II

A. $\sum_{0=1}^{n} \left(\frac{x_i - m}{\sigma_x}\right)^2$

B. $\frac{\pi}{\sqrt{\pi}} \arcsin n$

C. $\frac{n!}{\pi x!} e^{x^2}$

D. $\frac{(\frac{\sqrt{n}}{2})}{\sqrt{n-1}\sqrt{\pi}(\frac{\sqrt{n-1}}{2})(1+\frac{x^2}{n-1})^{\frac{n}{2}}} dx$

E. $\frac{1}{\sqrt{2\pi} n} e^{-\frac{1}{2}(\frac{x}{n})^2}$

F. $_mC_x\, n^x (1-n)^{m-x}$

G. $\frac{n^x}{x!} e^{-n}$

16.____

17.____

18.____

19.____

20. Two different companies manufacture serum XYZ. An analysis of 100 samples from each company yields the following data:

Company	Main Potency	Standard Deviation
A	7.84	.04
B	7.56	.05

    The values of $\frac{x}{\sigma}$ for a normal probability curve (where x is the deviation from the mean) which correspond to confidence coefficients of 90%, 95%, and 99% are 1.645, 1.960, and 2.576, respectively.
    The difference in mean potency between the two sets of samples is

    A. significantly different from zero at the 99% level
    B. significantly different from zero at the 95% level but not at the 99% level
    C. significantly different from zero at the 90% level but not at the 95% level
    D. not significantly different from zero at the 90% level
    E. probably equal to zero

21. If random samples are drawn from a normal bivariate population with coefficient correlation ρ, and are then grouped, the statistic r equal to the covariance divided by the geometric mean of variances

    A. is not an appropriate estimate of ρ as it does not approach ρ as n increases
    B. is neither an unbiased (consistent) nor appropriate estimate of ρ
    C. though unbiased (consistent), is not an appropriate estimate of ρ
    D. is an unbiased (consistent) and appropriate estimate of ρ
    E. though not unbiased (consistent), is an appropriate estimate of ρ

22. The flowers blossoming from a sample of 1000 seeds have the following characteristics:

ATTRIBUTE	WHITE	RED	TOTAL
TALL	300	250	550
SHORT	250	200	450
TOTAL	550	450	1000

    If it is assumed that the two attributes color and size are independent, chi-square for this sample is MOST NEARLY equal to

    A. .001   B. .1   C. 1   D. 10   E. 100

23. The sum of any number of quantities, chi-square, is distributed in the

    A. chi-square distribution with n equal to the mean of the values of n corresponding to the values of chi-square used
    B. normal distribution with m equal to the mean of the values of chi-square used and a equal to their standard deviation
    C. Poisson distribution with m equal to the mean of the values of chi used
    D. chi-square distribution with n equal to the sum of the values of n corresponding to the values of chi-square used
    E. normal distribution with m equal to the mean of the values of chi used and a equal to their standard deviation

24. In medicine the mean income is 30% higher than in dentistry. But both the median and the first quartile incomes are approximately the same in the two professions. The mean income for both doctors and dentists is higher than the respective median income. It may be most accurately concluded from this statement that

    A. the proportion of doctors having incomes above the median is larger than among dentists
    B. the range of income is higher among the doctors than among the dentists
    C. the percentage of doctors having incomes above the mean of the medical profession is higher than the percentage of dentists having incomes above the mean of the dental profession
    D. dentists with incomes lower than the median tend to earn less than doctors with incomes lower than the median
    E. doctors with incomes higher than the median tend to earn more than dentists with incomes higher than the median

25. May I point out that if technical employees are given assignments only in their special fields, there will be an immediate gain in conserving special skills. And, if we are to make optimum use of the abilities of the technical employees, it is necessary that these skills be conserved. Assuming the correctness of this analysis, it follows that

    A. if we are not making optimum use of the abilities of technical employees, we have been giving technical employees assignments outside of their special fields
    B. we are making optimum use of the abilities of technical employees if we conserve special skills
    C. we are making optimum use of the abilities of technical employees if we give them assignments only in their special fields
    D. we are not making optimum use of the abilities of technical employees if we give them assignments out-side of their special fields
    E. if we are making optimum use of the abilities of technical employees, there is no need to conserve special skills

26. Statistics having efficiency less than 100 percent may be legitimately used for many purposes. It is conceivable, for example, that it might in some cases be less laborious to increase the number of observations than to apply a more elaborate method of calculation to the results.
    It may be properly inferred from the above passage that a statistic having less than 100 percent efficiency

    A. becomes more useful if the number of observations is increased
    B. is generally more difficult to compute than a statistic of 100 percent efficiency
    C. is generally less difficult to compute than a statistic of 100 percent efficiency
    D. becomes more efficient if the number of observations is increased
    E. is not affected by the number of observations

Questions 27-29.

DIRECTIONS: Questions 27 through 29 are to be answered on the basis of the following paragraph.

When the structure of an experiment consists of a number of independent comparisons between pairs, our estimate of the error of the average difference must be based upon the discrepancies between the differences actually observed. Consequently, we must determine what precautions are needed in the practical conduct of the experiment to guarantee that such an estimate shall be a valid one; that is to say that the very same causes that produce our real error shall also contribute the materials for computing an estimate of it.

27. The requirement *that the very same causes that produce our real error shall also contribute the materials for computing an estimate of it* is

    A. *necessary;* the causes which produce our real error cannot fail to contribute the materials for computing an estimate of it
    B. *not necessary;* the causes which produce our real error obviously must also contribute the materials for computing an estimate of it
    C. *necessary;* if causes of variation affect the real error in such a way as to make no contribution to our estimate, this estimate will be of little value
    D. *not necessary;* if the causes which produce the real error do not contribute to the estimate, we can always change the estimate
    E. *necessary;* if causes which produce the real error do not contribute to the estimate, causes which contribute to the estimate may not be the real causes

28. The one of the following which the above paragraph assumes to be a characteristic of the experimental method is that

    A. estimates may not be valid
    B. precautions cannot guarantee that our estimate will be valid
    C. differences are actually observable
    D. observation may yield only an approximation
    E. it may not be possible to make any prediction

29. On the basis of the assumptions expressed and implied in the above paragraph, our estimate of an error will not be a valid one if causes

    A. are allowed to determine what precautions are needed
    B. affect the estimate in the same way that they influence the real error
    C. are not allowed to determine what precautions are needed
    D. which do not affect the estimate have not produced the real error
    E. which do not influence the real error affect the estimate

30. Randomization is often necessary to avoid biases in experiments involving several treatments. The result of such specific randomization may favor any one of the treatments but only to an extent that is allowed for in the calculations used for tests of significance and confidence limits. According to the above statement, randomization will tend to

    A. reduce bias to such a degree that tests of significance will be valid
    B. eliminate bias completely
    C. not reduce bias significantly
    D. not be effective unless all bias can be eliminated
    E. be ineffective unless tests of significance are used

Questions 31-32.

DIRECTIONS: Questions 31 and 32 are to be answered on the basis of the following statement.

The process of validating a factual proposition is quite distinct from the process of validating a value judgment. The former is validated by its agreement with the facts, the latter by human authority.

31. According to the above statement, the one of the following methods which is most acceptable for determining whether or not a proposition is factually correct is to   31.____

    A. prove that a related proposition is factually correct
    B. derive it logically from accepted assumptions
    C. show that it will lead to desired results
    D. compare it with experience
    E. refer to some recognized authority

32. Assuming the correctness of the above statement, the statement that *the correctness of all ethical propositions can be tested empirically* is   32.____

    A. *correct;* testing empirically is validating by agreement with facts
    B. *not correct;* ethical propositions are value judgments
    C. *correct;* ethical propositions are based on rational hypotheses
    D. *not correct;* a factual proposition is validated by its agreement with facts
    E. *correct;* the process of validation used depends upon what is being validated

33. Cyclical movements of general activity could be generated by a concurrence of the same cyclical phase in the activity of many important industries or they might be generated by interferences of a major type from outside the business world. On the basis of the above statement, the one of the following which would be most likely to cause general cyclical movements is   33.____

    A. concurrence of twenty year cycles in manufacturing industries using cotton as raw material
    B. a local draught
    C. concurrence of ten year cycles in iron and steel industries
    D. ten year cycles following each other at three-year intervals in paper, steel, glass, and woolen industries
    E. a war involving several countries

34. The rejection of the theory of inverse probability was for a time wrongly taken to imply that we cannot draw, from knowledge of a sample, inferences respecting the corresponding population. Such a view would entirely deny validity to all experimental science. According to the above statement,   34.____

    A. the theory of inverse probability cannot be applied to an entire population
    B. making deductions from a sample is consistent with experimental science
    C. making deductions from a sample is inconsistent with experimental science
    D. the theory of inverse probability is based on the study of samples
    E. the principles of experimental science are not applicable to the theory of inverse probability

35. When a number of quite independent tests of significance have been made, it sometimes happens that, although few or none can be claimed individually as significant, yet the aggregate gives an impression that the probabilities are on the whole lower than would often have been obtained by chance. On the basis of the above statement, a combination of several tests of significance

    A. may indicate results contrary to the results obtained from single tests of significance
    B. is required before a difference can be considered significant
    C. will usually give results which are different from results obtained from independent tests
    D. may not yield true probabilities
    E. should be employed in all tests of significance involving probabilities

35.____

KEY (CORRECT ANSWERS)

1. B	11. D	21. E	31. D
2. C	12. C	22. B	32. B
3. D	13. A	23. D	33. E
4. B	14. B	24. E	34. B
5. D	15. A	25. D	35. A
6. C	16. F	26. A	
7. C	17. A	27. C	
8. B	18. G	28. D	
9. D	19. E	29. E	
10. B	20. A	30. A	

SOLUTIONS TO PROBLEMS

1. **CORRECT ANSWER: B**
   In general, fewer points for a scatter diagram lead to a weaker correlation between the variables. Thus, the correlation coefficient would become smaller.

2. **CORRECT ANSWER: C**
   $Z = x-m/\sigma$ represents a standard score. If all scores of a distribution are converted to standard scores, the resulting mean would be zero.

3. **CORRECT ANSWER: D**
   The standard deviation of the distribution in #2 would be 1. As an example, consider the distribution 1, 2, 3, 6. The mean m = 3 and $\sigma = \frac{\sqrt{14}}{4} \approx 1.87$. The z values would be -1.069, 4 -.535, 0, 1.604. The standard deviation for these z values =
   $$\sqrt{[(-1.069)^2 + (-.535)^2 + 0^2 + (1.604)^2]/4} \approx \sqrt{1.00045} \approx 1$$
   Error is due to rounding.

4. **CORRECT ANSWER: B**
   Because the sets are added, $X_1 + X_2 = X_3$ will be positively correlated with X_1 (or with X_2).

5. **CORRECT ANSWER: D**
   If $Y_i = X_i + a$, then the value of each Y is a constant added to the value of each a. The variance of the X_i's must equal the variance of Y_i's.

6. **CORRECT ANSWER: C**
   The probability required = (Probability of bag 1)(Probability of a black ball) + (Probability of bag 2)(Probability of a black ball) = (1/2)(1/10) + (1/2)(3/6) = 3/10.

7. **CORRECT ANSWER: C**
   Assuming independence of size and color, the number of plants which should be tall and red is found by (600)(600)/1000 = 360.

8. **CORRECT ANSWER: B**
   The mean of the sampling distribution of means would approach the mean of the population, which is 3.

9. **CORRECT ANSWER: D**
   Correlation coefficients for samples with a size less than 30 are identified with a student t-distribution.

10. **CORRECT ANSWER: B**
    The original distribution is normal and the size of the population (1000) is certainly considered large.

11. **CORRECT ANSWER: D**
    In tests of the difference of the means of two populations, each of size less than 30, the student's t-distribution is used.

10 (#2)

12. CORRECT ANSWER: C
This type of distribution does not depend on a normal distribution of data. It depends on the ratio of *arriving* entities, such as shipments of lightbulbs, planes at an airport, people at a line in a store, etc. The mathematical model measures some characteristic x as P(x) = In this example, x could be number of actual defective lightbulbs, whereas is the expected number of defective lightbulbs. e = 2.718, approximately.

13. CORRECT ANSWER: A
This distribution can be used when the probability for success (or failure) remains the same for each of a fixed number of trials. If x = number of successes, P(x) = C(n,x)Px(1-p)n-x, where n = number of trials, C(n,x) = n!/[(n-x)!x!] and p = probability of success on any trial.

14. CORRECT ANSWER: B
It is certainly possible that by choosing two other samples, we could show that the populations are alike.

15. CORRECT ANSWER: A
Once the number of cases increases to 30, the Normal Distribution may be used.

16. CORRECT ANSWER: F
In this Binomial Distribution, the probability of success is n, the probability of failure is 1-n, and m is the number of trials.

17. CORRECT ANSWER: A
In this distribution, which is X^2, X ,...,X_n denote a random sample of size n with mean = μ , variance = σ_x^2 .

18. CORRECT ANSWER: G
In this Poisson Distribution, the mean is n. The expression represents the probability of x successes.

19. CORRECT ANSWER: E
This is a Normal Distribution with a mean of zero and a standard deviation of n.

20. CORRECT ANSWER: A
The test statistic z = 7.84 - 7.56 = 43.75 $\frac{\sqrt{(.04)^2}}{100} + \frac{\sqrt{(.05)^2}}{100}$ and this value far exceeds the 99% critical value of 2.576.

21. CORRECT ANSWER: E
The correlation coefficient p = $\frac{\sigma x,y}{\sigma x \cdot \sigma y}$, which is the co-variance divided by the product of the individual standard deviations of x,y.

11 (#2)

22. CORRECT ANSWER: B
The expected values for each quantity is as follows:
Tall and white: 302.5   Tall and red: 247.5
Short and white: 247.5   Short and red: 202.5
The chi-square statistic becomes: $(300 - 302.5)^2/302.5 + (250 - 247.5)^2/247.5 + (250 - 247.5)^2/247.5 + (200 - 202.5)^2/202.5 = .1$.

23. CORRECT ANSWER: D
Let $Y = \sum_{i=1}^{n} Z_i^2$, where each $Z_i = (X_i - \mu)/\sigma_x$. These X_i's are a random sample of size n taken from a normal distribution with mean y and variance σ_x^2. Y is X^2.

24. CORRECT ANSWER: E
Since the mean of each profession is higher than the respective median and since the entire medical profession mean is higher than that for dentists, we can infer that the mean for doctors is higher than the mean for dentists. (Medians are about equal.)

25. CORRECT ANSWER: D
From the first sentence, it can be inferred that by giving these employees outside their fields, there is little gain (probably a loss) in conserving special skills. According to the second sentence, when skills are not conserved, there is not optimum use of the abilities of the employees.

26. CORRECT ANSWER: A
According to the second sentence of the passage, it is less laborious to increase the number of observations than to apply a more complicated statistical method to fewer observations, in order to be more useful.

27. CORRECT ANSWER: C
These causes of variation must also contribute to the elements affecting the estimate of the real error. Otherwise, the estimate will have little value.

28. CORRECT ANSWER: D
Since our estimate of the error of the average difference is based upon discrepancies observed, we recognize that observations may not be exact.

29. CORRECT ANSWER: E
The last 3 lines of the passage verify this statement.

30. CORRECT ANSWER: A
Randomization cannot eliminate all biases, but will certainly reduce them. The significance tests will still be valid.

31. CORRECT ANSWER: D
By comparing, we can validate its agreement with facts. This comparison would be based on experience.

32. CORRECT ANSWER: B
Ethical Propositions, being value judgments, are only validated by human authority.

33. **CORRECT ANSWER: E**
    This would qualify as a concurrent activity generated by interferences of a major type from outside the business world.

34. **CORRECT ANSWER: B**
    The statement beginning *such a view would entirely...* confirms this statement.

35. **CORRECT ANSWER: A**
    In the paragraph, it is mentioned that *...the aggregate gives an impression that...chance.* Thus, the aggregate would appear to be significant.

EXAMINATION SECTION
TEST 1

DIRECTIONS: Each question or incomplete statement is followed by several suggested answers or completions. Select the one that BEST answers the question or completes the statement. *PRINT THE LETTER OF THE CORRECT ANSWER IN THE SPACE AT THE RIGHT.*

1. The difference between the lowest and the highest measure in any distribution is statistically known as the

    A. mean difference
    B. interquartile range
    C. range
    D. distribution
    E. maximum difference

    1.____

2. In computing index numbers from raw data, the FIRST step is to determine the

    A. base
    B. mean
    C. standard deviation
    D. median
    E. mean difference

    2.____

3. The one of the following measurements which would yield *discrete* data is

    A. men by height
    B. families by children
    C. marriages by duration
    D. people by age
    E. automobiles by speed

    3.____

Questions 4-8.

DIRECTIONS: Questions 4 through 8 are to be answered on the basis of the following table.

DISTRIBUTION OF SCORES ON X TEST
FOR 1,000 PUPILS

Scores	Frequency
0 -19.99	36
20 -39.99	199
40 -59.99	421
60 -79.99	276
80 -100	68

4. If all scores are considered to be at the midpoint of the interval, the mean score was MOST NEARLY

    A. 40   B. 45   C. 50   D. 55   E. 60

    4.____

5. The median is MOST NEARLY

    A. 40   B. 45   C. 50   D. 55   E. 60

    5.____

6. The mode is MOST NEARLY

    A. 40   B. 45   C. 50   D. 55   E. 60

    6.____

7. If we assume the true mean to be 50, the standard deviation is MOST NEARLY

    A. 0   B. 5   C. 10   D. 15   E. 20

    7.____

8. The distribution is BEST described as being

   A. normal
   B. U-shaped
   C. J-shaped
   D. linear
   E. bimodal

9. The type of data which would be MOST useful in determining if a decline in the general business index is followed by a fall in prices is that which would indicate that a _____ by a _____ in the business index.

   A. rise in prices is never preceded; decline
   B. fall in prices is not always followed; decline
   C. fall in prices is not always preceded; decline
   D. fall in prices is never preceded; rise
   E. rise in prices may be preceded; rise

10. The data indicate that an increase in the cost of living results in an increased number of applicants for relief. On the basis of these data, we can CORRECTLY state that if the

    A. number of relief applicants increases, the increase is preceded by an increase in the cost of living
    B. number of relief applicants is decreasing, the cost of living cannot be increasing
    C. cost of living is increasing, the number of relief applicants cannot be increasing
    D. cost of living is decreasing, the number of relief applicants cannot be increasing
    E. cost of living changes, the number of applicants for relief will change

11. The one of the following results which would MOST NEARLY prove that the *well baby clinics* tend to decrease the infant mortality rate is

    A. the infant mortality rate varies as the general mortality rate
    B. increased attendance at the clinics frequently follows a period with high infant mortality rates
    C. increased attendance at the clinics is never followed by a period with increasing infant mortality rates
    D. decreased attendance at the clinics frequently follows a period with low infant mortality rates
    E. attendance at the clinics during any period is a function of the infant birth rate of the preceding period

12. Data proving which of the following statements would be MOST informative in a study of the relationship between juvenile delinquency and employment conditions?

    A. During periods of changing employment conditions, juvenile delinquency is variable.
    B. Juvenile delinquency does not decrease during periods of poor employment conditions.
    C. The number of new cases of juvenile delinquency is not a linear function of the number of juvenile delinquents.
    D. The number of cases of juvenile delinquency and the number of persons gainfully employed both show seasonal variations.
    E. Juvenile delinquency and the number of persons gainfully employed both decrease during periods of bad weather.

13. It is less costly to replace old equipment than to repair it. 13._____
Which of the following statements tends to prove this hypothesis MOST conclusively?

    A. The repair of old equipment is frequently as costly as the purchase of new equipment.
    B. Continuance in service of old equipment is at least as costly as its replacement by new equipment.
    C. The replacement of old equipment is more desirable than its repair.
    D. The cost for repairing old equipment is not a onetime cost while the cost of new equipment is a onetime cost.
    E. The operating time lost as a result of repairs being required increases the actual cost of operating old equipment.

14. The following information about sections of railroad track has been accumulated: manufacturer, manufacturer's lot number, specifications, result of a sample test for specifications, date of purchase, date section was put into use, date section was withdrawn and reason for withdrawal. 14._____
The one of the following questions which we could BEST answer, having this data, is:

    A. Does track replacement follow a seasonal trend?
    B. Is track wear a function of its location?
    C. Are track costs increasing?
    D. How much of the wear of the track is caused by flat wheels and how much by loose tracks?
    E. Is it more desirable to order large quantities of track than small quantities of track?

15. On the basis of the information in Question 14 above, which of the following questions could be LEAST satisfactorily answered? 15._____

    A. What is the life expectancy of a section of track at the moment it is put into use?
    B. Considering only manufacturer and specifications, which type of track has given us longest service?
    C. How are differences from the set specifications in track reflected in the length of time it is in use?
    D. On the average, how much money is tied up in track which has been purchased but not put into use?
    E. Neglecting accidents, which manufacturer's track gave the longest satisfactory service?

16. In order to study the relationship between the number of weekly treatments with Drug X required to cure a particular disease and the amount of Drug X administered at each treatment, the method which should be adopted is to 16._____

    A. increase the amount of drug administered to any one patient by regular amounts until he is cured
    B. give each patient a fixed amount weekly but do not give any two patients the same amount
    C. divide the patients into several groups. Start each group with a small amount of the drug and increase the amount administered at a different rate for each group.
    D. divide the patients into several groups. Give each member of any one group the same fixed amount of drug weekly but give members of different groups different amounts of the drug
    E. treat each subject independently until he is cured

17. An increasing birth rate will be followed by an increased school registration. On the basis of this statement only, it would be MOST accurate to state that

    A. school registration does not change during a period with a level birth rate
    B. an increasing school registration is preceded by a period with an increasing birth rate
    C. a period with an increasing birth rate is sometimes followed by a decreasing school registration
    D. a period with a decreasing birth rate is sometimes followed by a decreasing school registration
    E. a decreasing school registration is never preceded by a period with an increasing birth rate

18. Of the following *averages,* the one which is MOST influenced by infrequent extreme variations in the data is the

    A. mode
    B. median
    C. geometric mean
    D. arithmetic mean
    E. harmonic mean

19. Of the following *averages,* the one which is LEAST influenced by infrequent extreme variations in the data is the

    A. mode
    B. standard deviation
    C. geometric mean
    D. arithmetic mean
    E. harmonic mean

20. When the standard deviation is computed from grouped data, a correction is frequently made to account for the distribution within the class interval.
    This correction is MOST commonly known as

    A. Pearson's Correction
    B. Chadwick's Error
    C. Witticker's Law
    D. Yule's Correction
    E. Sheppard's Adjustment

21. The equation of the normal curve, with the mean of the distribution taken as the origin, is

    $$Y = \frac{1}{t\sqrt{2\pi}} e^{-\frac{x^2}{2t^2}}$$

    In this equation, t is the

    A. variance
    B. correlation coefficient
    C. amplitude
    D. standard deviation
    E. probable error

22. We know the values of the standard deviations S_x and S_y for two variables and the regression coefficient b_{yx} and wish to calculate the correlation coefficient r_{xy}. This is

    A. *impossible;* b_{xy} is not known

    B. *possible;* $r_{xy} = b_{xy} \frac{Sx}{Sy}$

    C. *impossible;* the respective means are not known

    D. *possible;* $r_{xy} = byx \frac{Sy}{Sx}$

    E. *impossible;* the distributions are not known

23. The coefficient of variation (the standard deviation divided by the mean) is calculated for a set of measures. This coefficient is ALWAYS

    A. *increased* if 5 points are added to each measure
    B. *decreased* if each measure is divided by 5
    C. *unchanged* if 5 points are added to each measure
    D. *increased* if each measure is multiplied by 5
    E. *decreased* if 5 points are added to each measure

24. In order to obtain a relationship of the type y = bx between the correlated variables x and y, where both x and y are deviations from the means of their respective distributions, the sums $A = \sum_{i=1}^{0} y_i$ and $B = \sum_{i=1}^{0} x_i$ § Xi are calculated and then b is set equal to A/B. This value for b is

    A. meaningless
    B. correct
    C. not accurate for small values of N but approaches the correct value as N increases
    D. accurate only for small values of N
    E. a helpful approximation to the least square formula

25. For each person taking a typing course, the number of hours of training required to acquire a given standard of proficiency is noted. All students are grouped into 3 year age groups, and for each age group, the mean number of hours noted above is calculated.
    If the mean number of hours for all age groups is approximately the same, we may conclude that the correlation between age and the number of hours required to learn typing is

    A. close to -1
    B. close to -.5
    C. approximately zero
    D. greater than .5
    E. any value between -1 and +1

26. From the regression equation Y = 22.232 + .943X, we can conclude that the coefficient of correlation between X and Y, except for sampling variations, is

    A. close to +1
    B. positive, but the specific value cannot be estimated
    C. either positive or negative
    D. negative, but the specific value cannot be estimated
    E. close to -1

27. If two characteristics (x_i) and (y_i) of a population have the same variance a σ^2 and if the coefficient of correlation between them is p, then the correlation p(x+y)(x-y) between ((x_i + y_i)) and ((x_i - y_i)) is

   A. $\dfrac{\sqrt{1-p}}{1+p}$ B. Zero   C. $\sqrt{\dfrac{1-\sigma}{1+\sigma}}p$

   D. $.6745\dfrac{1-p^2}{\sqrt{p}}$ E. $\sigma\sqrt{1-p^2}$

27._____

28. The sine and cosine curves are MOST likely to be useful in statistics in the

   A. study of population forecasting
   B. measuring of cyclical variation
   C. smoothing of frequency distributions
   D. studying of linear correlation
   E. measuring of significance of differences

28._____

29. We have a sample population consisting of the income earned by each member of a large group of professional men.
   If we wish to compare the income earned in each profession with that earned in every other profession, it is MOST appropriate to

   A. calculate a regression coefficient between income and profession and to determine its significance
   B. calculate the correlation coefficient and test it for significance
   C. calculate the multiple correlation coefficients between income and profession
   D. use chi square to test for differences among the means of the income
   E. calculate the mean income for each profession and test for significance of differences by means of analysis of variance

29._____

30. For each of five different types of crime, a random sample of 20 cases is selected; and for each of the 100 criminals involved, the age at first conviction is ascertained. Which of the following tests of significance is MOST appropriate for determining the significance of the differences among the mean ages for each of the five types? The

   A. t test, using student's distribution
   B. Chi Square test
   C. F test
   D. test comparing areas under the normal curve
   E. contingency test

30._____

31. For each of 16 neighborhoods in the city, the death rate and a coefficient of population density have been determined. The coefficient of correlation r_1 for the two sets of data has been calculated.
   In order to determine if the correlation coefficient of .5 obtained from the sample indicates a real relationship between these variables, it is BEST to test by calculating

31._____

A. $\dfrac{\sigma r}{r_1}$ and using a normal distribution

B. S_r for the sample and using a normal distribution

C. $r_1\sqrt{14}/\sqrt{1-r_1^2}$ and then using student's distribution

D. $\int_{-r_1}^{r_1} re^{-r}\,dr$ and then using the distribution re^{-r}

E. biserial r

32. In order to determine from two samples if the two populations represented by these samples differ in the percentage of each having the mutually exclusive and exhaustive characteristics A, B, C, and D, it would be BEST to   32.____

    A. use a Chi Square test
    B. calculate the correlation coefficient between the samples and use student's distribution
    C. calculate the mean of the differences and test for significance
    D. use an F test
    E. calculate the median for each characteristic and compare the two samples

33. Two drugs are administered to each of 12 patients in order to determine which is preferable in its ability to induce sleep. The drugs are administered at different times, and their effects are measured in terms of hours of sleep induced.   33.____
    In order to determine if the effects are significantly different from each other, the statistician should

    A. calculate the mean hours of sleep induced by each drug and test the difference by

       the formula $t = \dfrac{\bar{x}1-\bar{x}2}{\dfrac{\sqrt{\Sigma(x1-\bar{x}1)^2 + \Sigma 1x^2-\bar{x}2^{12}(1/6)}}{22}}$

    B. calculate the mean hours of sleep for each drug and test the differences by means of the formula

       $t = \dfrac{\bar{X}_1 - \bar{X}_2}{\sqrt{\hat{j}^2_{1/12} + \hat{j}^2_{2/12}}}$

    C. calculate the correlation coefficient and test whether it is significantly different from zero
    D. use either of the methods in A or C because they give equivalent results
    E. calculate the difference for each patient and test the mean of the differences by student's distribution to determine if it is significantly different from zero

Questions 34-38.

DIRECTIONS: Questions 34 through 38 are to be answered on the basis of the following table.

THE NUMBER OF DEATHS DURING THE YEAR FOR EACH OF TWO POPULATION GROUPS SUBDIVIDED BY CAUSE, AGE GROUP, AND SEX

CAUSE

		X M	X F	Y M	Y F	Z M	Z F	R M	R F
Number of	Under 1 year	6	4	2	1	1	3	–	–
Deaths in	1 to 4	15	12			20	14	–	–
Group A	5 to 14	9	6	–	–	27	16	–	–
	15 to 24	53	82	1	2	25	28	1	1
	25 to 44	485	316	36	20	349	657	78	43
	45 to 64	892	137	191	45	2918	2826	221	67
	65 plus	276	77	88	26	2831	2473	45	9
	Total	1736	634	318	94	6171	6017	345	120
	Number of Under 1 year	4	1	11	11	–	–	–	–
Deaths in	1 to 4	9	7	–	–	2	1	–	–
Group B	5 to 14	5	8	–	1	1	–	–	–
	15 to 24	66	124	2	5	1	3	–	1
	25 to 44	259	189	60	31	44	96	15	8
	45 to 64	190	54	104	36	207	223	11	3
	65 plus	32	13	19	14	85	91	1	–
	Total	565	396	196	98	340	414	27	12

Assume that on January 1, the number of men was equal to the number of women in each of the two populations, but do NOT assume that the number of persons in Group B was equal to the number of persons in Group A.

34. With respect to deaths from Cause Y, the disproportion between the sexes is GREATEST in Group

    A. A, age 25 to 44
    B. B, age 25 to 44
    C. A, age 45 to 64
    D. B, age 45 to 64
    E. A, age 65 and over

35. With respect to deaths from Cause Y, the median age at death is LOWEST in Group

    A. A, males
    B. B, males
    C. A, females
    D. B, females
    E. A, considered as a single unit

36. It is MOST likely that a person dying from Cause X is a man rather than a woman if the person is

    A. younger than 25
    B. younger than 25 in Group B
    C. 25 to 44 in Group A
    D. 25 to 44 in Group B
    E. over 65

37. A person whose death was caused by Z is MOST likely to have been a female if the age group was   37._____

    A. 1 to 4
    B. 5 to 14
    C. 15 to 24
    D. 25 to 44
    E. 45 to 64

38. The median age at death is LOWEST in Group A for   38._____

    A. Males, Cause Z
    B. Females, Cause R
    C. Males, Cause Y
    D. Females, Cause X
    E. Males, Cause X

Questions 39-43.

DIRECTIONS: Column I below lists five sequences. Column II lists five amounts. In the space at the right, for each of the sequences in Column I, write the letter of the amount in Column II which is MOST NEARLY equal to the ninth term of that sequence.

COLUMN I	COLUMN II	
39. 3, 9, 19, 33, 51,.....	A. 163 or less	39._____
40. -90, -89, -87, -83, -75, ..	B. 164	40._____
41. -18, -23, -20, -9, 10.....	C. 165	41._____
42. 151, 157, 155, 165, 159, 173......	D. 166	42._____
43. -341, -341, -335, -317, -281, ...	E. 167 or greater	43._____

Questions 44-53.

DIRECTIONS: Questions 44 through 53 are to be answered on the basis of the following information.

It is proposed to make a study for the City of New York which would yield the following information:

1. The number of unoccupied buildings which could be used for residential purposes.
2. The number of these which could be put into usable condition at a cost of
    (a) $15,000 or less per room
    (b) more than $15,000 but not more than $30,000 per room
    (c) more than $30,000 per room
3. The amount and types of material which would be required by a program to make all houses of types (a) and (b) inhabitable.
4. The total cost of making all houses of (a) and (b) inhabitable.
5. The effect on the new housing program which has been instituted by private companies of removing from the market the materials which would be used in this rehabilitation program.
6. For the purpose of this study, consider a building inhabitable if all violations of pertinent city codes charged against it are removed.

44. Which of the following pieces of information is the MOST important for beginning your study? 44.____

    A. The types of material available
    B. The number of homes required
    C. The location of each unoccupied house
    D. The exact number of unoccupied buildings in New York City
    E. What each type of renovation will cost

45. In order to get information to work with as quickly as possible about unoccupied buildings, it would be MOST desirable to 45.____

    A. send questionnaires to all real estate owners and operators
    B. request a list of unoccupied or condemned buildings from city departments such as the Department of Housing & Buildings
    C. check the census for empty buildings
    D. send a number of investigators into the field
    E. advertise in the newspapers requesting citizens to submit the addresses of unoccupied buildings

46. Under the conditions of the study, the MOST important question to be answered about any unoccupied building investigated is 46.____

    A. How long has the house been empty?
    B. How much will it cost to make the house habitable?
    C. Who is the owner?
    D. How old is the house?
    E. If renovated, how many years of service will the house give?

47. In a preliminary study to approximate costs, the BEST procedure would be to get contractors' 47.____

    A. bids for the complete renovation of each house
    B. estimates for the complete renovation of each house of a sample
    C. bids for enough renovation to remove all code violations from each house
    D. estimates for removing typical code violations
    E. None of the above

48. In order to determine cost, it is decided to make a preliminary study on a sample of the population. 48.____
    Of the following, the BEST sample for this purpose would be

    A. one stratified by the cost of renovating
    B. one stratified by the name of the owner
    C. a random sample
    D. one stratified by the type of code violation against the building
    E. stratified by the number of rooms in the building

49. In order to determine how the renovating program will affect the new building program, a questionnaire is being prepared which is to be distributed to firms engaged in the construction of new buildings. 49.____
    It is of LEAST importance in the construction of these questionnaires that

A. it be known whether or not the data is to be put into punch cards
B. some idea be obtained in advance of possible points at which the renovating program may affect the new building program
C. the type of person filling out the questionnaire be considered
D. the questionnaire be tested for unambiguity in advance of general distribution
E. a control group be set up so that answers can be compared to a standard

50. To discuss the above questionnaire, after it has been prepared, with a construction group, in advance of general distribution, would be

    A. *desirable;* the more persons with whom the project is discussed, the better the chances for success
    B. *undesirable;* it is pointless and consumes valuable time
    C. *desirable;* it is the best way of getting cooperation and uniform interpretation from the people who will fill out the questionnaire
    D. *undesirable;* it may bring up arguments and ill feeling which can be avoided
    E. *desirable;* it will make the construction group feel that they are part of the project

51. A great deal of data about the houses under consideration has been assembled. These data are: address, type of violations against the building, number of rooms, total cost for making the building inhabitable, age of building, and owner or agent.
    In setting up a punch card which will contain this information, the one of the following which it is LEAST desirable to code before punching is the

    A. address
    B. types of violations
    C. age of building
    D. number of rooms
    E. average cost per room to make the building inhabitable

52. If all data in Question 51 above is put on a card without coding, the one of the following pieces of information which could NOT be obtained by only sorting and tabulating the cards is

    A. the total cost of making all the buildings inhabitable
    B. the number of violations of each kind for each age separately
    C. the number of rooms available in houses for which the total repair costs would be less than $500,000
    D. the most frequent type of violation in houses for which the total cost of repairs would be less than $100,000
    E. maximum amount of floor space which could be made habitable for $5,000,000

53. In presenting the finished study, it is MOST desirable that

    A. only recommended courses of action be given
    B. the statistical techniques used be shown in detail in order to prove the validity of the study
    C. the report be presented without any mention of the statistical techniques used as the persons reading the report will not understand them
    D. the conclusions reached be presented along with a general statement of the methods used and that all data and technical methods used be placed in an appendix
    E. a chronological narrative of the investigation be presented, with the conclusions reached highlighted in the narration

54. Three balls are drawn, without being replaced, from a bowl containing six white balls and seven black balls. The probability that exactly two of the balls are white is MOST NEARLY

   A. .4   B. .3   C. .5   D. .2   E. .1

55. Two red markers and three black markers are arranged in a linear order.
The probability that someone guessing the arrangement will make at least one mistake is MOST NEARLY

   A. .9   B. .8   C. .7   D. .6   E. .5

56. A random selection showed that within the given period, 720 male children and 684 female children were born.
If the frequencies of male and female births are assumed to be equal, the probability of obtaining a sample deviating from the expected by more than the amount which the given sample deviates is MOST NEARLY

   A. .8   B. .7   C. .5   D. .3   E. .2

57. Two judges have been selected to rank five essays in order of merit. Each judge independently assigns one of the ranks 1, 2, 3, 4, 5 to each essay.
On the basis of pure chance, the probability that the judges will agree on the exact positions of more than three essays is MOST NEARLY

   A. .05   B. .04   C. .03   D. .02   E. .01

58. In an effort to determine whether a given coin is biased, the coin is tossed 100 times. Head appears 42 times.
If the usual criteria for the acceptance or rejection of hypothesis are applied, it may be concluded that the experiment

   A. does not prove that the coin is biased as the probability of obtaining a deviation from 50 as great or greater than the one indicated is greater than 1/20
   B. proves that the coin is biased since the difference between .58 and .42 is significantly greater than zero
   C. proves that the coin is biased since the probability of obtaining a deviation from 50 as great or greater than the one indicated is less than 1/50
   D. proves that the coin is biased since it is more probably, on the basis of Bayes Theorem, that the next 100 tosses of the coin will yield head 42 times rather than 50 times
   E. does not prove that the coin is biased since all combinations of heads and tails are equally probable

59. The statistical unit in which you are employed is preparing a handbook of instructions for the construction and preparation of statistical tables and charts.
A handbook of this type is

   A. *unnecessary*; each table or chart must be constructed and prepared individually
   B. *necessary*, time and work are saved by conforming to uniform procedures
   C. *unnecessary*, such handbooks are never followed
   D. *necessary*, if procedures are not uniform, the same procedures may be used for essentially different types of work
   E. *unnecessary*, restrictions on the work of the statisticians may result in poor morale

60. Of the following considerations in determining the order of items in a table, LEAST consideration should be given to

    A. order of importance
    B. associations among items
    C. number of items
    D. convenience in reading
    E. the existence of a standard order

61. In tables of index numbers or of relative prices, the actual price or absolute value for the period or year used as a base should be clearly stated.
    This is important MAINLY because if it is not stated, the

    A. table is valueless
    B. table loses most of its value
    C. accuracy of the table cannot be checked
    D. absolute value for any one year cannot be calculated
    E. relative value for any one year cannot be calculated

62. Of the following statements concerning the statement of sources used in constructing a chart or table, the MOST correct is

    A. source material should generally not be indicated
    B. important sources should be clearly identified; the less important ones may be omitted
    C. sources in the public domain should be indicated; for the rest, such a heading as *Departmental Data* may be employed
    D. only sources in which you have confidence should be listed
    E. sources should be so definitely described that a person using the data may retrace every step taken

63. A questionnaire is being prepared, to be distributed to all persons having contact with a large city department, in which they will be asked to indicate their attitudes toward the department.
    Of the following questions in the questionnaire, the one which will be LEAST helpful for comparing attitudes toward the department with other factors about the person answering the questionnaire is

    A. sex   B. name   C. age
    D. place of birth   E. education

64. The form on which the employees of Department X report the work they have performed during the week provides no space for reporting units of each type of work performed but requires instead a narrative statement of accomplishment for the week.
    This procedure is justified if

    A. each employee performs as many as five different kinds of work during the week
    B. the department has many functions
    C. the completion of a unit of work may take several weeks
    D. several units of work are completed each week
    E. most work units are started on Friday and completed on Thursday

Questions 65-66.

DIRECTIONS: Questions 65 and 66 are to be answered on the basis of the following information.

One hundred observations are distributed over a range extending from 0 to 70 in class intervals of five units. The class intervals are zero to, but not including, 5; 5 to, but not including 10, etc. The mean of the distribution is 32.5 and the median is 30.

65. If five observations are added to the interval *25 to but not including 30* and five to the interval *50 to but less than* 55, the new mean is MOST NEARLY

    A. 32.5   B. 32.85   C. 33.20   D. 33.55   E. 33.90

66. If there are ten cases in the interval *30 but less than 35* and if ten observations are added to the interval *65 to but not including 70*, then the new median is MOST NEARLY

    A. 32.5   B. 33   C. 35   D. 34   E. 34.5

67. If each x score is obtained from the x_1 score given below it,

x score	65	70	70	45	80	40	45	55
x_1 score	1	2	2	-3	4	-4	-3	-1

    then from S_1, the standard deviation of the X_1 set, S, the standard deviation of the x set is
    A. calculable; $S = 5S_1$
    B. not calculable; the scores are not grouped
    C. calculable; $S = 5S_1 + 60$
    D. not calculable; the mean of the x_1 set is different from the mean of the x set
    E. calculable; $S = 25S$

68. If the vertical distance between two time series when plotted on semi-logarithmic paper is constant, then the

    A. ratio between the functions is increasing
    B. difference between the functions is increasing
    C. ratio between the functions is constant
    D. difference between the functions is constant
    E. ratio between the functions is decreasing

69. If the probability that b<x<a is given by $\int_b^a w(x)dx$, then the statistic of the distribution w(x) given by $\int_{-\infty}^{\infty} xw(x)dx$ is the

    A. standard deviation   B. variance   C. mode
    D. median   E. mean

70. The distribution $p(x:m) = \frac{m^x}{x!} e^{-m}$ is USUALLY called the _____ Distribution.

    A. Poisson   B. Normal   C. Binomial
    D. Chi Square   E. Student's

KEY (CORRECT ANSWERS)

1. C	16. D	31. C	46. B	61. D
2. A	17. E	32. A	47. D	62. E
3. B	18. D	33. E	48. C	63. B
4. D	19. A	34. C	49. E	64. C
5. D	20. E	35. D	50. C	65. C
6. C	21. D	36. E	51. A	66. A
7. E	22. B	37. D	52. E	67. A
8. A	23. E	38. D	53. D	68. C
9. A	24. A	39. A	54. A	69. E
10. B	25. C	40. C	55. A	70. A
11. C	26. B	41. D	56. D	
12. B	27. B	42. E	57. E	
13. B	28. B	43. A	58. A	
14. A	29. E	44. C	59. B	
15. D	30. C	45. B	60. C	

SOLUTIONS TO PROBLEMS

1. **CORRECT ANSWER: C**
   In any distribution, the range equals the highest score minus the lowest score.

2. **CORRECT ANSWER: A**
   The base must be determined before an index number can be assigned to raw data. For example, if 50 is the base, it is assigned an index number of 100. Then, a value of 60 would be assigned an index number of $(60/50)(100) = 120$.

3. **CORRECT ANSWER: B**
   The only allowable values of the data would be 0, 1, 2, 3,..., that is, only integral values. Each of the other selections could contain fractional values, so the data would not be discrete.

4. **CORRECT ANSWER: D**
   The mean score = $[(9.995)(36) + (29.995)(199) + (49.995)(421) + (69.995)(276) + (90)(68)] \div 1000 \approx 52.8$, which is closest to 55.

5. **CORRECT ANSWER: D**
   The median is the 500th score. The first two intervals contain 235 scores. To find the median, which lies in the 3rd interval, we calculate $39.995 + (265/421)(20) \approx 52.58 \approx 55$.

6. **CORRECT ANSWER: C**
   The mode would be the midpoint of the interval with the highest frequency. Thus, the mode = $(40 + 59.99)/2 = 49.995 \approx 50$.

7. **CORRECT ANSWER: E**
   $$\sqrt{[(9.995-50)^2 \cdot 36 + (29.995-50)^2 \cdot 199 + (49.995-50)^2 \cdot 421 + (69.995-50)^2 \cdot 276 + (90-50)^2 \cdot 68]/1000}$$
   $$\approx \sqrt{(57{,}614 + 79{,}640 + .01 + 110{,}345 + 108{,}800)/1000}$$
   $$\approx \sqrt{356.4} \approx 18.9,$$ which is closest to 20.

8. **CORRECT ANSWER: A**
   Since the middle interval has the highest frequency, and since the frequencies become lower as the scores move further from the mean, the distribution resembles the normal distribution.

9. **CORRECT ANSWER: A**
   This would imply that each time there is a rise in prices, the business index preceding it is either constant or also rising.

10. **CORRECT ANSWER: B**
    Let P = an increase in the cost of living Let Q = an increased number of applicants for relief. Then, we have $P \rightarrow Q$. Statement B would translate as not Q $\rightarrow$ not P, which follows logically.

11. **CORRECT ANSWER: C**
    Let P = attendance at baby clinics
    Let Q = infant mortality rates decrease
    Then, we have $P \rightarrow Q$. Statement C translates to P never $\rightarrow$ not Q,
    which is equivalent to $P \rightarrow Q$.

12. **CORRECT ANSWER: B**
    This would imply that when employment conditions worsen, juvenile delinquency either remains steady (unlikely) or that it increases (more likely).

13. **CORRECT ANSWER: B**
    The original statement means that replacing is cheaper than repairing, with respect to old equipment. Statement B is equivalent to this concept.

14. **CORRECT ANSWER: A**
    The information provided includes dates pertaining to purchase, initial use, and withdrawal for sections of the track.

15. **CORRECT ANSWER: D**
    No information concerning cost of any section of the track is included in the paragraph for Question 14.

16. **CORRECT ANSWER: D**
    In this manner, we can observe the length of time required for treatment for each group separately, then compare times between any two groups.

17. **CORRECT ANSWER: E**
    Let P = increasing birth rate
    Let Q = increased school registration
    Then, we have $P \rightarrow Q$. Statement E translates to not $Q \rightarrow Q$ not P,
    which is equivalent to $P \rightarrow Q$.

18. **CORRECT ANSWER: D**
    This value is influenced by all data, even more so than other types of means.

19. **CORRECT ANSWER: A**
    The mode can only be influenced by repetition of given data. By altering extreme values, the probability is strong that the mode remains unchanged.

20. **CORRECT ANSWER: E**

21. **CORRECT ANSWER: D**
    In this formula, e is the natural logarithm and t is the standard deviation.
    (Replace N by 1)

22. CORRECT ANSWER: B
This can be proved algebraically by using the definitions of each variable, using formulas.

$$r = \frac{n(\sum xy) - (\sum x)(\sum y)}{\sqrt{n(\sum x^2) - (\sum x)^2} \cdot \sqrt{n(\sum y^2) - (\sum y)^2}}$$

$$by_x = \frac{n(\sum xy) - (\sum x)(\sum y)}{n(\sum x^2) - (\sum x)^2}$$

S_x and S_y are the standard deviation formulas for x and y.

23. CORRECT ANSWER: E
If 5 points are added, the mean will be increased by 5 points, but the standard deviation will remain the same. Thus, the new coefficient of variation will have the same numerator, but a larger denominator. This will decrease its value.

24. CORRECT ANSWER: A
$\sum_{i=1}^{n} y_i$ and $\sum_{i=1}^{n} x_i$ must be zero for <u>any</u> distribution if y_i and x_i represent deviations from the mean. Example, let y's consist of the numbers 2, 3, 10. Then $\bar{y} = 5$. Then, $y_1 = 2 - 5 = -3$, $y_2 = 3 - 5 = -2$, $y_3 = 10 - 5 = 5$, and $\sum_{i=1}^{3} y_i$ -3-2+5=0

25. CORRECT ANSWER: C
Since the mean number of hours remains unchanged for each age group, the correlation is about zero.

26. CORRECT ANSWER: B
Since the slope of the regression equation is +.943, the correlation coefficient will be positive. Its specific value is unknown since we don't know how far from the regression line the actual points lie.

27. CORRECT ANSWER: B

28. CORRECT ANSWER: B
Cyclical variations are long-term oscillatory patterns of upswings and downswings. Sine and cosine curves also exhibit oscillatory movements.

29. CORRECT ANSWER: E
In analysis of variance (ANOVA), the F statistic can be used to test whether the means of two or more groups are significantly different. F = MST/MSW, where MST = between-treatments mean square and MSW = within-treatment mean square.

30. CORRECT ANSWER: C
Same explanation as for Question 29.

31. CORRECT ANSWER: C
If the variables under consideration are normally distributed, the t-distribution is used to test whether the population correlation coefficient is statistically significantly different from zero. The formula is: $t_{n-2} = r \cdot \sqrt{n-2}/\sqrt{1-r^2}$. Here, $r = r_1$ and n = 16.

32. CORRECT ANSWER: A
This application is called the homogeneity of proportions test. As samples are selected from different populations, proportions for common characteristics are checked to see if they are statistically different.

33. CORRECT ANSWER: E
This t-distribution can be used when the sample sizes are small (less than 30). The actual formula is:

$$t = \frac{\bar{x}_1 - \bar{x}_2}{s \cdot \sqrt{\frac{1}{n_1} + \frac{1}{n_2}}}$$, where $\bar{x}_1$ and $\bar{x}_2$ are the sample means (of these differences) and

$$s = \frac{\sqrt{(n_2-1)s_1^2 + (n-1)s_2^2}}{n_1 + n_2 - 2}$$

34. CORRECT ANSWER: C
The numerical difference = 191 - 45 = 146. This number exceeds the differences of the other selections.

35. CORRECT ANSWER: D
The median is located in the 98/2 = 49th position. Beginning with the lowest age bracket, there are 48 deaths, counting up through the age bracket 25 to 44. The age for the 49th death = $44.5 + \frac{1}{36}(64.5 - 44.5) \approx 45.06$. This value is lower than that of the other selections.

36. CORRECT ANSWER: E
In this age bracket, 398 people died from Cause X. Of these, 308 were men, while 90 were women. Thus, the probability that a randomly selected person dying from Cause X would be a man = 308/398 $\approx$ 77%. This percent is higher than that of the other selections.

37. CORRECT ANSWER: D
In this age bracket, 1146 people died from Cause Z. Of these, 753 were women, while 393 were men. Thus, the probability that a randomly selected person dying from Cause Z would be a woman = 753/1146 $\approx$ 66%. This percent is higher than that of the other selections.

38. CORRECT ANSWER: D
There are a total of 1030 females who died from Cause X. We need to locate the 1030/2 = 515th position to find the median age. There are 244 females, up through age 24 in this category of deaths. Counting up through age 44, there are 749 females who died from Cause X. Thus, the median = 24.5 + 271/505(20) $\approx$ 35.23. This value is lower than that of the other selections.

39. CORRECT ANSWER: A
In this sequence, the successive differences between terms are 6, 10, 14, 18, ... Thus, the next difference should be 22. The sixth term = 51 + 22 = 73. The ninth term would be 73 + 26 + 30 + 34 = 163.

40. CORRECT ANSWER: C
    In this sequence, the successive differences between terms are 1, 2, 4, 8,.... Following this pattern, the next four differences would be 16, 32, 64, 128. Thus, the ninth term would be - 75 + 16 + 32 + 64 + 128 = 165.

41. CORRECT ANSWER: D
    In this sequence, the successive differences between terms are -5, 3, 11, 19,.... Following this pattern, the next four differences would be 27, 35, 43, 51. Thus, the ninth term = 10 + 27 + 35 + 43 + 51 = 166.

42. CORRECT ANSWER: E
    The pattern for successive differences is: add 6, subtract 2, add 10, subtract 6, add 14,.... To continue this pattern for four more numbers, subtract 10, add 18, subtract 14, add 22. The ninth number = 173 - 10 + 18 - 14 + 22 = 189.

43. CORRECT ANSWER: A
    The pattern for successive differences is: add 0, add 6, add 12, add 18, ... To continue this pattern, add 24, add 30, add 36, add 42. The ninth number is - 281 +24+30+36+42 = - 149.

44. CORRECT ANSWER: C
    Before the study can begin, each unoccupied house must be identified.

45. CORRECT ANSWER: B
    Each of the other options would be very time-consuming and probably inaccurate.

46. CORRECT ANSWER: B
    This relates to condition #4, the total cost involved.

47. CORRECT ANSWER: D
    Unless code violations are removed, the buildings cannot be actually used for residential purposes.

48. CORRECT ANSWER: C
    The difficulty with using stratified samples is that the categories of stratification cannot easily be determined. A random sample will probably include high-priced as well as low-priced renovation costs.

49. CORRECT ANSWER: E

50. CORRECT ANSWER: C
    This will ensure the best chance for a successful project.

51. CORRECT ANSWER: A
    The address is just used for identification purposes. It has no direct bearing on the cost of the project.

52. CORRECT ANSWER: E
    The punch card would contain the total cost to make the building inhabitable, but no data on floor space.

53. CORRECT ANSWER: D
    The average reader will appreciate the general methods used in the study.

21 (#1)

54. **CORRECT ANSWER: A**
The probability is given by $({}_6C_2)({}_7C_1)/{}_{13}C_3 = (15)(7)/286 \approx .367 \approx .4$

55. **CORRECT ANSWER: A**
The number of distinguishable arrangements = $\dfrac{5!}{2! \cdot 3!}$. The probability of not guessing the exact arrangement = $1-\dfrac{1}{10}=.9$

56. **CORRECT ANSWER: D**
684 + 720 = 1404, so we would expect 1/2(1404) = 702 males. We are seeking the probability of at least 720 males or fewer than 684 males. We'll use the Normal approximation to the Binomial Distribution where the mean = 1/2(1404) - 702 and the standard deviation is $\sqrt{(1404)(.5)(.5)} \approx 18.735$. More than 720 means at least 720.5. Convert 720.5 to a z-score of (720.5 - 702) ÷ 18.735 .99. In the Normal Distribution, Prob(z>.99) = .1611. Now, less than 684 means no greater than 683.5. Change 683.5 to a z-score of (683.5 - 702) ÷ 18.735 ≈ .99. Prob(z<-.99) = .1611. The combined probability is 2(.1611) = .3222 ≈ 3.

57. **CORRECT ANSWER: E**
If the judges agree on more than 3, this means they agree on all 5. There are 5! = 120 ways to judge the essays. Prob(perfect match) = 1/200 = $.008\overline{3} \approx .01$. Note: A match on 4 essays automatically means a match on the 5th essay.

58. **CORRECT ANSWER: A**
To find the probability of a deviation as large as 8, (50-42), we need Probability (42<x<58) and subtract from 1. The z-scores for 42 and 58 are -1.6 and 1.6. P(-1.6<z<1.6) = .8904, so Prob(z>1.6) or Prob(2<-1.6) = .1096, well above 1/20.

59. **CORRECT ANSWER: B**
In this manner, all individuals will follow the same guidelines in using the tables and charts. Results will be consistent.

60. **CORRECT ANSWER: C**
Of importance would be readability and listing the items in order of importance. The actual number of items in the table doesn't matter.

61. **CORRECT ANSWER: D**
Relative values will still be accurate, but the base year is always necessary to assign absolute values.

62. **CORRECT ANSWER: E**
This allows the reader to understand how the chart values were obtained.

63. **CORRECT ANSWER: B**
The survey may consider other factors such as sex, age, education, and even birthplace in analyzing responses. However, a person's name would not be relevant.

64. **CORRECT ANSWER: C**
If this is the case, reporting units of work done for each week would be impossible, so a narrative statement of accomplishments would be more useful.

65. **CORRECT ANSWER: C**
The total of the initial 100 observations = (32.5)(100) = 3250. Since the middle of the intervals 25-29 and 50-54 are 27 and 52, respectively, the new total of 110 observations = 3250 + (5)(27) + (5)(52) = 3645. Then, 3645 ÷ 110 ≈ 33.14, which is closest to 33.20.

66. **CORRECT ANSWER: A**
Since there are already 10 observations in the interval 30-34, the addition of 10 more observations in the interval 65-69 will shift the median to the 55.5th position. With 100 observations, the median was in the 50.5th position. The new median will most likely be 30 + (5/10)(5) = 32.5.

67. **CORRECT ANSWER: A**
It can be shown that $x = 5x_1 + 60$. Then, the standard deviation of the x set, S, is equal to $5 \cdot S_i$, where S_1 is the standard deviation of the x_1 set. In this example, S ≈ 14.577 and Si ≈ 2.915.

68. **CORRECT ANSWER: C**
If $f(x) = K \cdot g(x)$, then Log $f(x)$ = log K + log $g(x)$ and the distance Log $f(x)$ - Log $g(x)$ = constant. On semi—log paper, x is plotted against $f(x)$ or $g(x)$.

69. **CORRECT ANSWER: E**
If $Pr(b<x<a) = \int_a^b w(x)dx$, then E(x) = expected value of a x = mean = $\int_{-\infty}^{\infty} xw(x)dx$.

70. **CORRECT ANSWER: A**
The probability of X occurrences, where m = mean number of occurrences is:

$p(x,m) = m^x e^{-m}/x!$

BASIC FUNDAMENTALS OF STATISTICS

TABLE OF CONTENTS

		Page
I.	SCORES: THEIR MEANINGS AND FORMS	1
	a. Discrete and Continuous Scores	1
	b. Raw and Derived Scores	1
II.	THE ARRANGEMENT	1
	a. Rank Order	1
	b. Tabulation	2
	c. Graphical Representation	2
III.	MEASURES OF CENTRAL TENDENCY, OR AVERAGES	2
	a. The Median (Mdn.)	2
	b. The Mean (M)	3
	c. The Mode	3
IV.	MEASURES OF THE DISTRIBUTION OF SCORES	3
	a. The Normal Curve	3
	b. Importance of Measures of Distribution	3
	c. Measures of Distribution	4
	i. The Range	4
	ii. The Average Deviation (A.D.)	4
	iii. The Standard Deviation (S.D.)	4
	iv. The Probable Error (P.E.)	5
	v. The Quartile Deviation (Q)	5
V.	DERIVED SCORES	5
	a. Percent Scores	5
	b. Distance from the Average	5
	c. Percentile Scores	5
	d. T Scores	6
	e. Mental Age (M.A.)	6
	f. Intelligence Quotient (I.Q.)	6
	g. Educational Age	7
	h. Educational Quotient (E.Q.)	7
	i. Achievement Quotient (A.Q.)	7
	j. Norms	7
VI.	COMPARISONS OF GROUPS	7
VII.	CORRELATION	7
	a. Interpretation of the Coefficient of Correlation	8
	b. Uses of Correlation	8
	c. Reliability	8
	d. Validity	9
APPENDIX		10
	Table 1 – Calculation of the Mean, Median and Q	10
	Table 2 – Calculation of the A.D., S.D., and P.E.	12
	Table 3 – Calculation of the Rank-Difference Coefficient of Correlation	12

Basic Fundamentals of Statistics

I. SCORES: THEIR MEANINGS AND FORMS

"Whatever exists, exists in some amount."

As soon as measurements of any sort advance beyond the primitive statement that one thing is greater than, equal to, or less than another thing, we find the attempt to state results in numerical terms.

The meaning of such numerical statements should be clearly understood.

  A. Discrete and Continuous Scores

There are certain kinds of measurement that result in scores that are *discrete* in the sense that there exist real gaps between the possible measurements that one can obtain. Thus the number of children in a family, or bills in a purse, increases only by whole numbers; one cannot find 5 1/2 children, or 7 1/4 bills, unless one practices mutilation. Other measures give *continuous* scores in the sense that the scores are theoretically capable of any degree of subdivision. Scores on tests are usually given in units, as 68 or 75; but with more accurate tests, scores of 77.4 or 86.273 would also be possible. Nearly all measurements in psychology and education deal with continuous series of scores rather than with discrete series, and the following discussion deals throughout with the statistical treatment of continuous series. Some modification of the formulas used with continuous series is necessary before one can apply them to discrete series.

  B. Raw and Derived Scores

The score actually obtained in making a measurement is called a *raw score*. If a pupil makes a score of 59 on a test, that is his raw score. Raw scores do not by themselves indicate if they are high or low; a score of 59 might be high on one test and low on another. If a pupil made a score of 59 on an intelligence test, that might be translated to mean that he achieved a mental age of 12 years, an IQ of 108, a percentile rank of 78, etc. All these interpretative measures would be called *derived scores*, as they are derived from the raw score. A derived score tells us much more about the quality of a performance than the raw score does. Many kinds of derived scores will be described below.

II. THE ARRANGEMENT

Suppose that a certain class takes a test and makes the following scores: 92, 88, 97, 95, 100, 58, 90, 94, 72, 91, 83, 88, 83, 87, 82, 78, 64, 69, 97, 95, 86, 85, 85, 89, 77, 61, 74, 59. Until we arrange them in some different way we cannot tell much about these scores. (Note: most of the computations in the Appendix are based on this series of scores.)

  A. Rank Order

With a small number of scores, it is often profitable to arrange them in rank order, with the highest at one end and the lowest at the other. From the rank order one can very easily determine the highest score, the lowest score, the midscore and percentile scores. One method of correlation is based on the rank order. Confusion will be avoided if the lowest score is always given rank one. The only difficulty that arises in constructing a rank order is in regard to tie scores. In such a case, the ranks covered by the tied scores are averaged, and that average rank is given to each. Example: If two scores are tied for second rank, they cover ranks two and three; $\frac{2+3}{5} = 2.5$, and than rank is given to each. The next following score is given rank four. If the ranking is done properly, the last score should come out with a rank equal to the number of scores, except where there is a tie for last place.

B. Tabulation

Tabulation consists essentially in dividing the scores into groups, all groups covering equal portions of the total range of scores, and arranging the groups in rank order. When the groups, which are called *classes,* are arranged in a vertical column, and the number of scores falling in each class is indicated by a number, the tabulation is called a *frequency distribution.* A frequency distribution gives us a fairly clear picture of the way the scores are distributed. It is necessary to get the frequency distribution before one can represent the results graphically, or use any of the shortcut methods of computation. It usually takes less time to tabulate scores than it does to rank them, unless the number of scores is very small.

Before tabulating, it is necessary to choose the size of the class interval to be used. To do this, first subtract the lowest from the highest score, getting the range. Choose as the size of the interval a number that will divide the range into not less than 10 or more than 20 classes. Arrange the classes in a vertical column, with the highest at the top. In table 1, Appendix, a class interval of 5 has been used. Note that the lowest class, 55-59.99, means anything from 55.0 up to but not including 60; and that its midpoint is 57.5, not 57.0. Often the class is written simply as 55-59; in that case, it really means 55.0-59.99. For each score in the series, place a tally (/) to the right of the class in which the score belongs. The frequency column simply states in numbers the number of tallies, or scores, in each class.

C. Graphical Representation

A graph, or pictorial representation, often tells a story much more vividly than a table. There are two main kinds of graphs for representing score distributions, the histogram and the frequency polygon. In both, the classes are represented by equal distances along a horizontal line, with the lowest at the left. The difference is that in the histogram a horizontal line is drawn above the class to indicate the number of scores, and these lines are connected by vertical lines; while in the frequency polygon the number of scores is represented by a dot above the midpoint of the class, and the dots are joined by straight lines. Note that the histogram represents each score by a similar unit of area; the frequency polygon does not. The frequency polygon is generally used when two or more distributions are to be compared graphically, as similarities and differences in shape stand out more clearly, due to the oblique lines, than they do with histograms. The Appendix contains a histogram and a frequency polygon for the same set of scores.

III. MEASURES OF CENTRAL TENDENCY, OR AVERAGES

There are several kinds of averages, or measures of central tendency, of which only three -- the median, the mean, and the mode -- are used to any extent in psychological and educational measurement. All averages represent the whole distribution of scores by a single number. It must be remembered that most score distributions contain some scores that are far from the average. Nevertheless, the average is the most useful single statistical measure that one can find out about a group of scores.

A. The Median (Mdn.)

The median is that value such that half of the scores are greater than or equal to it, and half of the scores are less than or equal to it. If the scores are arranged in rank order, the median is the middle score, or mid-score, and can be obtained by counting from either end of the rank order. Note that the extreme scores can be either close to or far from the median without affecting its computation.

The median is preferable to the mean when quick computation is desired; when extreme or inaccurate scores should not influence the average; and when percentile scores are to be obtained. The norms (see below for the meaning of this term) of many intelligence and educational tests are stated in terms of median and percentile scores, and when using such tests the median is to be preferred to the mean.

   B. The Mean (M)

The mean is the measure popularly called "the average" and can be simply obtained by adding together all of the scores and dividing by the number

$M = \frac{\Sigma m}{N}$ In the Formula means "sum of," m refers to an individual score, and N means the number of scores. The exact size of each score counts in finding the mean, while only the scores near the middle of the distribution are important in determining the median. The mean should be used when a standard deviation or coefficient of correlation is to be found, and when every score should count in the average. It involves somewhat more arithmetical computation than the median.

Unless the number of cases is small, time can be saved by computing the mean from scores grouped in a frequency distribution, rather than from ungrouped scores. Multiply the midpoint of each class by the frequency in that class; i.e.,

$M = \frac{F \times Midpoint}{N}$. A still shorter method is available, in which one takes the midpoint of some class as a guessed mean, and then calculates a correction which is added to the guessed mean. This is profitable when the number of scores is fairly large. For details of this "short method," consult a standard text.

   C. The Mode

The mode is simply the score that occurs the greatest number of times. There may be more than one mode in a score distribution. When the scores are grouped, the midpoint of the class that contains the greatest frequency is called the crude mode. The mode is greatly influenced by chance factors, and so is ordinarily of not much significance. It should be used when one wants the most frequent score, or when one wants a very rough average without calculation.

IV. MEASURES OF THE DISTRIBUTION OF SCORES

   A. The Normal Curve

Scores in a great many human traits distribute themselves so as to form a symmetrical, bell-shaped frequency polygon, which is called a normal curve, normal distribution curve, normal probability curve, etc. Normal curves are obtained when the results are influenced by a large number of factors, each acting separately in an apparently chance way. For instance, if one tosses 20 pennies 1000 times, and plots the number of times each possible combination of heads and tails comes out, the results will form a normal curve. The normal curve is very important statistically, because all normal curves have similar statistical properties. Knowing the mean and standard deviation of a normal curve, one can deduce all of the other characteristics of the distribution. In a perfectly normal curve the mean, median, and mode all fall on the same score. Very often distributions are obtained which closely approximate normal distributions, but are not exactly normal; if the difference is slight, they may be treated as normal curves. When a distribution is lop-sided, with the scores piled up more on one side of the mean than on the other, it is said to be skewed. A large departure from the true normal curve may be due to a small number of cases, or may indicate that the trait is distributed in a way that is not fundamentally normal.

   B. Importance of Measures of Distribution

Two groups may have the same average scores on a test, but be widely different. All the members of one class may make very similar scores, while the members of the other class may differ widely. For instance, 3, 6, 9, 12, and 15 have the same mean as 7, 8, 9, 10, and 11. This matter of the spread, scattering, variability, or distribution of scores is often very important. It can be roughly estimated from a graph, but for accuracy one of several available statistical measures should be used. These measures of distribution are really valid only for distributions that are fundamentally normal.

C. Measures of Distribution
   1. The Range is simply the difference between the highest and lowest scores. It is the easiest measure of distribution to obtain, but the least dependable, because factors that have little effect on the distribution as a whole may have a marked effect on the on the extreme scores.
   2. The Average Deviation (A.D.), sometimes called the mean deviation, is the mean of the deviations of the separate scores from the mean. The deviation of any score is the difference between that score and the mean. In getting the mean of the deviations, no attention is paid to plus and minus signs. Although relatively easy to obtain, the A.D. is less useful than the standard deviation, and. is being used less and less.

   With grouped scores, the A.D. can be obtained by getting the deviation of each class midpoint from the mean. Each deviation is then multipled by the corresponding frequency. The mean of these deviations is then obtained, disregarding plus and minus signs. A "short method," in which deviations are taken from a guessed mean and a correction applied afterward, saves arithmetic because it eliminates multiplying by numbers containing decimals.
   3. The Standard Deviation (S.D. or the Greek letter sigma (6). In calculating this measure, the deviation of each score from the mean is obtained, as with the A.D. Instead of simply averaging the deviations, however, each deviation is squared before averaging, and the square root of the average is extracted. This square root is the standard deviation -- it is the square root of the mean of the squared deviations.

$$S.D. = \sqrt{\frac{\Sigma D^2}{N}}$$

The S.D. has many uses. It has a constant relationship to the shape of the normal curve. Knowing the mean and the S.D. of a normal distribution, one can determine the percent of the total number of scores that lie between any two scores, by referring to a special table. Approximately 68% of the scores in any normal curve lie between the mean and the scores 1 S.D. above and below the mean; approximately 95% lie between the mean and the scores 2 S.D.'s above and below the mean; and over 99% of the scores are less than 3 S.D.'s above or below the mean (see the illustration of a normal curve in the Appendix). If we wanted to compare the variability of one set of scores with that of another, we simply compare their S.D.'s; the one with the larger S.D. has the greater spread of scores. The S.D. is the most valuable of the various measures of distribution, although its computation takes longer than that of the A.D. or Q. It must be computed if one wants to get T Scores or a product-moment coefficient of correlation (These are explained below).

As with the M and A.D., arithmetic can be lessened by computing

$$S.D. = \frac{\Sigma (F D^2)}{N}$$

the S.D. from grouped scores. See Table 2 in the Appendix for examples of the calculation of the A.D. and S.D. from grouped scores. There is also a "short method" of computing the S.D., in which deviations are taken from a guessed mean, and a correction applied.

4. The Probable Error (P.E.). The P.E. is obtained by multiplying the S.D. by .6745. In a normal distribution exactly 50% of the cases lie between the mean and the scores one P.E. above or below the mean; the other 50% of the scores are more than one P.E. away from the mean. Practically all cases in a normal distribution are less than 4 P.E.'s away from the mean.

5. The Quartile Deviation (Q). One often wants to locate the middle 50% of a group of scores. The first quartile point, Q_1, is that score below or equal to which are 25%

of the scores in the distribution. The third quartile point, Q_3, is that score below or equal to which 75% of

the scores lie. The middle 50% of the scores can be found by subtracting Q_1 from Q_3

$$Q = \frac{Q_3 - Q_1}{2}$$

The quartile deviation is half of the range of scores. It is one-half of the range covered by the middle 50% of the scores. In a perfectly normal distribution Q and P.E. are identical. It is customary to use Q as the measure of variability when the median is used as the measure of central tendency.

V. DERIVED SCORES

If one is told that a person has made a score of 43 on a test, that in itself means very little, as the meaning of a score depends on many factors. The test itself may have a total possible score of 50, 100, or 150. The mean may be below 30 or above 70. The scores may be grouped closely together or spread over a wide range. For this reason a raw score must be interpreted in some way before it tells much about the goodness of the performance.

A. Percent Scores

Teachers often express scores in terms of the percent of the total possible score. An easy way to do this is to score the test so as to have a total possible score of 100. This is fairly satisfactory, but has some shortcomings. One teacher may give harder tests than another, or score of 85%. This sometimes happens when the students in the two classes have equal knowledge; sometimes the better class may get the lower average.

B. Distance from the Average

If we know that a score is 5 points above or below the mean or median, we know more about it than if we simply know the raw score or percent score. However, 5 points may be a big difference on one test and a small difference on another test.

C. Percentile Scores

A percentile score states the percent of the total number of scores that are below or equal to a particular score. For instance, the statement that the raw score of 67 on a test stands at the 83rd percentile means that 83% of the scores in the distribution are at or below 67. The median is the 50th percentile; Q_1 is the 25th percentile; Q_3 is the 75th percentile. The percentile score tells us not merely whether a score is above or below the median, but gives us also its exact place in the rank order. Because percentile scores are easy to compute and help greatly in the interpretation of scores, most psychological and educational tests designed for general use are accompanied by tables giving the percentile values of all of the possible raw scores on the test.

These values are based on results previously obtained with the test. Often separate percentile tables are given for each age or grade, so that one can determine just how each pupil in a group stands in comparison with the much larger group used in determining the tables.

Since in a normal distribution the scores are much more frequent near the median than they are near the extremes, percentile scores are not directly proportional in size to raw scores. For instance, there is more of a difference between the raw scores of two pupils with percentile ranks of 90 and 95 than there is between the ra.w scores of two pupils with percentile ranks of 50 and 55. For this reason one cannot combine a pupil's scores on different tests by averaging his percentile scores. The best way to average scores on different tests, with different averages and different variabilities, is to use T Scores, which are explained below.

To find the raw scores corresponding to any percentile value, first multiply N by the percentile value, and then count up that many scores from the bottom of the rank order, or down from the top. The median is the 50th percentile; to locate it, count 50% of the scores from either end of the rank order. The 60th percentile, in a group of 25 scores, is the 15th from the lowest. When the desired score is fractional, and when the percentile score is calculated from grouped scores, interpolation is necessary. In Table 1, Appendix, illustrations are given of the calculation of the Median, 25th percentile, 75th percentile, and Q. The calculation of the median may be explained as follows: 50% of N is 14. There are 12 scores below the 85 - 89.99 class, and 7 scores in that class; therefore the median is 2/7ths of the way up in that class. Since the class covers 5 scores, multiply 2/7ths by 5; add this to 85.0, the lower limit of the class, and the result is the median. Other percentiles are calculated in the same way.

D. T Scores

Since the S.D. has a constant relation to the shape of the normal curve, a score which is a certain distance above the mean on one test has the same relative value as a score which is the same distance above the mean on another test, if the distances are divided by the S.D. in each case, and equated on that basis. In other words, a score which is two S.D.'s above the mean on one test is equivalent to a score which is two S.D.'s above the mean on another test. T Scores are scores stated in terms of what fraction of an S.D. a score is above or below the mean. Because T Scores are always proportional to the raw scores, the T Scores of the same individual on different tests can be combined by simple averaging. This is the best way to combine scores from several different tests into a total score.

To translate raw scores into T Scores, first subtract the mean from each score, and divide each remainder by the S.D. This will be plus if the score is above the mean and minus if below the mean. Such scores are called "standard deviation scores." Multiply the standard deviation score by 10, and add 50; the result is a T Score. The possible range of T Scores is from 0 to 100, and the mean always has a T Score value of 50.

E. Mental Age (M.A.)

Mental age is a kind of derived score used with intelligence tests. The M.A. corresponding to any raw score may be defined as the age of the group of children who on the average make that raw score. Example: A child makes a score of 43 on an intelligence test. 43 is the average raw score on this test of children 9 years, 3 months old. The child's M.A. is therefore 9 years, 3 months. A child's mental age increases as he gets older. Children of different chronological ages (C.A.'s) may have the same M.A.'s.

F. Intelligence Quotient (I.Q.)

The I.Q. is the M.A. divided by the C.A. A child who is above average mentally always has an I.Q. above 100, and a child below average has an I.Q. below 100. The I.Q. remains roughly constant as a child grows older; it is an indication of the rate of mental growth, or brightness.

G. Educational Age (E.A.)

This is similar to the M.A., except that it applies only to tests of educational achievement or knowledge. A child has an E.A. of 10 years when he makes a score on an educational test equal to the average score of 10 year old children.

H. Educational Quotient (E.Q.)

This is the E.A. divided by the C.A. It indicates the rate of educational progress, while the E.A. indicates the present educational attainment. The E.A. and E.Q. are obtained from standardized tests covering several subjects. Ages and quotients can also be obtained for individual subjects, as reading age, reading quotient, arithmetic age, etc.

I. Achievement Quotient (A.Q.)

This is an indication of how a child's educational achievement compares with his intelligence. It is obtained by dividing the E.A. by the M.A., or by dividing the E.Q. by the I.Q. A child with an E.A. of 8 years an an M.A. of 10 years has an A.Q. of 80; a child with an E.Q. of 120 and an I.Q. of 100 has an A.Q. of 120.

J. Norms

Norms are groups of scores for a particular test which have been obtained from large groups of subjects, and which are used for interpreting new results obtained with the test. Percentile scores, T Scores, mental and educational ages and quotients are all different ways of stating the norms. Usually the author of an intelligence or achievement test states his norms in more than one of these ways. Another kind of norm sometimes used is the *grade norm,* where the average score given is for a grade rather than for a chronological age.

VI. COMPARISONS OF GROUPS

One often wants to compare the results of two groups on the same test. A simple statement of the means or medians of the two groups is not sufficient, because there may be much or little overlapping between the two groups (see examples at the right.) A commonly used device is to state the percent of one group that exceeds the median of the other group. If this is close to 50%, the amount of overlapping is great; if close to 0 or 100, the overlapping is relatively slight.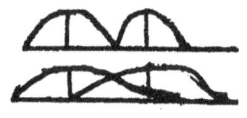

A problem that occurs frequently in psychological and educational measurement is the question whether a difference that has been found between two measures is reliable; in other words, would a similar difference be found again and again if the measurements were repeated. This is determined by comparing the obtained difference with the standard error of the difference, or the probable error of the difference. The exact meaning of these two statistical measures need not be explained here. Differences are not considered to be completely reliable unless they are at least three times their standard error or four times the probable error. Example: The mean I.Q. of another class; the standard error of the difference is 1.3 points. Since the difference is less than 3 times its standard error, it is not reliable -- it may be due purely to chance, and a repetition may show no such difference.

VII. CORRELATION

One often wants to know whether there is any relation between two sets of results obtained from the same subjects. The most frequently used method of measuring such a relationship is to calculate a coefficient of correlation. This is a quantitative measure of the degree of relationship between two sets of measures for the same group of individuals. There are two widely used methods of measuring correlation. The simpler of these is the rank-difference method, devised by Spearman. This is based on the comparison of the rank orders in the two sets of measures, disregarding the actual size of the raw scores. It is much easier to calculate, and is usually used when the number of cases is small. It is somewhat less accurate than the product-moment method, devised by Pearson, which uses the raw scores. The symbol for the coefficient of correlation obtained by the rank-difference method is the Greek letter rho; for the product-moment coefficient, the letter r.

The student who wishes to learn how to compute r should refer to a basic reference. The computation of rho is relatively simple, and will be briefly outlined. The rank order for each set of measures is first obtained. For each subject the two ranks are placed side by side. The D or difference column records the difference between the two ranks, for each subject. These differences are then squared, and the squared differences are added up. This total is multipled by 6, and is the numerator of a fraction. The denominator of the fraction is $N(N^2-1)$. Rho is obtained by subtracting the fraction from 1.00. Consult Table 3 for an illustration.

    A. Interpretation of the Coefficient of Correlation

Coefficients of correlation range in size from plus 1.00 to minus 1.00. Both of these values indicate a perfect relationship or correspondence. Plus 1.00 indicates that the person with the highest score on one trait also has the highest score on the other, the second highest is also second highest on the second, etc. Minus 1.00 means that the highest on one trait is the lowest on the other, the second highest on one is next to the lowest on the other, etc. An r of zero indicates that there is a complete absence of relationship between the two sets of measurements; those high on one trait may be either high or low on the other. Intermediate values (+.53,-.40, etc.) are not percents, an an r of approximately .80 indicates only half as close a relationship an an r of 1.00. Customarily an r of less than .40 is considered low, .40 - .70 substantial, and above .70, high. But even an r of .80 contains an occasional marked exception to the general relationship. Before we can predict a person's score on one trait with accuracy from a knowledge of his score on another trait, we should have an r above .90 between the two traits.

It should be noted that the presence of a correlation between two traits does not prove that one is the cause of the other; it merely indicates the presence of a relationship between the two. For instance, in an 8th grade class there is a minus correlation between height and I.Q. Neither of these traits is the cause of the other; the relationship is due to the fact that the younger children in the class are both smaller and brighter than the older children.

    B. Uses of Correlation

One of the important uses of correlation is in *prediction*. If there is a high correlation between two traits, one can predict a person's score on one from a knowledge of his score on the other, with better than the chance success. A very high correlation, however, is necessary for accurate prediction.

    C. Reliability

In using a test, it is important to know if the results obtained are close to what would be obtained if the measurements are repeated. By reliability we mean the extent to which the same test (or two equivalent forms of the same test) will give similar results when used on the same subjects more than once. Reliability is indicated by correlation. *Retest reliability* is the correlation between two sets of scores on the same test obtained from the same subjects. *Split-half reliability* is the correlation between scores on the two halves of a test; to make this comparable to retest reliability, a special formula (the Spearman-Brown Formula) is applied. A test to be really reliable, should have reliability over .90 as measured in both ways. Reliability is essentially the consistency with which a test will give the same results on repeated administration.

D. Validity

The validity of a test is its most important characteristic, and also the one hardest to measure. By validity we mean the degree of perfection to which a test measures what it is supposed to measure. Students often confuse validity with reliability. Remember that reliability measures the consistency of a test, the extent to which it will give the same results over and over again. A test may be reliable, without measuring what it is supposed to measure. For instance, one could measure the circumference of the skull very reliably, but the result would be an exceedingly poor indication of intelligence-- as a measure of intelligence this measure, although reliable, would be totally invalid. A history test consisting entirely of dates to be identified might give very reliable results, but they could be invalid as a measure of understanding the significance of historical events.

The usual way of measuring the validity of a test is to correlate the results with some criterion -- that is, with some other measure of the trait in question, which is already known to be valid. The big difficulty in establishing the validity of a new test is to find a satisfactory criterion. For instance, one should not look for an extremely high correlation with teacher's marks and estimates, because the test is expected to be a better measure than the teacher's marks are. Also, a perfect correlation with other tests that are known to be only partly valid is not desirable. Ordinarily a test is correlated with each of a few partly satisfactory criteria, and its validity is estimated from the results.

APPENDIX
Table 1 - Calculation of the Mean, Median, and Q

SCORES	MIDPOINT	TALLIES	F (FREQUENCY)	F x MIDPOINT
100-104.99	102.5	/	1	102.5
95- 99.99	97.5	////	4	390.0
90- 94.99	92.5	////	4	370.0
85- 89.99	87.5	++++ / /	7	612.5
80- 84.99	82.5	///	3	247.5
75- 79.99	77.5	//	2	155.0
70- 74.99	72.5	/	2	145.0
65- 69.99	67.5	//	1	67.5
60- 64.99	62.5	//	2	125.0
55- 59.99	57.5		2	115.0
			N = 28	2330.0

HISTORGRAM

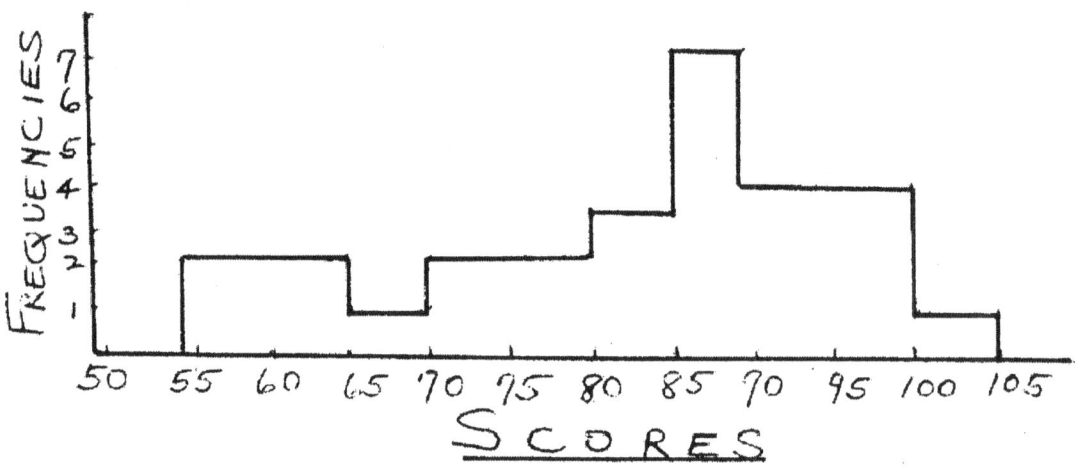

The Mean

$$M = \frac{(Fx\ Midpoint)}{N} = \frac{2330.0}{28} = 83.2$$

The Median

50% of N = 14. There are 12 scores below the 85-89.99 interval, leaving 2 scores to go. There are 7 scores in that class, and the class covers 5 scores. 2/7 X 5 = 1.4.

Median = 85.0 + 1.4 = 86.4

Frequency Polygon

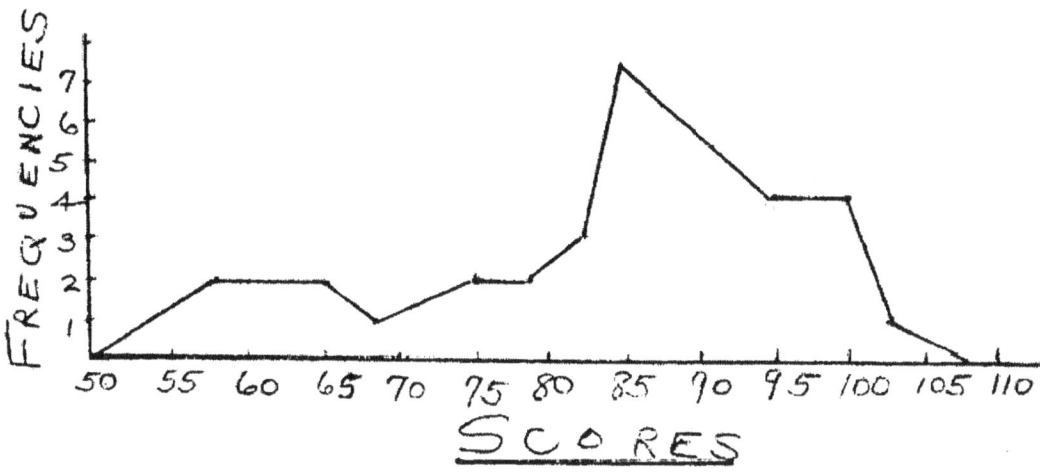

The Quartile Deviation

$$Q = \frac{Q_3 - Q_1}{2}$$

$$= \frac{92.5 - 75.0}{2}$$

$$= 8.75$$

$Q_3 =$ 75th percentile. 75% of 28 = 21. There are 19 scores below 90.0. 90.0 + 2/4 X 5 = 92.5

$Q_1 =$ 25th percentile. 25% of 28 = 7. 7 scores bring us exactly up to 75.0; therefore Q_1 = 75.0

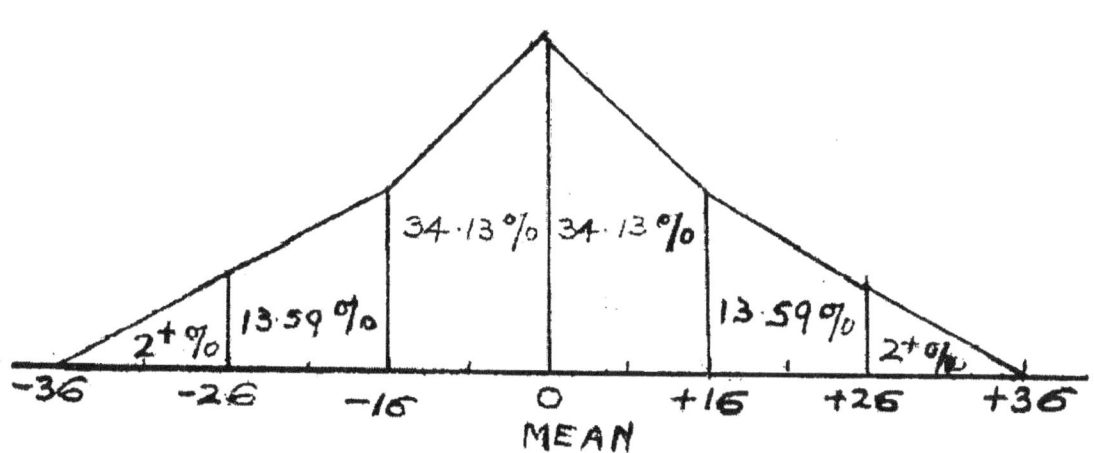

A THEORETICAL NORMAL CURVE

Table 2 - Calculation of the A. BY, S.D., and P.E.

SCORES	MIDPOINT	F	D(DEVTATION)	FD	FD²
100-104.99	102.5	1	19.3	19.3	372.49
95- 99.99	97.5	4	14.3	57.2	817.96
90- 94.99	92.5	4	9.3	37.2	345.96
85- 89.99	87.5	7	4.3	30.1	129.43
80- 84.99	82.5	3	- 0.7	- 2.1	1.47
75- 79.99	77.5	2	- 5.7	-11.4	64.98
70- 74.99	72.5	2	-10.7	-21.4	228.98
65- 69.99	67.5	1	-15.7	-15.7	246.49
60- 64.99	62.5	2	-20.7	-41.4	856.98
55- 59.99	57.5	2	-25.7	-51.4	1320.98
M= 83.2		N=28		257.2	4385.72

NOTES
1. For each class, the deviation is the difference between the mean and the midpoint of that class.
2. The FD² column is obtained by multiplying each FD by the corresponding D. It is F X D², not F² X D².
3. In adding up the FD column to get the A.D., the minus signs are disregarded. There are no minus signs in the FD²

The Average Deviation

$$A.D. = \frac{\Sigma FD}{N} = \frac{287.2}{28} = 10.29$$

The Standard Deviation

$$S.D. = \sqrt{\frac{\Sigma(FD^2)}{N}} = \sqrt{\frac{4385.72}{28}} = \sqrt{56.63} = 12.52$$

The Probable Error
P.E. = .6745 X S.D. = .6745 X 12.52 = 8.44

Table 3 - Calculation of the Rank-Difference Coefficient of Correlation

Individual	Score on Test 1	Score on Test 2	Rank on Test 1	Rank on Test 2	D	D
A	18	20	7	4	3	9
B	24	17	4	7	3	9
C	22	19	5	5.5	0.5	0.25
D	27	21	1.5	3	1.5	2.25
E	26	25	3	2	1	1
F	27	26	1.5	1	0.5	0.256
G	20	19	6	5.5	0.5	0.25
N = 7					ΣD²	=22.00

NOTES

1. Each entry in the "D" or difference column is the difference between the two ranks attained by that individual.
2. Note that, in getting the rank orders, two tied scores get the average of the two ranks covered; the following score gets the next rank.

$$\text{rho} = 1 - \frac{6 \Sigma D^2}{N(N^2 - 1)} = 1 - \frac{6 \times 22.00}{7(49-1)} = 1 - \frac{132}{336} = +.61$$

GLOSSARY OF STATISTICAL SYMBOLS

Σ: process of summation.

$\| \|$: the positive value of the quantity in between.

m: the value of an individual observation; the value of the mid-point of a class.

f: the number of observations (frequency) in a given class.

i: the width of the class interval, i.e., the difference between two consecutive class limits.

N: the total number of observations.

a: the value of an original observation (same as m); symbol a used in formula for the geometric mean; value of Y_c when $X = 0$ in equation of trend or in regression equation.

w: weight attached to a value entering into an average.

M: the arithmetic mean.

M': an assumed arithmetic mean.

c: the correction factor, the difference between an assumed mean and the actual mean $(M - M')$.

d: the deviation of a given observation from an average.

d': the deviation of the mid-point of a class from an assumed mean or arbitrary origin.

Md: the median.

Mo: the mode.

L_1: the lower limit of the modal class.

d_1: the difference between the frequency of the modal class and the frequency of the preceding class.

d_2: the difference between the frequency of the modal class and the frequency of the following class.

Mg: the geometric mean.

H: the harmonic mean.

Q_1: the first quartile.

Q_2: the second quartile; the median.

Q_3: the third quartile.

$Q.D.$:	the quartile deviation or semi-interquartile range.
K:	the value of a point which lies halfway between quartile one and quartile three.
$A.D.$:	the average or mean deviation.
σ:	the standard deviation.
V:	the coefficient of variation.
Coef. $Q.D.$:.	the coefficient of quartile deviation.
σ_M:	the standard error of the mean.
σ_s:	the standard deviation of the original observations in the sample.
σ_D:	the standard error of the differences between sample means.
σ_{md}:	the standard error of the median.
σ_{Q1}:	the standard error of quartile one.
σ_{Q3}:	the standard error of quartile three.
σ_σ:	the standard error of the standard deviation.
σ_p:	the standard error of a sample percentage.
p:	the proportion in the population expressed as a decimal; the probability of success in a single trial of an event.
q:	$1 - p$; the probability of failure in a single trial of an event.
T:	the critical ratio.
M_h:	a hypothetical statement of the mean.
sk:	the coefficient of skewness.
p_0:	the price of a single commodity or service in the base year.
p'_0:	the price of a second commodity or service in the base year.
p''_0:	the price of a third commodity or service in the base year.
p^n_0:	the price of the nth commodity or service in the base year.
p_1:	the price of a commodity in a given year.
p'_1, p''_1, p^n_1:	the prices of other commodities or services in the given year.
q_0:	the quantity, i.e., the barrels, gallons, bushels, and so forth, produced, consumed, bought, or sold, in the base year.
q'_0, q''_0, q^n_0:	the quantities of other commodities in the base year.
q_1:	the quantity of a commodity in the given year.

q'_1, q''_1, q^n_1: other quantities in the given year.

$\Sigma p_0 q_0$: the summation of the products of the commodity prices times their quantity in the base year.

$\Sigma p_1 q_1$: the summation of the products of prices times quantity in the given year.

$\dfrac{p_1}{p_0}$: the ratio of prices in the given year to prices in the base year.

b: the "typical" change in the growth factor per X unit of time, or the "typical" change in Y for a given change in X, in functional analysis, least-squares straight line.

$\log a$: the log of the value of Y_c for a trend or regression line where $X = 0$.

$\log b$: the log of the "typical" rate of change in the growth factor per X unit of time, or the log of the "typical" rate of change in Y for a given change in X, functional analysis, least-squares geometric straight line.

r: the Pearsonian coefficient of correlation.

$\bar{r}$: the coefficient of correlation adjusted for the number of observations.

ρ: the index of correlation (rho).

$\bar{\rho}$: the index of correlation corrected for the number of observations.

σ_r: the standard error of r.

Sy: the standard error of estimate.

$\overline{Sy}$: the standard error of estimate corrected for the number of observations.

k: the coefficient of alienation.

X: an observed value of a variable quantity.

x: value of a variable quantity expressed as a deviation from the arithmetic mean of values of X.

Y: an observed value of a variable quantity, the dependent variable in functional analysis.

Y_c: values of Y computed by use of formula for trend, or regression equation.

y: value of a variable quantity expressed as a deviation from the arithmetic mean of values of Y.

GREEK ALPHABET

Letters		Names	Letters		Names
A	α	Alpha	N	ν	Nu
B	β	Beta	Ξ	ξ	Xi
Γ	γ	Gamma	O	o	Omicron
Δ	δ	Delta	Π	π	Pi
E	ϵ	Epsilon	P	ρ	Rho
Z	ζ	Zeta	Σ	σ	Sigma
H	η	Eta	T	τ	Tau
Θ	θ	Theta	Υ	υ	Upsilon
I	ι	Iota	Φ	φ	Phi
K	κ	Kappa	X	χ	Chi
Λ	λ	Lambda	Ψ	ψ	Psi
M	μ	Nu	Ω	ω	Omega

STATISTICAL TESTS
SAMPLE STUDIES

CONTENTS

		Page
1.	Binominal Test	1
2.	Chi-Square Two-Sample Case	2
3.	Cochran Q Test	3
4.	Contingency Coefficient: C	5
5.	Fisher Exact Probability Test	6
6.	Friedman Two-Way Analysis of Variance by Ranks	7
7.	Kendall Coefficiency of Concordance: W	8
8.	Kolmogorov-Smirnov One-Sample Tests	10
9.	Kruskal-Wallis One-Way Analysis of Variance by Ranks	11
10.	Mann-Whitney U Test	13
11.	Randomization Test for Two Matched Samples	11
12.	Sign Test	15
13.	The Spearman Rank Correlation Coefficient: Rank	16
14.	Wilcoxon Matched-Pairs Signed-Ranks Test	18

STATISTICAL TESTS
SAMPLE STUDIES

1. **Binominal Test**

    The Binominal is a goodness-of-fit test. It is useful in determining whether it is reasonable to believe that the portions (or frequencies) within a given sample could have been drawn from a population having a specified value of P. P is the proportion of cases in one class within a population. The data must be nominal level and separated into two discrete categories such as: male and female, in-school and out-of-school, member and non-member. There is no comparable parametric test which is applicable data measured at the nominal level. However, when the relative power of the Binominal test was measured, the results showed it to have 95% of the power of a parametric test to reject the null hypothesis when N-6. As N grew, power went down to 63%.

    Tom Reed is doing a study to determine whether the disruptive children in his class like the token economy system he established in the class.

    a. **Null Hypothesis:** There will be no difference between the number of disruptive students who like the token economy and the number of those who don't.
    Hypothesis: The disruptive student will like the token economy.

    b. **Statistical Test:** The binominal test is chosen because the data are in two discrete categories (disruptive/nondisruptive) and the design is of the one sample type (he only asks the pupil preference once).

    c. **Significance Level:** Let probability .-05, N = the number of disruptive students = 10.

    d. **Data 1**

Names	Disruptive	Non-Disruptive
John	✓	
Susie		✓
Fred	✓	
Larry	✓	
Mary	✓	
Tina		✓
Tom		✓
Kathy	✓	
Dan	✓	
Pam	✓	
Bill		✓
Terry	✓	
Jean	✓	
Joan		✓
Rob	✓	

    Disruptive student = N 10 N = 10
    P = the expected number of disruptive students who like the token economy occurring by chance
    Q = 10 disruptive students − P

The Equation $\sum_{i=0}^{N} \binom{N}{t}() P^i Q^{N-i}$
i = 0

Table D gives the probabilities associated with the occurrence under the Null Hypothesis.

e. **Rejection Region:** He will find support for his hypothesis if the number of disruptive students who don't like the token economy is so small that the probability of that number of students occurring under the Null Hypothesis is equal to or less than P = .05.

f. **Decision:** Only one of the 10 did not like the token economy. Looking up in Table D with N = 10 and X = 1, we find P = .011. Since .011 < .05, the hypothesis is supported. Mr. Reed's students did enjoy using the token system.

2. **Chi-Square Two-Sample Case**

This test is used to compare the number of scores in two or more categories with the expected number of scores in those categories, based on the null hypothesis. This goodness-of-fit-test can be used with nominal level data. There is no information in the literature as to the power of Chi-Square to reject the false null hypothesis. However, it is suggested that if the statistician's data is ordinal level or higher, the Kolmogorov-Smirnov or some other test be used because they use more information and, therefore, would have more power to reject the null hypothesis.

Example: Helen McBride felt that her second graders who were read to by their parents enjoyed reading more than those whose parents did not read to them. Some of her students' parents did not read to them but had allowed their children to attend Story Hour at the library. Helen decided to find out if there was a difference between the three groups' preference for reading.

a. **Hypothesis:** The students whose parents read to them will have a higher score on the reading enjoyment test than those whose parents do not.
Null Hypothesis: There will be no difference in reading preference among the three groups.

b. **Statistical Test:** The Chi-Square test is chosen because the data is categorical or nominal level of measurement and because Mrs. McBride wants to compare a theoretical distribution with the distribution of scores which actually occurred.

c. **Level of Significance:** Let a (alpha) = .05, N = 30 students.

d. **Computation:** Data

	Parent Read to Children	Children Attend Library Hour	Children Not Read To	Total
Like to read	Expected 5 (under the null hypothesis) Observed 9	5	5	15
Don't like to read	Expected 5 (under the null) Observed 1	5 4	5 8	15
Total	10	10	10	30

Equation:

i. $x^2 = \sum^r \sum^k \frac{(O-E)^2}{E}$

x^2 = chi square
O = observed scores
E = expected scores
$\sum^r \sum^k$ = add the sums of each cell

ii. $x^2 = \frac{(9-5)^2}{5} + \frac{(6-5)^2}{5} + \frac{(2-5)^2}{5} + \frac{(1-5)^2}{5} + \frac{(4-5)^2}{5} + \frac{(8-5)^2}{5}$

$x^2 = \frac{16}{5} + \frac{1}{5} + \frac{9}{5} + \frac{16}{5} + \frac{1}{5} + \frac{9}{5} = \frac{52}{5}$

$x^2 = 10.4$ df = (r-1)(k-1) = (2-1)(3-1) = 2

iii. Consult Table C. df = 3   5.99 = critical value of Chi-Square

e. **Region of Rejection:** In order to reject the null hypothesis, Ms. McBride must have 5.99 or more.

f. **Decision:** Chi-Square = 10.4, which is greater than 5.99. Therefore, Ms. McBride may reject the null hypothesis at the .05 level. She finds support for her hypothesis that the children who have someone read to them will enjoy reading more. She decided to start reading aloud to her class.

3. **Cochran Q Test**

The Cochran Q tests for significance difference among three or more matched sets of data that are at the nominal or dichotomized ordinal level of measurement. The test can be used to compare the same subjects under three or more conditions, or three or more different sets of subjects under the same condition. The power of this test is not known; however, the fact that it should be used with nominal or ordinal level data makes comparison between the Cochran Q and parametric tests meaningless. Parametric tests must have an interval level of measurement. The statistician is cautioned, however, not to use the Cochran Q if the data is an interval level of measurement, as some of the information may be wasted.

Example: Mary Stewart was interested in finding out what teaching method would increase reading enjoyment for the children in her 6th grade Title 1 reading program. The three methods she employed were as follows: 1) a traditional round-robin oral reading approach; 2) educational comic books were used in class as supplementary reading materials; and 3) time was provided during class to go to the library for selection of books. Mary would like to know if there is any difference in enjoyment for the three methods of instruction.

The following is an outline of Ms. Stewart's study.

a. **Hypothesis:** There will be a significant difference of reading enjoyment for the three different methods of instruction.
   Null Hypothesis: There will be no difference in the reading enjoyment for the three methods.

b. **Statistical Test:** The Cochran Q is chosen because the data are for three related groups and are dichotomized as yes and no reading enjoyment.

c. **Significance Level:** Let a (alpha) = .01, N = 14 (students).

d. **Computation:** Data: 0 = no enjoyment; 1 = enjoyment

Names	Traditional	Educational Comics	Library Time	L1	L2
Tod	0	0	0	0	0
Anna	0	1	1	2	4
Sue	0	1	0	1	1
Kenny	0	0	0	0	0
Steven	0	1	0	1	1
Marie	0	0	1	1	1
Mike	0	0	1	1	1
Barry	0	1	1	2	4
Lenore	1	1	1	3	9
Kathy	0	0	1	1	1
Craig	0	0	1	1	1
Terry	1	0	1	2	4
John	0	1	0	1	1
Joey	0	1	1	2	4
	$G_i = 2$	$G_j = 7$	$G_l = 9$	$L_1 = 18$	$L_1^2 = 33$

$$Q = \frac{(k-1)[k\sum G_i^2 - (\sum G_1)^2]}{k\sum L_i - \sum L_1^2}$$

$$Q = \frac{(3-1)3(4+49+81)-(18)}{(3)(18)=33}$$

$$Q = \frac{23(134)-18}{54-33} \quad Q = \frac{768}{21}$$

Consult Table C, with df = k - 1 = 3 – 1 = 2
The figure under .05 column in row 2 = 5.99.

e. **Rejection Region:** One may reject the null hypothesis when the value of Q is larger than the figure listed for the significance level of .05.

f. **Decision:** Since Ms. Stewart's data yielded a Q = 3657 which is larger than the necessary 5.99 for significance at the .05 level, she can reject the null hypothesis. She finds support for her hypothesis that there is a significant difference among methods of teaching for increasing reading enjoyment.

4. **Contingency Coefficient: C**

The Contingency Coefficient: C is a measure of relationship or the extent of association between two sets of attributes. It is the only test of its kind for data which is nominal scale, that is of an unordered series of frequencies. This test is not powerful in rejecting the false null hypothesis, but is uniquely useful with its ease of computation and freedom from restrictive assumptions about the population.

Example: John Stock felt that there was a relationship between low achievement and disruptive behavior. He wanted to determine the strength of this relationship in his fifth grade students. This part of his study follows.

a. **Hypothesis:** There will be a significantly strong positive relationship between the low scores obtained on the achievement test and ratings of disruptiveness.
   Null Hypothesis: There will be no relationship between low achievement and disruptiveness.

b. **Statistical Test:** The Contingency Coefficient: C was chosen because the data of one of the variables was categorical (disruptive/nondisruptive) and also Mr. Stock was seeking to discover the strength of the relationship.

c. **Level of Significance:** Let a (alpha) = .05, N =15 students.

d. **Computation:** Data

	Below 50 Percentile		Above 50 Percentile		Total
Disruptive	5	8	5	2	10
Nondisruptive	3	2	3	4	6
Total		10		6	16

Equations

$$x^2 = \sum^r \sum^k \frac{(Oi_1 Ei_1)^2}{Ei_1} \quad \sum^r \sum^k = \text{add the sum of differences of each cell.}$$

Oi_1 = observed number of cases in a cell.
Ei_1 = expected number of cells in a cell, all chances being equal

$$x^2 = \frac{(8-5)}{5} + \frac{(2-5)}{5} + \frac{(2-3)}{3} + \frac{(4-3)}{3}$$

$$x^2 = \frac{9}{5} + \frac{9}{5} + \frac{1}{3} + \frac{1}{3} = \frac{27}{15} + \frac{27}{15} + \frac{5}{15} + \frac{5}{15} = \frac{64}{15}$$

$$C = \sqrt{\frac{x^2}{N+x^2}}$$

x^2 = value of x^2 for data
N = number of subjects

$$C = \sqrt{\frac{4.26}{16+4.26}} = \sqrt{\frac{4.26}{20.26}} = \sqrt{.21} = .458$$

Consult Table C. .46 is significant at .5 level.

e. **Rejection Region:** The null hypothesis will be rejected. C = .05 significance or less.

f. **Decision:** Since C was not significant at the .05 level, Mr. Stock cannot reject the null hypothesis. Therefore, Mr. Stock does not find support for his hypothesis that there is a significant relationship between disruptiveness and low achievement.

5. **Fisher Exact Probability Test**

This test is used to determine if one of two independent samples has significantly more scores in one of the two mutually exclusive categories than the other. The two groups must be small in size and be measured at the nominal or dichotomial ordinal level. The Fisher test is the most powerful one a teacher can use on data that meets these specifications.

Example: Joan Mitchell noticed that the children in her first grade class who seemed least well adjusted were also the youngest children chronologically. She wanted to discover if there was a significant difference between the adjustment ratings between the group of children whose birthdates fell between October 1 and December 1 and those born in other months. An outline of her study follows.

a. **Hypothesis:** The children born between October 1 and December 1, 2012 will be rated as having adjustment problems significantly more frequently than the other group.
Null Hypothesis: There will be no difference in adjustment ratings between the two groups.

b. **Statistical Test:** The Fisher Exact Probability Test was selected because the categories—adjusted and maladjusted—are mutually exclusive, and since the N is small.

c. **Computation:** Data

	Adjusted		Maladjusted		Totals
Youngest Children	A	1	B	8	9
Older Children	C	6	D	0	6
		7		8	15

Refer to Table 1
A + B = 9, C + D = 6. Go to this row under Totals in the right-hand column.
B = 8, therefore, go to 8 under the B (or A) column.
D = 0, therefore, go across the 0 to find the level of significance, which is 0.1.

d **Rejection Region:** The null hypothesis will be rejected if D = a .05

e. **Decision:** Since D = 0 which is less than the 2 needed for significance at the .05 level, Mrs. Mitchell's hypothesis is supported. She can reject the null hypothesis. She can therefore conclude that there was a significant difference in adjustment between the two age groups.

6. **Friedman Two-Way Analysis of Variance by Ranks**

The Friedman test is to be used to determine if three or more samples differ significantly from one another and thus come from different populations. The samples must be matched and be measurable at the ordinal level of data. This matching may be achieved by studying the same group of subjects under three or more conditions or by assigning matched groups to the different conditions. Although the exact power of the Friedman test is not reported, Friedman compared the results of his test with the results of the F test, a parametric test, and the comparison shows the Friedman statistical test to be equally as powerful as the F test.

Example: John McGee was interested in discovering which of three methods of teaching was most effective in helping his fifth graders to learn vocabulary words. The first method he tried was to have each child look up the definitions of the words only. In the second method, he divided the children into groups with each group giving a report on the etymology of each word. The third type was to have the students write stories using the words. His study follows.

a. **Hypothesis:** There will be significant difference among the group's performance under different conditions.
   Null Hypothesis: There will be no significant difference among the treatments.

b. **Statistical Test:** The Friedman Two-Way Analysis of Variance was used in this case because the data was ordinal level in measurement with matched samples.

c. **Significance Level:** Let a (alpha) = .05, N = 9 (the number of students in Mr. McGee's reading class)

d. **Computation:** Data

	Scores					
Names	Definitions	Ranks	Etymology	Ranks	Stories	Ranks
Mary	5	1	8	2	9	3
Greg	8	2	9	3	7	1
Tom	7	2	6	1	9	3
Renee	6	2	7	3	5	1
Tony	8	2	9	3	7	1
Ray	8	1	10	3	9	2
Ann	9	3	8	2	7	1
Rick	5	1	9	3	8	2
Martha	10	3	9	2	7	1
	$R_i =$	17	$R_j =$	20	$R_l =$	15

$$Xr^2 = \frac{12}{Nk(k+1)} \Sigma (r_i)^2 - 3N(k+1)$$

N = number of rows
k = number of columns
R, = sum of ranks in each individual column 2 = directs one to sum the squares of the sums of ranks over all three teaching methods

$$Xr^2 = \frac{12}{9(3)(3+1)} (289+400+225) - 3(8)(3+1)$$

$$Xr^2 = \frac{12}{108} 918 - 108$$

$$Xr^2 = .11(806)$$

$$Xr^3 = 88.66$$

Consult Table N where K = 3, N = 9.
Significant at the .05 level = 6.22 = Xr^2

e. **Rejection Region:** The rejection region for the Null Hypothesis of all values of Xr^2 which are so large that the probability associated with their occurrence under the null hypothesis is equal to or less than a (alpha) = .05(6.222)

f. **Decisions:** Since the Xr^2 = 88.66 is considerably larger than the 6.222 to considerably larger than the 6.222 to find significance at the .05 level, Mr. McGee finds support of his hypothesis. He can reject the null hypothesis, that all the treatments help his students equally.

7. **Kendall Coefficient of Concordance: W**

The Concordance W is used to measure correlation or strength of relationship among three or more sets of scores. Such a measure may be particularly useful in studies of interest or inter-judge reliability or in studies of clusters of variables. A high or significant value of W may be interpreted as meaning that the tests or judges are applying the same standards in ranking the variables under study. Clusters of variables are studied in the example below.

Example: Mrs. Dema Jane Martin had the idea that some of her students felt that the work she assigned was too difficult to perform; therefore, they didn't even try to listen or make their best efforts. She wants to find out if there is a relationship among the variables lack of self-esteem, reading comprehension scores, and fear of failure scores.

a. **Hypothesis:** There will be a significant strong relationship among the three variables: self-esteem (as measured by the Self-Esteem questionnaire); fear of failure (as measured by the test of that same name) and achievement (as measured by the SRA Reading Comprehension Test).
   Null Hypothesis: There will be no significant relationship among the variables.

b. **Statistical Test:** The Kendall Concordance W was used in this study to find the strength of relationship among three variables and the data is ordinal level in measurement.

c. **Significance Level:** Let a (alpha) = .05, N = 15.

d. **Computation:** Data

Student	SRA Rank	Self-Esteem Rank	Fear of Failure Rank	R_j	$R_v - \frac{R}{N}$	$(R_j - \frac{R_j}{N})^2$
Debbie	12	14	12	38	13.73	188.51
Linda	3	4	4	11	-13.27	176.09
Patrick	2	6	3	11	-13.27	176.09
Allen	11	10	8	29	4.73	22.37
Steve	13	12	14	39	14.73	216.97
Alice	1	3	5	9	15.27	233.17
William	7	6	7	20	4.27	18.23
Pam	8	9	10	27	2.73	7.45
Terry	10	8	9	27	2.73	7.45
Joan	4	1	2	7	17.27	298.25
Mike	14	13	13	40	15.73	247.43
Fred	5	2	1	8	16.27	264.71
Marty	6	7	6	19	5.27	27.77
Sue	9	15	15	39	14.73	216.97
Kevin	15	13	12	40	15.73	247.43

$\frac{R_1}{N} = 24.2$ $\frac{(R_1 R_1)_2}{N} = 2348.89s$

Equation: $w = \dfrac{s}{1/12 k^2 (N^3 - N)}$

$s = \sum (R_i - \dfrac{\sum R_t}{N})^2 =$ sum of observed deviations from the mean of R_t = 2348.89

k = number of sets of rankings = 3
N = number of subjects (students) = 15

$W = \dfrac{2348.89}{1/12(3)^2(15^3-15)}$

$W = \dfrac{2348.89}{1/12(9)(3360)} = \dfrac{2348.89}{2520}$

W = .932 since N 7 find x^2 (chi square)

$x^2 = K(N-1)W$

$x^2 = 3(15-1).932$

$x^2 = 39.144$

df = N-1 = 15 – 1

Consult Table C. (If N 7 consult Table R)
df = 14 Critical value for .05 = 23.68

e. **Rejection Region:** In order to reject the null hypothesis, x^2 must be equal to or greater than 23.68.

f. **Decision:** 39.144 is greater than 23.68; therefore, Mrs. Martin may reject the null hypothesis at the .05 level of significance. She finds a significant relationship among the three variables of achievement, self-esteem and fear of failure. The data must be ordinal or ordered in level of measurement.

8. **Kolmogorov-Smirnov One-Sample Test**

This is a goodness-of-fit test. It is used to determine the degree of agreement between the distribution of a set of sample values (observed scores) and some specified theoretical distribution. The Kolmogorov-Smirnov test is useful with ordinal or ordered level of data, particularly if the number of scores in each category is small. This test is more powerful than its counterpart, the chi-square test, in rejecting the null hypothesis when it is false, so the statistician has a better chance of getting significant results by using the Kolmogorov-Smirnov test than by using the chi-square test.

Example: John Stock's 5th grade students are classified as having the lowest language arts ability of all fifth graders in the school. Most of these students have been in his low grouping throughout grade school. Many of them have also been discipline problems throughout their grade school days. Consequently, John has instituted a point system to try and improve the discipline in his room. He wants to find out if the class likes the point system, so he administered a questionnaire to his students. His study follows.

a. **Hypothesis:** The students will rate the point system significantly higher as measured by the questionnaire.
   Null Hypothesis: The number of students who rate the point system high will equal those who rate it low.

b. **Statistical Test:** The statistical test which is appropriate to test this hypothesis is the Kolmogorov-Smirnov test because the data is of ordinal scale and it is compared with a theoretical distribution.

c. **Significance Level:** Let a (alpha) = .01, N = 20, number of students.

d. **Computation:** Data

   Score on Questionnaire (10 = High Preference)

	1	2	3	4	5	6	7	8	9	10
f = number of subjects choosing rank	0	0	1	0	2	4	3	2	4	4
f(x) = theoretical cumulative distribution under H	1/10	2/10	3/10	4/10	5/10	6/10	7/10	8/10	9/10	10/10
525(X) = observed cumulative distribution	0/20	0/20	1/20	i/20	3/20	7/20	10/20	12/20	16/20	20/20
$f(x) - S_{20}(X) =$	2/20	4/20	5/20	7/20	7/20	5/20	4/20	4/20	2/20	0

   Highest $F_0(x) - S_{20}(x)$

   Equation

   $F_0(x) - S_{20}(x) = D$ Highest D = 7/20 = 3.5/10 = .35
   Consult Table E: .01 probability, N = 20.
   Significant D = .356

e. **Rejection Region:** To reject the null hypothesis D .56

f. **Decision:** John's data shows .35 which is less than .356. He can reject the null hypothesis and finds support for his hypothesis that his students like the point system.

9. **Kruskal-Wallis One-Way Analysis of Variance by Ranks**

This test is used to determine whether two or more independent samples comes from the same population or whether they can be said to be significantly different from one another. The test assumes that the variable under study be at least ordinal level of measurement and have an underlying continuous distribution. This means that the variable may have any value in a certain interval, not restricted to isolated values. The Kruskal-Wallis Test has a relative power of 95.5% compared to the parametric F test.

Example: Joan Rollinson taught twenty-seven third graders, who had various levels of abilities. She is trying to find the most efficient mode of giving instructions for the children in her class.

a. **Hypothesis:** There will be significant difference in performance on the test among the three groups receiving oral instructions, written instructions, and both.
   Null Hypothesis: The performance of the different groups will be no different.

b. **Statistical Test:** The Kruskal-Wallis test is chosen because Joan is looking for statistical significance among two or more samples and the data is ordinal level in measurement.

c. **Significance Level:** Let a (alpha) = .05, N = 30 number of students

d. **Computation:** Data

Oral	Rank	Written	Rank	Both	Rank
17	7.5	10	15	20	1.5
18	5.5	14	12	19	3.5
15	1.1	13	13	20	1.5
17	7.5	16	9.5	18	5.5
16	9.5	11	14	19	3.5
$R_1 =$	41.0	$R_2 =$	63.5	$R_3 =$	13.5

Equation

$$H = \frac{\frac{12}{N(N+1)} \sum \frac{R_i^2}{N_1} - 3(N+1)}{1 - \frac{\sum T}{N^3 - N}}$$

N = number of scores
R_i = sum of the ranks of a column squared
N_i = number of scores in a column
$T = t^3 - t$ (when t is the number of tied scores in a tied group of scores)

Note: $\frac{1-T}{N_3-N}$ is only used to correct for ties. If there are no ties, delete this part from the equation.

$$H = \frac{\frac{12}{15(15+1)} \frac{(41)^2}{5} + \frac{(63.5)^2}{5} + \frac{(13.2)^2}{5} - 3(15+1)}{\frac{6+6+6+6+6}{(15)^3 - 15}}$$

$$H = \frac{\frac{12}{240} \frac{1681}{5} + \frac{3969}{5} + \frac{172.25}{5} - 48}{1 - \frac{30}{3360}}$$

$$H = \frac{\frac{1}{20} 336.2 + 793.8 + 34.45 - 48}{1 - \frac{1}{112}}$$

H = 10.12

Consult Table O, sample size = 5555, p = .049 = 5.78

e. **Rejection Region:** Ms. Rollinson can reject the null hypothesis if the H derived from her data is greater than the H on the chart (5.78).

f. **Decision:** Since her H = 10.12, which is larger than 5.78, she may reject the null hypothesis. Ms. Rollinson does find support for her hypothesis that there is significant difference in performance with different type of instruction. She would, therefore, use both oral and written instructions to facilitate her pupils' performance.

10. **Mann Whitney U Test**

    This test should be used to determine whether two independent groups have been drawn from different populations, and whether they are significantly different. The data must be at least ordinal level of measurement. Mann-Whitney U is one of the most powerful nonparametric tests. When compared to the parametric T-test, it had 95.5% of its power to reject the null hypothesis. Mann-Whitney U is a useful alternative to the T-test, then, when the assumptions of a parametric test cannot be made.

    Example: Marlene Piscitelli noticed that her students with dominance problems in the remedial reading clinic seemed to have more problems with reading comprehension than the other students. She decided to find out if there was a significant difference between the two groups. Her study follows.

    a. **Hypothesis:** There will be a significant difference in achievement between the students who have lateral dominance problems and those who do not.
    Null Hypothesis: The two groups were drawn from the same population; there will be no significant difference in performance.

    b. **Statistical Test:** The Mann-Whitney U Test is chosen because the data is at the ordinal level of measurement and Marlene is looking for significant difference between two independent groups.

    c. **Significance Level:** Let a (alpha) = .05, N = 2 students with dominance problems. N^2 = 6 students with no dominance problems.

    d. **Computation:** Data

N	1	41	45				
N	2	78	75	82	90	51	68

90	82	78	75	68	51	45	41
N_2	N_2	N_2	N_2	N_2	N_2	N	N_1

    U = number of N's preceding N_2's
    U = 0

    Table J, N_2 = 6, U = 0, N_2 = 2, Significant at .036

e. **Rejection Region:** The U has to be so small that there would only be .05 chance or less that it could have occurred by chance. In other words, the significant level must be .05 or less.

f. **Decision:** Since the significance level for Ms. Piscitteli's data is equal to .036, which is less than .05, she finds support for her hypothesis that students with laterality problems also have difficulty in reading. She may reject the null hypothesis.

11. **Randomization Test for Two Matched Samples**

    This test is a useful and powerful non-parametric technique for testing the significant difference between the means of two matched samples when the two samples are small. It requires at least interval measurement of the variable being studied. There is no assumption of normal distributions or homogeneity of variance (which means the two samples don't have scores equidistant from one another) like the comparable T test assumes. The Randomization test efficiently uses all information and, therefore, its power to reject the false null hypothesis is essentially 100%. An example is shown below. However, if the samples are large, the Wilcoxon test may be more efficient to use.

    Example: Mike Brown is concerned that some of his students aren't doing as well on his tests as they are capable of doing. He feels that they get too anxious and feel they will flunk the test. To verify this observation, he administered the Fear of Failure test and found a high negative correlation between the scores on that test and his own reading tests. Mike, therefore, decided to give the students an option to retake the test as often as they want. He wants to find out if the students will do better on the tests if they feel less pressure. His study is shown below.

    a. **Hypothesis:** There will be a significant increase in reading scores when the students are given an option to retake the tests.
    Null Hypothesis: There will be no difference in the two scores.

    b. **Statistical Test:** The Randomization Test for Matched Pairs is chosen because the interval level of measurement is used, the samples are matched, and Mike is looking for significant difference.

    c. **Significance Level:** Let a (alpha) = .05, N = number of pairs = 8.

    d. **Computation:** Data

Names	Differences Between Option/No Option
Tina	+19
Ed	+27
Marty	-1
Larry	+6
Pam	+7
Michelle	+13
Amy	-4
Tom	+3

    Six most extreme positive outcome (a (alpha) = .05)

	Outcomes	Ed.
1	+19 + 27 + 1 + 6 + 7 + 13 + 4 + 3	80
2	+19 + 27 − 1 + 6 + 7 + 13 + 4 + 3	78
3	+19 + 27 + 1 + 6 + 7 + 13 + 4 − 3	74
4	+19 + 27 + 1 + 6 + 7 + 13 − 4 + 3	72
5	+19 + 27 − 1 + 6 + 7 + 13 + 4 − 3	72
6	+19 + 17 − 1 + 6 + 7 + 13 − 4 + 3	70

e. **Rejection Region:** Mike's data falls into one of three six extreme outcomes than his scores represent a significant difference of a (alpha) = .047.

f. **Decision:** Since Mike's set of data did match one of these extreme outcomes, he achieved significant results at .05 probability (alpha). He can reject the null hypothesis and finds support for his hypothesis that giving a retake option on the tests will improve his students' scores.

12. **Sign Test**

The Sign Test uses plus and minus signs rather than quantitative measures as its data. It is particularly useful with data which cannot be quantitatively measured but in which it is possible to rank with respect to each other the two members of each pair. The only assumption is that the variable measured has a continuous distribution, that is, the data can take on any value. This test is to be used when the subjects are drawn from matched samples. This can be accomplished either by using the subjects as their own controls (test/retest) or by using different subjects which are matched in respect to the relevant variables. The power of the Sign Test to reject the false null hypothesis is about 95% when N = 6, and as the sample increases its eventual power is 63%. A sample problem is shown below.

Example: Joe Risk's sixth graders having been labeled "troublemakers" early in their grade school careers were constantly disrupting his reading class. As Mr. Risk felt these disruptions were not conducive to learning either for the troublemakers or the other class members, he decided to try a token economy in the class to decrease the acting out behavior. He put the class on a point system, in which the class as a whole could earn points for participating in class and points were taken away for disruptive behavior. The points earned went toward the privilege of getting out of class early on Friday. Mr. Risk wants to find out if this point system is an effective way of controlling behavior. A synopsis of his study follows.

a. **Hypothesis:** The children will receive a higher behavioral rating after the use of the point system, where 1 = disruptive and 5 = well behaved.
Null Hypothesis: There will be no difference before and after the use of the point system.

b. **Statistical Test:** The sign test was chosen because the measurement is ordinal and the samples matched.

c. **Significance Level:** Let a (alpha) = .05, N = 17 students. This may be reduced if there are ties.

d. **Computation:** Data

Name	Pre-rating	Post-rating	Direction of Difference	Sign
Martha	5	5	5 = 5	0
Frank	2	4	2 < 4	+
Eddie	1	3	1 < 3	+
Mitch	3	4	3 < 4	+
Rita	4	4	4 = 4	0
Suzanne	4	5	4 < 5	+
Leta	4	5	4 < 5	+
Tom	2	3	2 < 3	+
Rick	4	2	4 > 2	-
Mike	4	3	4 > 3	-
James	3	4	3 < 4	+
Chris	3	5	3 < 5	+
Bob	2	4	2 < 4	+
Barb	3	4	3 < 4	+
Allan	1	3	1 < 3	+
Joe	2	3	2 < 3	+
Ellen	4	5	4 < 5	+

N = 15 x = number of fewer signs = 2

Consult Table D, N = 15, x = 2, p = .004

e. **Rejection Region:** Joe may reject the null hypothesis if p = .05.

f. **Decision:** Since p = .004, which is less than .05, Joe can reject the null hypothesis and finds support for his hypothesis that the point system reduces disruptive behavior. He will continue to use the point system.

13. **The Spearman Rank Correlation Coefficient: Rank**

The Spearman test, sometimes called RHO, is one of the best known non-parametric tests. It was developed to determine the amount of relationship between variables which must be measured at the ordinal level. However, no relationships can be established using this test, only degree of relationship. The more the ranks within two sets of scores agree, the higher the positive correlation; the more they diverge from one another, the higher the negative correlation. If there is no discernable pattern to the variables' variance in relation to one another, then there is said to be low correlation or little relationship between the scores. The Spearman Rank Correlation Test has 91% of the power to reject the null hypothesis of the Pearson r, a comparable parametric test.

Example: John Stock wishes to find out if two tests he gives his class at the beginning and end of every year measure the same aptitudes. The two tests are the Woodstock Reading test and the reading section of the Metropolitan Primary II. He will determine this by finding the strength of relationship between the scores his fifth graders obtained on the two tests. A synopsis of this portion of his study follows.

a. **Hypothesis:** There will be a significantly strong positive relationship between the scores obtained on the Woodstock test and the Metropolitan Primary II.
   Null Hypothesis: There will be either no relationship or negative relationship between the scores obtained.

b. **Statistical Test:** The Spearman Rank Test will be used because Mr. Stock wishes to find the strength of relationship and the data is ordinal level of measurement.

c. **Significance Level:** Let a (alpha) = .05, N = 15 students or sets of scores.

d. **Computation:** Data.

Name	Woodstock Test Score Rank	Metropolitan Primary II Score Rank	Difference di	Difference di
Jean	14	14	0	0
Tony	4	4	0	0
Rachel	13	11	2	4
Tim	5	3	2	4
Ann	10	12	-2	4
Lela	3	2	1	1
Tammy	1	1	0	0
Rick	7	9	2	4
Ruth	8	6	2	4
Mary	2	5	-3	9
Phillip	12	10	1	1
Clark	12	10	2	4
Kevin	6	7	-1	1
Mike	15	15	0	0
Pam	11	13	-2	4
				dr = 40

Equation

$$r_s = 1 - \frac{6 \sum di^2}{N^3 - N}$$

$$r_s = 1 - \frac{6(40)}{(15)^3 - (15)}$$

$$r_s = 1 - \frac{240}{3375 - 15}$$

$$r_s = 1 - \frac{240}{3360}$$

$$r_s = 1 - .07$$

$$r_s = .93$$

Consult Table P. N = 15 significance level = .08, critical value of rs = .425.

e. **Rejection Region:** If our score is larger than the critical value of rs listed in P, then we can reject the null hypothesis.

f. **Decision:** Since Mr. Stock's value .93 was larger than the critical value .425, he can reject the null hypothesis and find support for his hypothesis that there is a relationship between the Metropolitan Primary and Woodstock Reading tests.

14. **Wilcoxon Matched Pairs Signed Ranks Test**

    This test is used to determine if there is significant difference in direction and magnitude between pairs of scores. For example, if a teacher is interested in ascertaining whether more achievement scores increased or decreased and whether there was a bigger difference in the scores which increased or those which decreased, then (s)he would use this method.
    The teacher will use Statistical Models 4, 5, or 6 in conjunction with this test. The data must be ordinal level, i.e., the teacher must be able to make a judgment of greater than between any pairs two performances.
    If all these criteria are met, then use this method rather than the Sign Test, as the Wilcoxon is more powerful than the Sign, that is, it uses more information than the Sign. When compared to the T-Test (a parametric test), it is found to be about 95% as efficient. This is powerful for a non-parametric test.

    Example: Kathleen Bergman is trying to determine if the PLATO programmed instruction technique improves children's learning.

    a. **Hypothesis:** There will be a significant increase in the achievement scores obtained on the pretests and post tests.
       Null Hypothesis: There will be no increase in the achievement scores obtained on the pre and post test given to the children before and after treatment.

    b. **Statistical Test:** The Wilcoxon Matched Pairs Signed Rank Test is chosen because the study employs two related samples (two sets of scores for each child) and it yields different scores which may be ranked in order of absolute magnitude (absolute difference in the two scores).

    c. **Significance Level:** Let a (alpha) = .025, N = number of pairs of scores or number of children minus any pairs of scores whose difference was zero.

Name	12-2 = 10 = N Pretest Data Score	Post Test Score	Difference d	Rank of L	Ran with Less Frequent Sign
John	63	82	19	8	(-) 1
Suzi	42	69	27	9	
Fred	55	55	-1	-1	
Larry	74	73			
Tim	37	43	6	5	
Mary	51	58	7	6	
Rob	43	56	13	7	
Terry	80	76	-4	-3	(-) 3
Joe	60	60			
Mac	79	82	3	2	
Lois	90	85	-5	-4	(-) 4
Ed	40	70	30	10	8T

Equation (None for N ≥ 25

(For N ≥ 25, the equation is

$$z = \frac{T - \frac{N(N+1)}{4}}{\frac{N(N+1)(2N+1)}{24}}$$

N in this study = 10 25. Therefore, go directly to Table G. Find .025 under one tailed test. Find 10 under N.

e. **Rejection Region:** Since the direction of the difference is predicted (i.e., the scores will increase), a one-tailed test is appropriate. The region of rejection consists of all values of T so small that the probability associated with their occurrence under the Null Hypothesis is less than or equal to a (alpha) = .025 for one-tailed test.

f. **Decision:** Only three children in the study regressed while using PLATO. Looking at Table G with N = 10 and T = 8, so a T = 8 allows us to reject the Null Hypothesis at a (alpha) = .025 for a one-tailed test. We find support for Kathleen's hypothesis. The children do show significant increase in the achievement scores obtained on the pretest and post test.